Cambridge International AS and A Level

Economics

Revision Guide
Second edition

Susan Grant

CAMBRIDGE UNIVERSITY PRESS

CAMBRIDGE
UNIVERSITY PRESS

University Printing House, Cambridge CB2 8BS, United Kingdom

One Liberty Plaza, 20th Floor, New York, NY 10006, USA

477 Williamstown Road, Port Melbourne, VIC 3207, Australia

4843/24, 2nd Floor, Ansari Road, Daryaganj, Delhi - 110002, India

79 Anson Road, #06 -04/06, Singapore 079906

Cambridge University Press is part of the University of Cambridge.

It furthers the University's mission by disseminating knowledge in the pursuit of education, learning and research at the highest international levels of excellence.

www.cambridge.org

Information on this title: www.cambridge.org/ 9781316638095

First published 2013
Second edition 2016
20 19 18 17 16 15 14 13 12 11 10 9 8 7 6 5 4

Printed in Great Britain by CPI Group (UK) Ltd, Croydon CR0 4YY

A catalogue record for this publication is available from the British Library

ISBN 978-1-316-63809-5 Paperback

Table of Contents

Introduction

The structure of the book

This book is designed to help students revise both AS Level and A Level Economics. Chapters 1 to 5 are devoted to AS Level Economics, while chapters 6 to 10 cater to A Level. Each of these chapters contains a number of common features. They start with a summary of the key economic content that will help students to recall the topics covered during the course. Throughout the chapter there are progress checks designed to provide a quick assessment of students' knowledge and understanding. There are also a number of tips and revision activities. The tips give guidance on key points. The revision activities seek to allow students to apply the skills they have developed to a range of different situations and tasks.

At the end of each chapter there are two mind maps, data response, multiple choice and essay questions. The mind maps are designed to show links within certain topics, provide another way of summarising key points and encourage students to draw more mind maps as part of their revision.

The multiple choice questions help students to check their understanding and the skills they have gained, as well as giving them practice in answering the types of questions they will face in the examination. The data response and essay questions also provide examination practice. In addition, they assess students' ability to explore topics in more detail and to demonstrate their analytical and evaluative skills.

Answers for all the questions are provided at the end of the book for the benefit of the students. Students are encouraged not to look at the answers to a chapter until they have attempted all the questions in that chapter. They should also bear in mind that the answers to the essay questions are suggested answers. No answer can cover all the possible points and equally valid answers can be structured in a slightly different way.

The difference between IGCSE and AS/A Level

Some AS/A Level candidates have previously studied IGCSE Economics whilst others are new to the subject. In either case, it is important to remember that AS Level is a step up from IGCSE and, in turn, A Level is a step up from AS Level. As students progress up the levels, they are required to demonstrate higher order skills. At IGCSE Level there is, for instance, more emphasis on knowledge and understanding than at AS/A Level. The skills that become more important at AS/A Level are analysis, evaluation and judgement making.

The weighting given to the skills assessed at AS Level and A Level are 30% for knowledge and understanding, 20% for application, 30% for analysis and 20% for evaluation.

At AS/A Level students are beginning to work as economists. Economists working for a government, an NGO, bank or multinational company, for instance, analyse economic data, make judgements about the best strategies to follow and write reports which analyse the significance of events and government policy changes for their organisations. They will be able to write clearly, carry out numerical calculations and interpret and use statistics, graphs and diagrams. Through the examination questions students will be able to exhibit all of these skills.

At AS Level, the multiple choice questions have a 40% weighting as a means of assessment, the data response question a 30% weighting and the structured essay a weighting of 30%. The AS Level papers provide half the weighting for A Level with the remaining 50% being made up of 15% for the multiple choice questions, 10% for the data response questions and 25% for the essay questions. The overall weighting for the A Level is 35% for the multiple choice questions, 25% for the data response questions and 40% for the essay questions.

When revising the A Level part of the syllabus, it is important not to forget the AS Level part of the syllabus. For instance, in considering the reasons for market failure, students also have to consider public goods, merit and demerit goods which are first encountered at AS Level.

Coverage

The book follows the Cambridge International Examinations syllabus closely. Chapter 1 covers some key concepts and resource allocation. It includes scarcity, opportunity cost, positive and normative statements, factors of production, different economic systems, production possibility curves, money and different types of goods and services. Chapter 2 focuses on demand and supply. It covers the nature and determinants of demand and supply, elasticities, changes in market conditions and consumer and producer surplus. Chapter 3 concentrates on how the government intervenes in markets. It examines the effects of maximum and minimum prices, taxes, subsidies, transfer payments, the direct provision of goods and services and nationalisation and privatisation. In Chapter 4 the focus switches from the micro to the macro economy. It examines aggregate demand and supply analysis, inflation, balance of payments, exchange rates, the terms of trade, principles of absolute and comparative advantage and protectionism. Chapter 5 covers the three types of macroeconomic policies and then concentrates on policies to correct balance of payments disequilibrium, inflation and deflation.

Chapter 6 starts the A Level coverage. It covers the efficient allocation of resources and then externalities, market failure, social benefits, social costs and cost-benefit analysis. In Chapter 7 the price system and the roles of consumers and firms in the workings of the price system are explored. The law of diminishing returns, indifference curves, budget lines, costs of production, profit, different market structures, the growth and survival of firms and the different objectives of firms are covered.

Chapter 8 examines government microeconomic intervention, labour market forces and government intervention in the labour market and government failure in microeconomic intervention. In terms of government microeconomic intervention, it covers policies to achieve the efficient allocation and correct market failure, the concept of equity and policies towards income and wealth distribution. Among the labour market issues explored are the demand and supply of labour and wage determination in perfect and imperfect markets. Chapter 9 is a wide ranging chapter. It starts by examining economic growth, economic development, sustainability, national income and the classification of countries. Then it covers employment, unemployment, the circular flow of income and the money supply. It finishes by examining the Keynesian and Monetarist schools, the demand for money and interest rate determination and policies towards developing economies including policies of trade and aid.

The final chapter, Chapter 10 covers macro policy aims, the inter-connectedness of macroeconomic problems and the effectiveness of policy options to meet all macroeconomic objectiveness. Among the concepts explored are the Phillips curve and the Laffer curve.

Study skills

This book aims both to strengthen students' understanding of the economics they have covered during their course and to develop their study skills. It is designed to improve their ability to interpret and draw diagrams, interpret other forms of data, undertake numerical calculations and to write lucid and well-structured answers.

This book is designed to make revision more effective and hopefully increase the students' enjoyment of the subject, enabling them to excel in the examinations.

How to use this book: a guided tour

Learning summary –
A summary list of key topics and concepts that you will be looking at in this chapter, to help with navigation through the book and give a reminder of what's important about each topic for your revision.

TERMS

Market economy: resources are allocated by the price consumers are willing to pay for products.

Planned economy: government decides how resources are allocated.

Terms – clear and straightforward explanations are provided for the most important words in each topic. Key terms appear in blue bold type within the main text.

TIP

It is useful to give examples of taxes in your own country in assessing the effects of taxation.

Tip – quick suggestions to remind you about key facts and highlight important points.

Multiple Choice Questions

1 Which of the following is an example of an external benefit of increased train travel?

   A Increased overcrowding on trains

   B Reduced fares for train passengers

   C Reduced congestion on roads

   D Higher profits for train operating firms

2 After carrying out a cost-benefit analysis, a government decides to go ahead with a hospital building scheme as there is a net social benefit. Private costs were calculated to be $500m, private benefits at $600m and external benefits at $700m. What does this information indicate about the external costs of the scheme?

Multiple Choice Questions – Exam-style multiple choice questions for you to test your knowledge and understanding at the end of each chapter. The answers are provided at the back of the book.

Revision Activity C

a Categorise the following effects of building and operating a new airport into private benefits, private costs, external benefits and external costs.

   1 Air and noise pollution generated by flights to and from the airport

   2 Air fares collected by the airlines that use the airport

   3 A fall in the price of houses close to the airport

   4 Destruction of wildlife habitats

   5 Increased custom for local taxi choice

   6 Insurance paid by the airport operators

   7 Revenue for airport operators

   8 Traffic congestion near the airport

   9 Wages paid to workers building the airport

b Using the information in Table 6.01, calculate the marginal social benefit and the marginal social cost. What is the allocatively efficient output?

Revision activity – Practice questions in each chapter to help with your revision.

Progress check A

Explain two reasons why a fall in profit levels may reduce investment.

Progress check – check your own knowledge and see how well you are getting on by answering regular questions.

Revision Tips – Useful tips to help you with your revision.

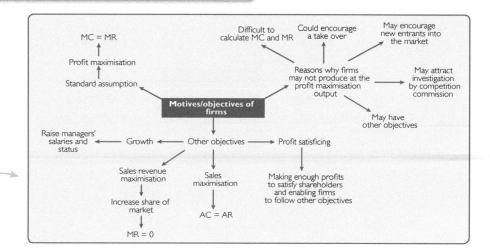

Mind Maps – To help consolidate key topics.

Essay Questions

1   a   Explain the difference between a maximum price and a minimum price.   [8]

    b   Discuss whether the introduction of an effective minimum price will benefit producers.   [12]

2   a   Explain the characteristics of a good tax.   [8]

    b   Discuss the effectiveness of government policy measures to correct market failure in the case of merit goods and demerit goods.   [12]

Essay Questions – Exam-style questions for you to test your knowledge and understanding at the end of each chapter. The answers are provided at the back of the book.

Data Response Questions

1 Measuring inflation

Many countries use consumer price indices to measure inflation. These are weighted price indices which reflect both changes in prices and changes in household spending patterns. There are a number of reasons why household spending patterns alter over time. These include changes in tastes and relative prices. As these factors vary from country to country, weights also vary. Table 4.06 compares some of the weights in the consumer price indices of India and Pakistan.

	India	Pakistan
Category	Weight (%)	Weight (%)
Food and beverages	45.86	34.83
Alcohol and tobacco	2.38	1.41

Data Response Questions – Exam-style questions for you to test your knowledge of analysing data at the end of each chapter. The answers are provided at the back of the book.

Section 1:
AS LEVEL

Basic economic ideas and resource allocation

Learning summary

After you have studied this chapter, you should be able to:

- ☐ define the fundamental economic problem

- ☐ explain the meaning of scarcity, opportunity cost and the basic economic questions

- ☐ define ceteris paribus

- ☐ recognise the importance of decision making at the margin

- ☐ distinguish between positive and normative statements

- ☐ outline the characteristics of factors of production

- ☐ distinguish between the rewards and the factors of production

- ☐ define specialisation

- ☐ assess the advantages and disadvantages of division of labour

- ☐ compare different economic systems

- ☐ explain the role of the factor enterprise in a modern economy

- ☐ draw and interpret production possibility curves

- ☐ explain how constant and increasing opportunity cost determine the shape of the production possibility curve

- ☐ explain the functions and characteristics of money

- ☐ distinguish between money and barter

- ☐ define liquidity

- ☐ explain free goods, economic goods, private goods and public goods

- ☐ distinguish between merit goods and demerit goods

1.01 The fundamental economic problem

The fundamental economic problem is that there are never enough resources to produce all the products people would like to have.

Resources are limited in supply (finite) whilst wants are unlimited (infinite).

1.02 Meaning of scarcity and the inevitability of choices at all levels

As there is scarcity of resources, choices have to be made. Consumers have to decide what to buy, workers – which jobs to do, firms – what to produce, governments – what to spend tax revenue on.

> ### Progress check A
>
> Will the economic problem ever be solved?

1.03 Opportunity cost

Having to select one option involves an opportunity cost. Opportunity cost is the best alternative forgone.

Due to the economic problem of wants exceeding resources, economies have to decide what to produce, how to produce it and who will receive what is produced.

What to produce, how to produce and who will receive what is produced are sometimes referred to as the three basic questions which all economies have to answer.

> **TERM**
>
> Opportunity cost: the best alternative sacrificed when an option is selected.

> **TIP**
>
> Opportunity cost is a concept that you can use in analysing and evaluating a significant number of topics, e.g. whether a government should spend more on healthcare.

1.04 Ceteris paribus

Ceteris paribus means other things being equal.

Economists often make use of ceteris paribus to consider the possible effects of a change in one variable on another variable. For instance, an increase in real disposable income would be expected to lead to an increase in demand for gold watches, on the assumption that the other influences on demand for gold watches are not changing.

> **TERM**
>
> Ceteris paribus: other things being equal.

1.05 Decision making at the margin

Individuals, households, firms and governments often have to make marginal decisions. These involve considering whether to make slight changes. For instance, whether to buy one more apple, produce one more car or to reduce the number of teachers employed in state schools.

1.06 Positive and normative statements

A positive statement is a statement of fact. It can be tested to assess whether it is right or wrong.

A normative statement is a statement based on opinion. It is a value judgement and, as such, cannot be proved right or wrong.

There are both positive and normative statements in economics. 'The unemployment rate in a country is 6%' is a positive statement. In contrast, 'the government's key priority should be reducing unemployment' is a normative statement.

> **TIP**
>
> Much of what you write will be based on positive statements. In coming to a conclusion in an answer you may, however, be making a value judgement e.g. on what might be the most appropriate government policy measure to reduce unemployment. The conclusion should be based on economic analysis and not on uninformed opinion.

> **TERMS**
>
> Marginal decision: whether to make slight changes.
>
> Positive statement: a fact that can be tested.
>
> Normative statement: a value judgement based on opinion that cannot be tested.

1.07 Characteristics of factors of production and their rewards

Factors of production are resources used to produce goods and services:

- Land covers all natural resources – for example, the surface of the earth, the sea, rivers, minerals below the earth. Most land is geographically immobile but occupationally mobile. The reward to land is rent.

- Labour is human effort, mental or physical, used in the production of goods and services. Labour may be geographically immobile due to differences in housing costs and because of family ties. It may be occupationally immobile if workers lack education and training. Spending on education and training increases human capital. Wages are the reward to labour.

- Capital is human made goods used to produce other goods and services. Investment is spending on capital goods. Net investment occurs when firms purchase more capital goods than are needed to replace those capital goods which have become obsolete – gross investment exceeds depreciation. Capital varies in its occupational and geographical mobility. A photocopier, for instance, can be used in most types of industries and can be moved from one part of the country to another. In contrast, an operating theatre is likely to be occupationally immobile and a gold mine is geographically immobile. The reward for capital is interest.

- Enterprise is the willingness and initiative to organise the other factors of production and, crucially, to bear the uncertain risks of producing a product. Entrepreneurs are the people who have the willingness and initiative to make decisions and to take the risks involved in production. In a public limited company, the role of the entrepreneur is divided between the managers (who make the business decisions) and shareholders (who bear the risks). Entrepreneurs tend to be relatively, occupationally and geographically mobile. The reward for enterprise is profit.

TERMS

Factors of production: resources used to produce goods and services.

Land: natural resources both on the surface and beneath the earth.

Labour: human effort used in production.

Capital: goods used to produce other goods.

Enterprise: organising the factors of production and bearing the risks of producing a product.

Revision activity A

a Identify an example of each factor of production that is employed in the film industry.

b Give an example of a capital intensive industry and a labour intensive industry.

c What factors influence the supply of labour to a particular occupation?

d Explain the link between enterprise and opportunity cost.

e Why is the rent on land in city centres usually higher than that on land in rural areas?

TIP

The two factors of production that students most commonly get confused about are land and capital. Remember land is any natural resource and not just land as soil, and capital refers to capital goods i.e. human-made goods and not money.

1.08 Specialisation

Specialisation involves concentrating on particular tasks or products. Workers, firms, regions and countries can concentrate on producing one product.

Specialisation can increase output but there are risks attached. For instance, if a firm makes only one product and demand for that product falls, the firm would be in difficulty.

TERM

Specialisation: concentration on a particular task or product.

1.09 Division of labour

Division of labour involves breaking down the production into separate tasks and having each worker concentrate on a particular task.

One of the first economists to describe division of labour was Adam Smith. In his book *An Enquiry into the Nature and Causes of the Wealth of Nations* (often shortened to *The Wealth of Nations*), he described the 18 separate processes involved in producing a pin.

Advocates of division of labour claim that it increases output and reduces the average cost of production. This is because it enables workers to concentrate on what they are best at, increases their skill ('practice makes perfect'), reduces the time it takes to train them, reduces the equipment needed, cuts back on the time involved in moving from one activity to another and makes it easier to mechanise the process.

Critics of division of labour, in contrast, argue that it may reduce output and increase the average cost of production. They claim that workers can get bored, doing the same task time after time. Boredom can lead to workers making mistakes and leaving the firm after a short time. In addition, division of labour may mean that a firm does not find out what task a worker is best at and may mean that a firm will find it difficult to cover for workers who are absent from work due to illness or because they are undergoing training.

Progress check B

In what way do schools engage in division of labour?

TERM

Division of labour: breaking down production into separate tasks to be carried out by separate workers.

1.10 Different economic systems

An economic system is a way of allocating resources to answer the three fundamental questions of what to produce, how to produce it and for whom.

There are three main types of economic systems:

- a market economy
- a planned economy
- a mixed economy

TERMS

Market economy: resources are allocated by the price consumers are willing to pay for products.

Planned economy: government decides how resources are allocated.

Market economies

A market economy is one in which resources are allocated by means of the price mechanism. Consumers indicate what they are willing and able to buy through the prices they are prepared to pay. Private sector firms respond to changes in consumer tastes by altering what they produce. Property is privately owned and the government's role in the economy is minimal.

Among the advantages claimed for a market economy are consumer sovereignty, incentives for workers and firms to be efficient and innovative, and a lack of bureaucracy.

The possible disadvantages of a market economy include an inequitable distribution of income, a risk of unemployment of resources, under-consumption of merit goods, over-consumption of demerit goods, lack of provision of public goods, information failure, and abuse of market power.

TERM

Public good: a product that people cannot be stopped from consuming even if they are not willing to pay for it and once used can still be used by others.

Planned economies

A planned economy is one in which the government makes most of the decisions on how resources are allocated. Property is largely state owned and most workers are employed in state owned enterprises (SOEs). The private sector's role in the economy is minimal.

The advantages of a planned economy include:

- full employment of resources
- avoidance of wasteful duplication
- an equitable distribution of resources
- consideration of externalities
- provision of merit goods and public goods
- discouragement of demerit goods
- long term planning and support for vulnerable groups

Among the possible disadvantages of a planned economy are slow responses to changes in consumer demand, too much bureaucracy, a lack of incentives, and too much concentration on capital goods.

Mixed economies

In a mixed economy, both the private and public sectors play a key role. Resources are allocated using both the price mechanism and state planning.

A mixed economy seeks to gain the advantages of both a market and a planned economy whilst seeking to avoid the disadvantages. How successful it is depends on the effectiveness of government policies and how efficient the private sector is.

In the late twentieth and early twenty-first century, a number of economies moved from a planned towards a market economy.

There are a number of problems that can arise when central planning in an economy is reduced:

- Inflation may rise when price controls are removed.
- It may take time to build up entrepreneurial skills, to develop a financial sector (including a stock exchange) and implement a social welfare network.
- The removal of government support and trade restrictions can result in some enterprises going out of business and can cause unemployment.

1.11 The role of the factor enterprise in a modern economy

In many countries enterprise is playing an increasing role. As the size of the private sector increases relative to the size of the public sector, there is more opportunity for new businesses to be set up.

Enterprise can encourage invention, innovation and competition. Such effects can increase output and improve living standards.

Revision activity B

Complete Table 1.01.

A comparison of a market economy and a planned economy		
Features	Market economy	Planned economy
Allocative mechanism		State directives
Key sector	Private	
Key decision makers	Consumers	
Other names		Centrally planned, collectivist, command, state owned
Example	Hong Kong	
Ownership of means		State owned
Provision of public goods		
The profit motive	Present	

Table 1.01

1.12 Production possibility curves

A production possibility curve (PPC) shows the maximum output of two types of products that can be produced with existing resources and technology.

A production point on the curve represents full use of resources, a production point inside the curve indicates unemployed resources and a production point outside the curve is currently unattainable.

A shift to the right of a PPC is caused by an increase in the quantity or quality of resources. A change in the slope of a PPC will occur if the ability to produce only one of the two products alters.

> **TERM**
>
> Production possibility curve (PPC): a diagram showing the maximum output of two types of products that can be made with existing resources and technology.

The shapes of production possibility curves

A straight line PPC indicates a constant opportunity cost.

A PPC which is bowed out indicates an increasing opportunity cost. In this case, as more capital goods, for example, are produced, more consumer goods have to be sacrificed. This reflects the fact that the resources which are most suited to producing capital goods are used first.

> **TIP**
>
> In drawing PPC curves make sure that you draw the curve/line all the way to each axis – do not leave a gap. Also when drawing the PPC as a curve, make sure it is continuing to rise when it touches the vertical axis – do not have it turning down.

Revision activity C

Look at Figure 1.01 and answer the questions which follow.

a What does a straight line production possibility curve (PPC) such as AB indicate?

b What does the movement of the PPC from AB to AC show?

c Why may the PPC have shifted from AB to DE?

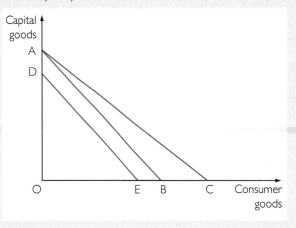

Figure 1.01

1.13 The functions and characteristics of money

Money covers any item which carries out the functions of money. The four functions of money are:

1 a medium of exchange

2 a store of value

3 a unit of account

4 a standard of deferred payments

Probably the best known function of money is as a medium of exchange. Money makes it easy for people to buy and sell products. In the absence of money, people would have to engage in barter.

A store of value means that money enables people to save. Money can be saved in a range of financial institutions to be used in the future.

Money acts as a unit of account, or a measure of value, as it permits the value of goods, services and assets to be compared.

A standard of deferred payments allows people to agree prices of future payments and receipts. This enables payments to be made and received in the future and allows people, firms and governments to lend and borrow.

To act as money, an item has to be generally acceptable. An item may have all the other characteristics needed for it to act as money but if people are not prepared to accept it in exchange for products and in its other capacities, it will not act as money. The other characteristics money should possess are durability, recognisability, divisibility, portability, limited in supply, stability in value and uniformity. There are links between the characteristics. For instance, to be stable in value it should be limited in supply.

TERMS

Money: any item that acts as a medium of exchange, store of value, unit of account or standard of deferred payments.

Barter: direct exchange of products.

Near money

Near money is a term for financial assets that can be converted into money relatively quickly. While such assets are not currently carrying out the essential function of money, that is acting as a medium of exchange, they have a high degree of liquidity. Examples of near money include treasury bills and short term government bonds. Commercial banks hold a range of these assets as they can be quickly turned into cash and so count in their liquidity ratios.

Money and barter

Barter is the direct exchange of products. Money has a number of advantages over barter. The key one is that it makes it easier and quicker to buy and sell products. As a result, money can encourage specialisation and trade.

Money also makes it easier for people to save, value products, borrow and lend. A system of barter would involve uncertainty as to which products other people will be prepared to accept and how they will value them.

Progress check C

Why do apples not act as money?

Liquidity

Liquidity means the ability to turn an asset into cash quickly and without loss. Cash is obviously the most liquid asset. Current (checking) accounts at commercial banks are more liquid than deposit (savings) accounts.

A commercial bank keeps some liquid assets to meet their customers' demand for cash.

TERM

Liquidity: being able to turn an asset into cash quickly without a loss.

Revision activity D

Fit the following terms into the sentences, using each term only once:

1 medium of exchange

2 store of value

3 unit of account

4 standard of deferred payments

5 general acceptability

6 durability

7 liquid

8 cheques

9 divisible

a .... are not money. They are a means of transferring a bank deposit from one person to another.

b The function of money which allows products to be bought on credit is a ....

c To act as a .... money has to be .... in order that payments of different values can be made and change can be given.

d A sight deposit (current account) is more .... than a time deposit (deposit account).

e The .... and .... of money allows it to act as a ....

f Money acts as a .... when the value of products is compared.

1.14 Economic goods and free goods

The vast majority of goods and services are what economists call economic goods. An economic good is one which takes resources to produce it. As a result, its production involves an opportunity cost.

Free goods are rare. They do not involve the use of resources to produce them and so they do not have an opportunity cost. Examples include sunlight and air.

Progress check D

A firm gives a present of a free cake to its customers just before a public holiday.
Explain whether the cake is a free good or an economic good.

TERMS

Economic good: takes resources to produce.

Free good: no resources are used to produce it.

1.15 Private goods and public goods

Most products are private goods. A private good is both excludable and rival. It is excludable in the sense that someone who is not prepared to pay for it can be prevented from consuming the product. It is rival in that if one person consumes the product, someone else cannot consume it. As private goods are excludable, they can be sold through the market. Private sector firms have an incentive to produce them as they can charge directly for them.

The two key characteristics of a public good are non-excludability and non-rivalry. It is not possible to stop non-payers from enjoying the product. As a result, people have no incentive to pay for a public good. Once provided, a public good is available for everyone including non-payers. So people can act as free riders, consuming the product without paying for it. When people consume a public good, they also do not reduce other people's ability to consume the product. For

instance, one more person walking down a street will not reduce the benefit other people receive from the street lighting.

Two other characteristics of a public good are non-rejectability and zero marginal cost. It is not possible for people to reject public goods such as defence. It is also often the case that once provided, it will not cost any more to extend the benefit of a public good such as sea defence to another person.

As it is not possible to charge people directly for public goods, private sector firms lack the financial incentive to provide them. As a result, the provision of public goods has to be financed out of taxation. The government can produce them or pay private sector firms to provide them.

A quasi-public good is a product which possesses some of the features of a public good. For instance, it may be difficult to restrict entry to a beach, making it non-excludable, but if it is crowded it may be rival. Some economists refer to products which are non-excludable but rival, such as a beach and fish in the ocean in some cases, as common resources.

It can be difficult for a government to determine the quantity of a public good to provide. This is because preferences are not revealed via the price mechanism.

TERM

Quasi-public good: has features of public and private goods, also called common resources.

Progress check E

Why does the development of electronic road pricing suggest that roads are changing from being a public good into a private good?

1.16 Merit and demerit goods

Merit and demerit goods are special categories of private goods.

A merit good is a product that a government considers people undervalue. It has two key characteristics. As well as people underestimating the benefit they receive from consuming the product, the consumption also provides external benefits. As a merit good is undervalued, it will be under-consumed and so under-produced if left to market forces. Output will be below the allocatively efficient (socially optimum) level. The existence of information failure and external benefits results in market failure.

To encourage greater consumption of a merit good a government may:

- provide it for free
- subsidise it
- set a maximum price combined with some state provision
- provide some information about its benefits

If the government thinks it is very important for people to consume the product, it may make its consumption compulsory.

A demerit good is a product that the government considers people overvalue. As with a merit good, a demerit good has two key characteristics. People fail to appreciate the harmful effects they experience from consuming the product and consumption of the product generates external costs. As a demerit good is overvalued, it will be over-consumed and over-produced if left to market forces. Output will be above the allocatively efficient level. The existence of information failure and external costs results in market failure.

To discourage consumption of a demerit good a government may: tax it, set a minimum price or provide information about its harmful effects. If the government thinks the product is very harmful, it may ban its consumption.

Governments differ as to what they consider to be merit and demerit goods. The US government, for instance, believes that people are fully and accurately informed about the benefits and risks of owning guns and so does not impose many restrictions on gun ownership. In contrast, the UK government makes it more difficult to own a gun as it thinks information failure and the negative externalities involved are more significant.

TERM

Private good: a product that people can be stopped from consuming and where one person's consumption does not reduce other people's ability to consume it.

Progress check F

Why may a product be treated as a demerit good in one country but not in another country?

TIP

Take care not to confuse public goods and merit goods. To decide whether a good is a public good, the key question is not whether people have to pay to consume it but whether it would be possible to charge for them.

Mind maps

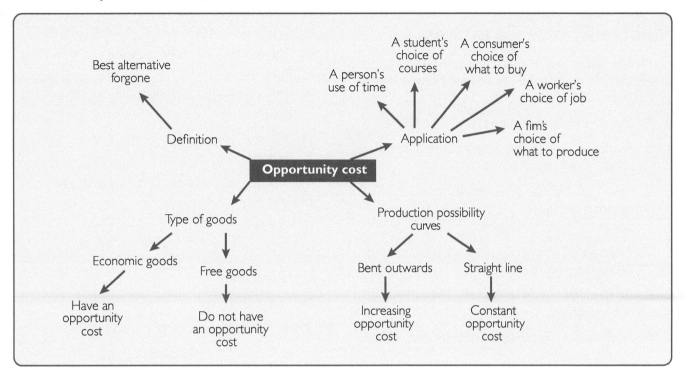

Mind map 1.01: Opportunity cost

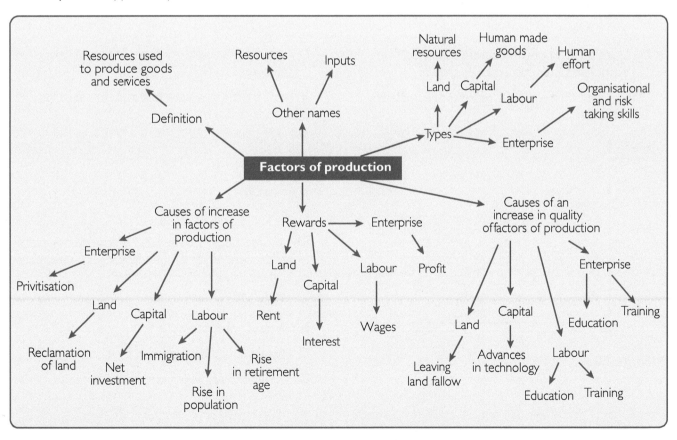

Mind map 1.02: Factors of production

Exam-style Questions

Multiple Choice Questions

1   In which circumstance would there be no opportunity cost involved in a country producing more agricultural products?

   A   Demand for manufactured goods has declined

   B   Previously unemployed resources are used to produce agricultural goods

   C   Resources that had been used to produce manufactured goods are transferred to producing agricultural goods

   D   The price of agricultural goods does not change as more are produced

2   Which question cannot be studied using positive economic analysis?

   A   How should products be distributed between households?

   B   In what sector are most workers employed?

   C   What is the gap between government spending and tax revenue?

   D   Does the economy is operate a planned economic system or a market system?

3   Which point on Figure 1.02 represents complete specialisation?

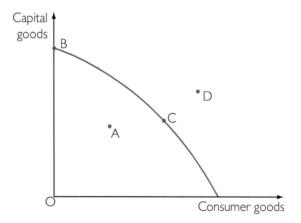

Figure 1.02

4   What is the key characteristic of a mixed economy?

   A   Some of the products produced are domestically produced and some are imported.

   B   The economy has both declining and expanding industries.

   C   There is both a private sector and a public sector.

   D   The sizes of the primary, secondary and tertiary sectors are equally balanced.

5   Who determines how resources are allocated in a planned economy?

   A   Consumers

   B   Managers

   C   Shareholders

   D   The government

6   What does the existence of scarcity mean?

   A   Economies are inefficient.

   B   Economies are developing.

   C   Households, firms and governments have to make choices.

   D   It is not possible to increase the quantity of resources.

7   What is the key characteristic an item needs to possess to act as money?

   A   General acceptability

   B   Intrinsic value

   C   Indivisibility

   D   Unlimited supply

8   The tourist industry makes use of a range of factors of production. Which of the following is an example of land used in the tourist industry?

   A   A hotel

   B   A beach near the hotel

   C   An air ventilation system in the hotel

   D   An indoor swimming pool in the hotel

9 Figure 1.03 shows the production possibility curve of an economy. What is the opportunity cost of the economy increasing the output of capital goods from 20 m to 50 m?

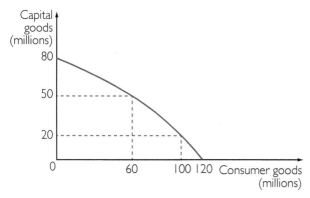

Figure 1.03

A   30 m capital goods

B   40 m consumer goods

C   70 m consumer goods

D   120 m consumer goods

10 What causes the free rider problem?

A   People avoiding paying fares on public transport

B   People who would have paid higher fares benefiting from government subsidies to producers of public transport

C   Public goods being non-excludable

D   Public goods being non-rival

Data Response Question

Since 1989 Eastern European countries have moved from operating planned economies towards operating market economies. This rate of change has varied. Russia and Kazakhstan, for instance, sold off its state owned enterprises (SOEs) and generally reduced government intervention at a quick rate. In contrast, Croatia, Poland and Slovenia removed price controls and subsidies and privatised relatively slowly.

Some economists claim that the 'shock therapy' swept away safety nets with state ownership. In a number of Russian towns, the SOEs provided not only jobs but also healthcare, childcare and pensions. When the SOEs were sold off unemployment rose and life expectancy fell. The lives of men were particularly badly affected with their lifespan falling even further than that of women.

The question of how fast to make the transition from a planned to a market economy is now facing China. The country is becoming more market orientated with the role of the private sector increasing. Structural change is also occurring with the proportion of output and employment accounted for by the secondary and tertiary sectors increasing.

The first decade of the twenty-first century witnessed a period of rapid economic growth in China boosted by high levels of investment and a low exchange rate which increased net exports. Although the country's economic growth slowed in the second decade of the twenty-first century it was still higher than most countries.

Table 1.02 shows some key social and economic data on China, Poland, Romania and Slovenia.

Key social and economic data				
Country	Life expectancy 2014		Annual growth (% change in real GDP) 2014	Unemployment (% in 2014)
	Male	Female		
China	73.4	77.7	7.3	4.1
Poland	73.5	81.5	3.4	12.3
Russia	64.7	76.6	0.6	5.2
Slovenia	74.4	81.9	3.0	13.1

Table 1.02

a   Identify from the extract three indicators of an economy moving from a planned to a market economy.   [3]

b   Which stage of production is not referred to in the extract?   [1]

c   Explain, using a production possibility curve, what happened to the Russian economy when the SOEs were sold off.   [5]

d   Using Table 1.02, comment on whether the Polish economy performed better in 2014 than the Russian economy.   [5]

e   Discuss whether the sale of state owned enterprises will benefit an economy.   [6]

Essay Questions

1   a   An economy can produce capital and consumer goods. Explain the possible effects on the economy's production possibility curve of an advance in technology affecting the production of capital goods.   [8]

b   Discuss whether a market economy or a planned economy is more effective in dealing with the economic problem.   [12]

2   a   Explain what is meant by the basic economic problem and the three fundamental questions that all economies face.   [8]

b   Discuss how useful the price mechanism is in tackling the basic economic problem.   [12]

REVISION TIPS

Engage in continuous revision. Many students think that revision is cramming facts just before an examination. The word 'revision' actually means to review work. This is something that you should do throughout your course. If you spend at least ten minutes after each lesson checking what you have just learned it will increase your understanding of the topics and help you to remember the key features. It may also encourage you to add notes on topics you feel uncertain about, or are particularly interested in, and to ask your teacher for clarification on some aspects. You should also review all your work on a regular basis, for example, every two weeks. By doing this, you should already be relatively familiar with the work you understand by the time you come to your final revision.

Chapter 2

Learning summary

After you have studied this chapter, you should be able to:

- define effective demand
- distinguish between individual demand and market demand
- explain the factors that influence demand
- distinguish between movements along and shifts in demand curves
- define and calculate price elasticity of demand (PED)
- explain the range of price elasticities of demand
- describe the factors that affect PED
- discuss the implications of PED for revenue and business decisions
- define and calculate income elasticity of demand (YED)
- distinguish between positive and negative YED
- discuss the implications of YED for revenue and business decisions
- define and calculate cross elasticity of demand (XED)
- distinguish between positive and negative XED
- discuss the implications of XED for revenue and business decisions

- distinguish between individual supply and market supply
- define price elasticity of supply (PES)
- explain the range of PES
- describe the factors that affect PES
- recognise the implications for speed and ease with which businesses react to changed market conditions
- distinguish between equilibrium and disequilibrium
- explain the effects of changes in supply and demand on equilibrium price and quantity
- apply demand and supply analysis
- outline demand and supply relationships
- explain the role of the price mechanism in rationing, signalling and transmitting preferences
- define consumer surplus and producer surplus
- explain the significance of consumer and producer surplus
- describe how consumer surplus and producer surplus are affected by changes in equilibrium price and quantity

2.01 Demand

Effective demand

Demand is the willingness and ability to buy a product. Economists sometimes refer to this as effective demand. This is to emphasise that the desire for the product has to be backed up by the money to buy the product.

When economists state that e.g. demand for a product is 600 at a price of $18, they mean people will buy that quantity at that price.

Individual and market demand

Individual demand is the amount of a product a person is willing and able to buy at each and every price. A demand curve can be plotted to show how much an individual would be prepared to buy at different prices. A demand curve is drawn up from a demand schedule. It shows the quantity demanded at different prices. Price and demand are usually inversely related.

A market demand curve shows the total demand for a product. The market demand is found by adding up the amount demanded by individual consumers at different prices.

> ## TERMS
>
> Effective demand: willingness and ability to buy a product.
>
> Individual demand: amount an individual will buy at each price.
>
> Demand curve: shows the demand at different prices.
>
> Market demand: the total demand for a product.

Factors that influence demand

Demand for a product is influenced by a number of factors including changes in:

- its price. As indicated above, a rise in price would be expected to result in a fall in demand.

- disposable income. A rise in disposable income increases purchasing power. Such a change is likely to alter the pattern of expenditure. For example, it may result in a fall in demand for bus travel but a rise in demand for car travel.

- the price of related products. A fall in the price of tea may result in a decrease in demand for coffee (a substitute) whilst it may increase demand for milk (a complement).

- tastes and fashion. For example, hairstyles go in and out of fashion. Advertising and healthcare reports can, in turn, influence tastes and fashions. Some firms spend a large amount of money in an effort to encourage people to buy their products and to build up brand loyalty. A report indicating, for example, that eating almonds may improve health may increase demand for almonds.

- population size. An increase in population size will increase demand for most products.

- age structure. An ageing population is likely to increase demand for healthcare.

> ## TERM
>
> Disposable income: the amount individuals have left after they have paid direct taxes.

> ## Progress check A
>
> Explain three factors that influence demand for air travel.

Movements along and shifts in demand curves

A movement along a demand curve can only be caused by a change in the price of the product itself. A rise in price will cause a contraction in demand. This movement can also be referred to as a decrease in quantity demanded. A fall in price will cause an extension in demand. This movement can also be called an increase in quantity demanded (see Figure 2.01).

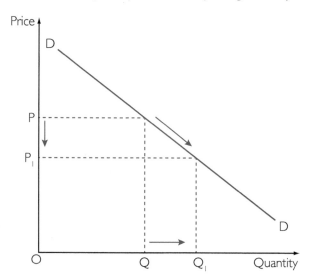

Figure 2.01

A change in any influence on demand for a product, other than its own price, will result in new quantities being demanded at each and every price. As a result, the demand curve will shift its position. A shift to the right of the demand curve is called an increase in demand, with higher quantities being demanded at each and every price.

A decrease in demand will lower quantities being demanded at each and every price and is illustrated by a shift to the left of the demand curve (as shown in Figure 2.02).

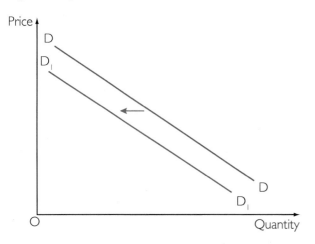

Figure 2.02

Progress check B

What is the difference between a contraction in demand for ice cream and a decrease in demand for ice cream?

2.02 Price elasticity of demand

Definition

Price elasticity of demand (PED) is a measure of the responsiveness of demand to a change in price. It is calculated by using the following formula:

$$PED = \frac{\text{percentage change in quantity demand}}{\text{percentage change in price}}$$

This can be abbreviated to: PED = %ΔQD/%ΔP.

TERM

Price elasticity of demand (PED): measure of responsiveness of demand to a change in price.

Range of price elasticities of demand

As price and demand are usually inversely related, PED is normally a minus figure. A PED figure (ignoring the sign) greater than one and less than infinity means that demand is elastic, with a change in price causing a greater percentage change in quantity demanded.

A PED figure (ignoring the sign) of less than one and greater than zero means that demand is inelastic. In this case, demand is not very responsive to a change in price, with a change in price resulting in a smaller percentage change in quantity demanded.

The three other degrees of PED are:

- perfectly inelastic demand
- unitary elasticity of demand
- perfectly elastic demand

Perfectly inelastic demand means that demand remains unchanged when price alters. In this case, PED is zero.

Unitary elasticity of demand occurs when a change in price causes an equal percentage change in quantity demanded, giving a PED figure of −1.

Perfectly elastic demand means that a change in price will cause an infinite change in quantity demanded, giving a PED of infinity.

Unitary price elasticity of demand is illustrated by a rectangular hyperbola, perfectly inelastic demand by a straight vertical line and perfectly elastic demand by a straight horizontal line (see Figure 2.03).

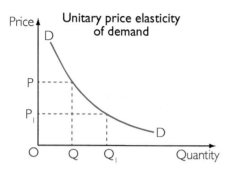

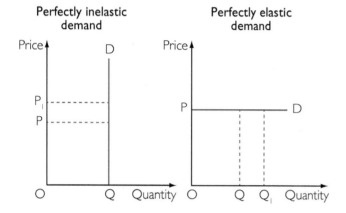

Figure 2.03

TERMS

Perfectly inelastic demand: demand remains unchanged when price alters.

Unitary elastic demand: change in price causes equal percentage change in demand.

Perfectly elastic demand: change in price causes infinite change in demand.

Factors affecting PED

- Availability of close substitutes – This is the main factor which influences the degree of PED. The existence of very similar products at a similar price would make demand elastic.

- The proportion of disposable income spent on the product – If the price of a product takes up a small proportion of income, demand is likely to be price inelastic. This is because a relatively large rise in price would not have much of an impact and so demand would be expected to fall by a smaller percentage.

- Whether the product is habit forming – If a product is habit forming, it will be relatively insensitive to price changes.

- Whether it is a luxury or a necessity – A luxury is likely to have elastic demand whereas a necessity is likely to have inelastic demand.

- Whether its purchase can be postponed or not – If its purchase cannot be delayed, demand will be inelastic.

- Time period – Demand tends to be more elastic over time as consumers have longer to recognise the price change and to find alternatives.

PED for the same products can vary between countries with, for instance, what is viewed as a necessity in one country being viewed as a luxury in another country and the availability of substitutes varying between countries.

Progress check C

Explain two factors that could make demand for a product more price inelastic.

Implications of PED for revenue and business decisions

If demand is inelastic, a rise in price will cause a rise in revenue and a fall in price will cause a fall in revenue.

In contrast, if demand is elastic, price and revenue will move in opposite directions.

Discovering that demand for its product is elastic, would usually indicate to a firm that close substitutes are available. This knowledge may make the firm reluctant to raise its price, as it will expect to lose a significant proportion of its sales. It may, however, be tempted to lower its price, as it may be able to capture more of the market.

Firms may try to make their products seem unique through, for instance, advertising and brand names. If successful, this would make demand more inelastic, giving firms greater market power.

Firms may estimate PED figures by examining past changes in price and demand and by carrying out market research. In basing their business decisions on PED estimates, however, firms have to take care. This is because the figures are only estimates and PED can change over time.

2.03 Income elasticity of demand

Definition

Income elasticity of demand (YED) is a measure of the responsiveness of demand to a change in income. It is calculated using the following formula:

$$YED = \frac{\text{percentage change in quantity demanded}}{\text{percentage change in income}}$$

This can be abbreviated to: $YED = \%\Delta QD/\%\Delta Y$.

> ### TERM
>
> Income elasticity of demand (YED): measure of the responsiveness of demand to a change in income.

Range of income elasticities of demand

If YED is greater than one, demand is income elastic. This means that a change in income will cause a greater percentage change in demand. A YED of less than one, in contrast, means demand is income inelastic. In this case, a change in income will result in a smaller percentage change in demand. If YED is zero, a change in income will have no impact on demand.

Positive, negative and zero YED

Most products have positive income elasticity of demand. This means that a rise in income will result in an increase in demand and a fall in income will cause a fall in demand (see Figure 2.04). So common is this positive relationship, that products which exhibit it are known as normal goods. One category of normal goods is superior or luxury goods. These products have positive YED greater than one.

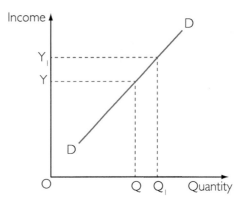

Figure 2.04

Products which have negative YED are called inferior goods. In the case of these products, income and demand are inversely related – an increase in income will cause a decrease in demand and a decrease in income will cause an increase in demand (see Figure 2.05) as shown below.

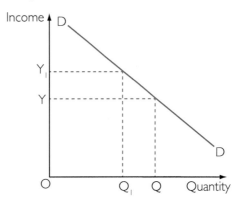

Figure 2.05

Over a certain income range, income elasticity of demand may be zero. For example, if a person's income rises from $30,000 to $35,000, she may not buy any more toothpaste than before.

Factors affecting YED

Products which have substitutes of a higher quality and a higher price are likely to be inferior goods. Expensive and desirable products may have positive income elasticity greater than one.

> ## Progress check D
>
> In most countries, services have an income elasticity of demand which is both positive and greater than one. Explain what this means.

Implications of YED for revenue and business decisions

As income usually rises, firms are likely to want to produce mainly normal goods. Producing a few inferior goods may protect firms from the risk of a recession; but usually the fear of the consumer finding out that they are making inferior goods will either stop the firms from producing them or will result in them trying to change their nature. To achieve the latter, firms may try to convince consumers that the products have, for instance, health benefits.

2.04 Cross elasticity of demand

Definition

Cross elasticity of demand (XED) is a measure of the responsiveness of demand for one product to a change in the price of another product. It is calculated using the following formula:

$$XED = \frac{\text{percentage change in the quantity demanded for another product}}{\text{percentage change in the price of one product}}$$

This can be abbreviated to:
XED = %ΔQD of Product A/%ΔP of Product B.

> ### TERM
>
> Cross elasticity of demand (XED): measure of the responsiveness of demand for one product to a change in the price of another product.

Positive, negative and zero cross elasticities of demand

Positive cross elasticity of demand means that a rise in the price of one product will result in an increase in demand for the other product. Similarly, a fall in the price of one product will cause demand for the other product to decrease. This is the case with substitutes (see Figure 2.06).

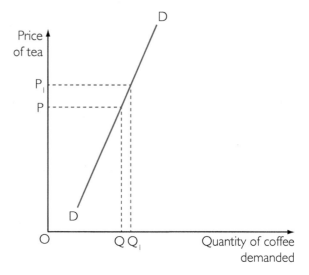

Figure 2.06

Negative cross elasticity of demand occurs when the change in the price of one product results in a change in the opposite direction of demand for the other product. Complements have negative XED. For instance, a rise in the price of PCs may result in a decrease in demand for printers, which are bought to be used with PCs (see Figure 2.07).

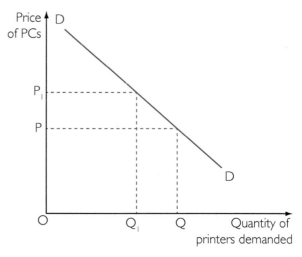

Figure 2.07

Zero cross elasticity of demand means that a change in the price of one product has no influence on demand for the other product. In this case the products are independent of each other.

Factors affecting XED

- The closer two products are as substitutes, the higher the positive XED figure will be.

- The higher the negative XED figure is, the closer the two products are as complements.

Progress check E

How does the cross elasticity of demand between models of car and petrol differ from the cross elasticity of demand between one model and another model of cars?

Implications of XED for revenue and business decisions

Firms have to be aware of the extent to which their products have close substitutes. The existence of close substitutes provides both a threat and a challenge for a firm. It has to be aware that raising its price may lose some of its customers. It may, however, be able to attract customers away from rivals by lowering price.

Knowledge about the existence of complements can help a firm to increase its revenue. A firm may offer one product at a lower price if it is purchased with a more expensive complement. For instance, a firm may seek to sell more TVs by offering to sell a CD player at a reduced price with every TV purchased.

Revision activity A

Data on a firm producing wrapping paper	
Luxury wrapping paper	Standard wrapping paper
PED = −0.5	PED = −2.0
YED = 2.5	YED = 0.5
XED in relation to rival brand = 0.2	XED in relation to rival brand = 1.5
XED in relation to own brand of luxury gift tags = −0.1	XED in relation to own brand of standard gift tags = −2.0

a   Why might the PED figures seem to be wrong, but why might they be right?

b   What should the firm do to the price of each of its products to raise revenue?

c   What should the firm do to the price of each type of gift tags?

d   In the long run, which type of wrapping paper should the firm specialise in?

2.05 Supply

Definition

Supply is the ability and willingness to sell a product.

Supply is not the same thing as production. A firm may, for example, produce 8,000 cars in a month but if the price has fallen, it may only offer 5,000 for sale. It may store the other 3,000 waiting for the price to rise.

Individual and market supply

Individual supply is the amount a firm is willing and able to sell at each and every price. A supply curve can be plotted to show how much an individual firm would be prepared to sell at different prices. A supply curve is drawn from a supply schedule. Price and supply are directly related.

A market supply curve shows the total supply for a product. The market supply is found by adding up the amount supplied by individual firms at different prices.

TERMS

Individual supply: the amount a firm is willing to sell at each and every price.

Market supply: the total supply of a product.

Factors that affect supply

Among the factors that affect supply are:

- price – As mentioned above a rise in price would be expected to cause a rise in supply. The higher price will provide a greater incentive to produce the product and will provide revenue to cover the extra costs involved in producing more.

- costs of production – An increase in costs of production, such as wages, will cause a decrease in supply.

- advances in technology – These are likely to increase the speed and ease of production. They are also likely to lower costs of production and so result in a higher supply.

- indirect taxes – The imposition of indirect taxes adds an extra cost on firms and so reduce supply.

- subsidies – A subsidy given to a producer is the equivalent of a fall in the cost of production and causes an increase in supply.

- weather conditions and diseases – A period of bad weather or a disease may cause a decrease in the supply of agricultural products.

Progress check F

Explain three factors that could increase the supply of rice in a country.

Movements along and shifts in supply curves

A movement along a supply curve can only be caused by a change in the price of the product itself. A rise in price will cause an extension in supply. This movement can also be referred to as a decrease in quantity supplied (see Figure 2.08).

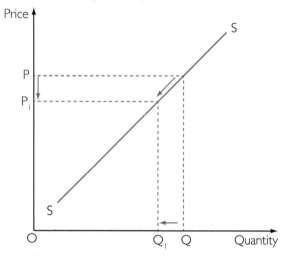

Figure 2.08

A change in any influence on the supply of a product other than its own price will result in new quantities being supplied at each and every price. As a result, the supply curve will shift its position. A shift to the right of the supply curve is called an increase in supply. Higher quantities are supplied at each and every price (see Figure 2.09).

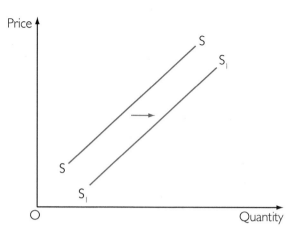

Figure 2.09

A decrease in supply with lower quantities being supplied at each and every price is illustrated by a shift to the left of the supply curve.

2.06 Price elasticity of supply

Definition

Price elasticity of supply (PES) is a measure of the responsiveness of supply to a change in the price of the product. It is calculated by using the formula below:

$$PES = \frac{\text{percentage change in quantity supplied}}{\text{percentage change in price}}$$

This can be abbreviated to: PED = %ΔQS/%ΔP.

TERM

Price elasticity of supply (PES): measure of the responsiveness of supply to a change in the price of a product.

Range of price elasticities of supply

As price and supply are directly related, PES is a positive figure. A PES figure greater than one and less than infinity means that supply is elastic, with a change in price causing a greater percentage change in quantity supplied.

A PES figure of less than one and greater than zero indicates inelastic supply. In this case, supply is not very responsive to a change in price, with a change in price resulting in a smaller percentage change in quantity supplied.

Supply may also be perfectly inelastic, unitary elastic and perfectly elastic. Perfectly inelastic supply means that a change in price has no effect on the quantity supplied. Unitary elasticity occurs when a change in price causes an equal percentage change in supply. Perfectly elastic supply means that a change in price will cause an infinite change in quantity supplied (see Figure 2.10).

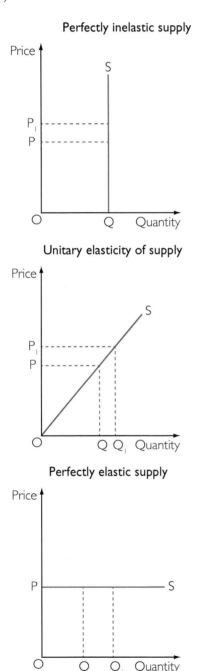

Factors that influence PES

The main factors that influence PES are whether the product can be stored, the time it takes to produce it and time itself. A product will have an elastic supply if it is non-perishable, can be stored at low cost, and is quick to produce. In this case, supply can be easily adjusted to changes in price.

Over time the supply of most products becomes more elastic as there is more opportunity to make adjustments to the factors of production being employed.

The supply of manufactured products is usually more elastic than agricultural products. Plants take time to grow and livestock to mature.

Firms benefit from making the supply more elastic. Their profits are likely to be higher if they can easily and quickly raise the quality supplied when the price rises and can easily withdraw supplies from the market when price falls.

Revision activity B

A rise in the price of a particular model of car from $12,000 to $15,000 results in an extension in supply from 500 to 600 a week.

a Calculate the price elasticity of supply.

b Is supply elastic or inelastic?

c Would the car firm want to change its price elasticity supply?

d If the car firm does want to change its PES, how could it achieve this?

TIP

In calculating any type of elasticity, remember that it is the variable that is causing the change that is at the bottom of the equation (the denominator) and the variable that is being influenced that appears on the top (the numerator).

Figure 2.10

2.07 Demand and supply analysis

Equilibrium price and disequilibrium

A market is in **equilibrium** when demand and supply are equal. In this situation, there will be no reason for price or quantity to change. The market will clear, with no surplus or shortage as shown in Figure 2.11.

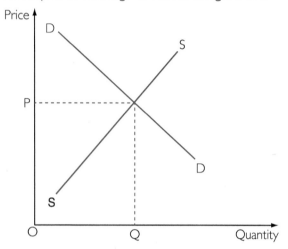

Figure 2.11

Disequilibrium occurs when demand and supply are not equal. If demand exceeds supply, a shortage will occur. This shortage is likely to result in price rising until demand and supply are again equal (see Figure 2.12).

In contrast, if supply is greater than demand, a surplus will result. The surplus will put downward pressure on price until equilibrium is restored, as shown in Figure 2.13.

TERMS

Equilibrium: when demand and supply are equal.

Disequilibrium: when demand and supply are not equal.

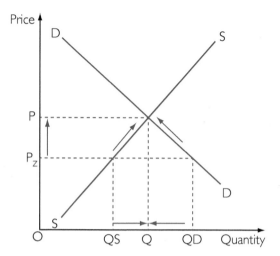

Figure 2.12

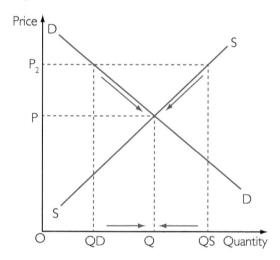

Figure 2.13

Effects of changes in supply and demand on equilibrium price and quantity

An increase in demand will result in a rise in price and an extension in supply. A decrease in demand will cause a fall in price and a contraction in supply.

An increase in supply will result in a fall in price and an extension in demand. A decrease in supply will push up the price which, in turn, will cause a contraction in demand.

Applications of demand and supply

Demand and supply analysis enables economists to make predictions about changes in market conditions.

Governments apply demand and supply analysis to consider the effects of taxes and subsidies. For instance, the imposition of an indirect tax effectively increases firms' costs of production. This will cause supply to decrease. The decrease in supply will cause price to rise and demand to contract. How much the price rises and the quantity bought and sold falls, will be influenced by the size of the tax and PED and PES.

Firms use demand and supply analysis to decide on their production and prices.

TIP

In analysing changes in demand and supply, it is important to get the order of events correct. Explain whether it is a change in demand or in supply that has started the move away from the initial equilibrium. Then explain what happened to price and finally how demand or supply has responded to the change in price.

Demand and supply relationships

Complements are said to be in joint demand. The two products are bought to be used together.

Substitutes are sometimes said to be in alternative demand. A person may switch from one product to a rival product.

Some products are in joint supply. This means that they are produced together e.g. lamb and wool. Most products are, however, in competitive supply. This means that if a firm produces more of one product, it will produce less of another.

Progress check G

A firm produces both blankets and duvets. Explain what effect a fall in the price of blankets is likely to have on its supply of blankets and duvets.

2.08 The role of the price mechanism

Prices allow consumers to transmit their preferences to producers. They signal to producers changes in their demand. If consumers want more of a product and are prepared to pay for it, the price of the product will rise. A higher price will provide an incentive for firms to respond by supplying more of the product.

Changes in prices reallocate resources away from producing products that are falling in demand towards those that are increasing in demand. If demand exceeds supply, price will rise and the products will be sold to those who can afford the higher price. Changes in price should ensure that the market clears with no products being unsold and no consumers who are willing and able to pay the market price, unable to purchase it.

Progress check H

How does the price mechanism ration products?

2.09 Consumer surplus and producer surplus

Definition

Consumer surplus is the difference between what consumers are willing to pay for a product and the amount they actually do. For instance, one person may be prepared to pay $20, another person $18, a third

$15 and a fourth $11. If the actual price charged is $11, the first person would enjoy $9 consumer surplus, the second person $7, the third $4 and the fourth zero. On a diagram, consumer surplus is the area above the price line and below the demand curve (see Figure 2.14).

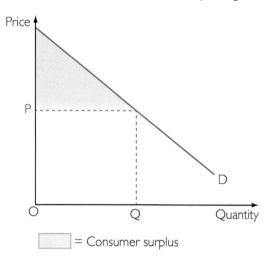

= Consumer surplus

Figure 2.14

Producer surplus is the difference between what firms are willing and able to sell a product for and what they are actually paid. For instance, a firm may have been prepared to accept $9 for a product but if it is paid $12, it will have received $3 in producer surplus. On a diagram, producer surplus is the area above the supply curve and below the price line (see Figure 2.15).

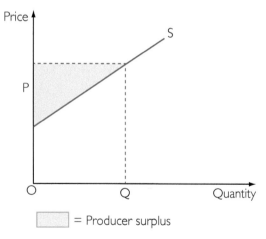

= Producer surplus

Figure 2.15

The significance of consumer surplus and producer surplus

Consumer surplus plus producer surplus (total surplus) is maximised when a market is in equilibrium as shown in Figure 2.16. The equilibrium outcome is an efficient outcome.

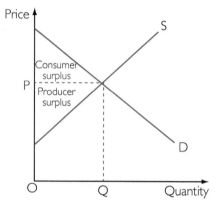

Figure 2.16

If the market is in disequilibrium total surplus will not be maximised. Figure 2.17 shows that at the disequilibrium price of PW total surplus is PWABC. Raising price to PX and increasing the quantity traded to QX would increase total surplus by BCD.

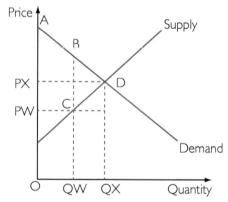

Figure 2.17

Progress check I

Why does the amount of consumer surplus received from the purchase of a product differ between consumers?

TERMS

Consumer surplus: the difference between the price consumers are willing to pay for a product and the price they actually pay.

Producer surplus: the difference between the price firms are willing to accept for a product and the price they actually receive.

More mutually beneficial transactions make society better off and so increases total surplus.

A decrease in supply will raise price, reduce the quantity traded and decrease consumer surplus and producer surplus.

A decrease in demand will reduce price, lower the quantity traded and decrease consumer surplus and producer surplus.

A decrease in the quantity traded lowers total surplus.

The effect on consumer surplus and producer surplus of changes in equilibrium price and quantity

An increase in supply will reduce price, increase the quantity traded and increase consumer surplus and producer surplus.

An increase in demand will raise price, increase the quantity traded and increase consumer surplus and producer surplus.

TIP

The concepts of consumer surplus and producer surplus can be used to assess the impact of changes in markets on economic welfare and to compare the performance of different market structures.

Mind maps

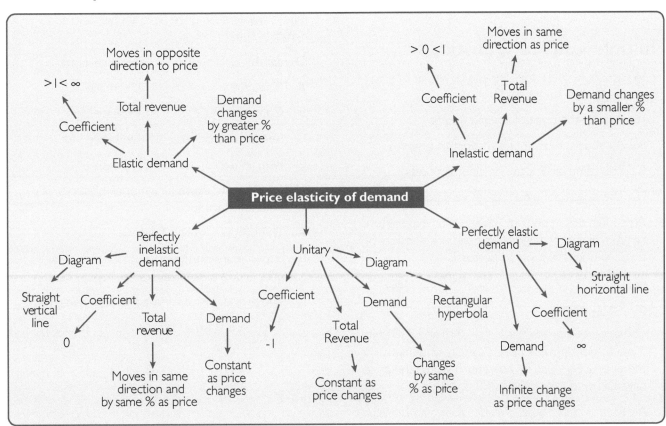

Mind map 2.01: Price elasticity of demand

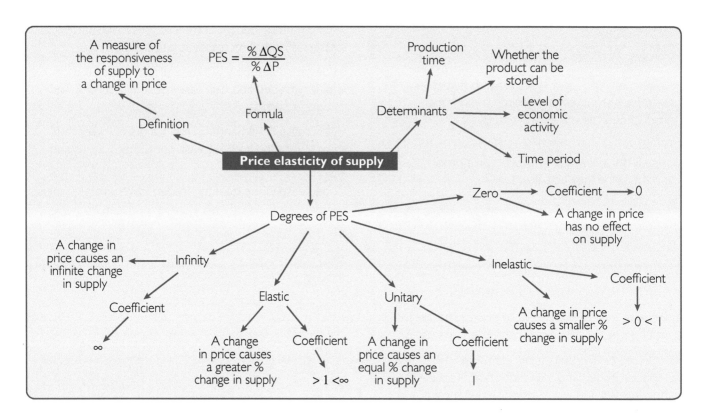

Mind map 2.02: Price elasticity of supply

Exam-style Questions

Multiple Choice Questions

1   What would cause the demand curve for cinema tickets to shift to the right?

   A   A fall in the price of cinema tickets

   B   A rise in the price of transport to cinemas

   C   The removal of a tax on cinema tickets

   D   The release of a number of very popular films

2   A product falls in price by 8% and total expenditure remains unchanged. What type of price elasticity of demand does the product possess?

   A   Elastic   C   Perfectly inelastic

   B   Perfectly elastic   D   Unitary

3   The price of a product is initially $10 and 200 units are sold per day. The price elasticity of demand for the product is −0.8. By how much would the price have to fall to raise sales by 80 units?

   A $1   B $3.2   C $5   D $8

4   Demand for a product is price inelastic. What effect will a rise in price have on demand and total revenue?

	Demand	Total revenue
A	Contract	Decrease
B	Contract	Increase
C	Remain unchanged	Decrease
D	Remain unchanged	Increase

5   What is likely to cause a high price elasticity of demand for a product?

   A   The product is habit forming.

   B   Expenditure on the product forms a small proportion of total spending.

   C   The product is considered to be a necessity.

   D   There are close substitutes to the product.

6

Price of Product X ($)	Quantity demanded of Product X	Quantity demanded of Product Y
10	200	500
15	180	600
20	120	800

Table 2.01

What is the cross elasticity of demand for Product Y when the price of Product X rises from $10 to $15?

A 0.2   B 0.4   C 0.6   D 0.8

7 What does a cross elasticity of demand figure of −0.2 indicate about the relationship between two products?

A Close complements

B Distant complements

C Close substitutes

D Distant substitutes

8 The price elasticity of supply of a product is 0.8. Initially the price of the product is $20 and the quantity sold is 2,000. The price then rises to $30. What will now be the firm's revenue?

A $36,000   C $84,000

B $40,000   D $108,000

9 Figure 2.18 shows the demand and supply curves of laptops. The initial equilibrium position is X.

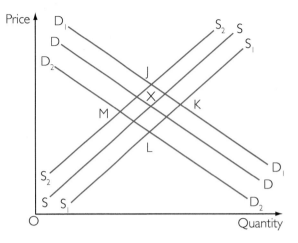

Figure 2.18

What will be the new equilibrium position if incomes rise and advances in technology reduce the cost of producing laptops?

A J   B K   C L   D M

10 Figure 2.19 shows the initial demand and supply curves of a product. The supply curve then shifts to S1. What is the change in consumer surplus?

A XYZ   C PP_1XZ

B PWZ   D Q_1YZQ

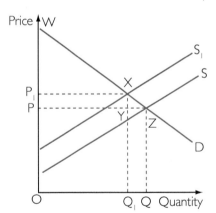

Figure 2.19

Data Response Question

Fluctuations in agricultural markets

Prices of agricultural products can fluctuate significantly. Two recent examples are changes in the prices of cotton and spices.

In 2015 the price of cotton fluctuated. It fell in the middle of the year. This was due to a bumper harvest in India caused by good weather conditions and due to China selling some of its stockpile of cotton. The price started to rise towards the end of the year.

Output of cotton in 2015 (millions of bales)	
China	30
India	30
USA	16
Pakistan	11
Brazil	7
World	120

Table 2.02

Spices are also produced by a number of countries that produce cotton. Pakistan, for instance, is a major producer of onions, garlic, chillies and coriander. The price of spices rose in 2015 because an increasing number of people, not only in Asia but also in the US and Europe, were buying spices to use in their cooking. Demand for spices also rose because of their increased use in health products and in natural colouring.

The higher prices in 2016 were encouraging more farmers to devote more of their land to spices but it was expected that it would take some time for this to increase the quantity supplied. For instance, it takes five years to grow nutmeg.

a   What was Pakistan's share of the global cotton market in 2015?   [1]

b   What might cause a fall in the price of cotton?   [2]

c   What effect would the rise in the price of spices have on the price of natural colouring?   [2]

d   Does the information suggest that the supply of spices is elastic or inelastic? Explain your answer.   [3]

e   Analyse, with a demand and supply diagram, why the price of spices rose in 2015.   [6]

f   Discuss whether farmers always benefit from a rise in the price of their products.   [6]

Essay Questions

1   a   Explain what cross elasticity of demand figures indicate about the relationship between products.   [8]

    b   Discuss whether a fall in the price of a product will always be accompanied by a reduction in the quantity traded of that product.   [12]

2   a   Explain why price moves towards equilibrium in a free market and why the equilibrium price may change over time.   [8]

    b   Discuss whether all firms in a country will welcome a change in people's income.   [12]

REVISION TIP

Remember the main purpose of revision in economics is not to learn facts. It is to develop your skills, including your ability to make links between causes and effects, problems and policies, theory and real world examples. For instance, you should recognise that a rise in aggregate demand would be expected to raise real GDP and lower unemployment. You also need to develop the ability to think critically about the sequence of events and to question the extent to which the events will happen and, indeed, whether they will happen at all. If you start to think like an economist, you will enjoy the subject more and you will perform better in examinations.

Government microeconomic intervention

3.01 Price controls

Maximum price controls

A maximum price is a price ceiling. The price is not allowed to go above this limit, although it can be below it.

To have any effect, a maximum price has to be set below the equilibrium price.

A government may impose a maximum price on a product for a number of reasons. These include:

- encouraging consumption
- to make it more affordable for the poor
- to counterbalance the power of monopolies

A maximum price can result in shortages as shown in Figure 3.01. Demand exceeds supply, giving rise to a shortage. Some willing buyers will be unable to purchase the product.

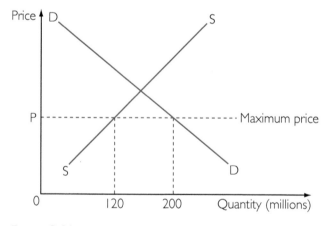

Figure 3.01

A rationing system may have to be introduced with a maximum price. There is a risk that a maximum price will result in a shadow market developing with producers selling the product illegally at higher prices.

Minimum price controls

A minimum price is a price floor. The price is not allowed to go below this limit, although it can be above it.

A government may set a minimum price to discourage consumption of a product or to increase the income of producers.

To have any effect, a minimum price must be set above the equilibrium price.

Among the disadvantages of a minimum price are that a surplus will be created as shown in Figure 3.02. Some of the supply will be unsold.

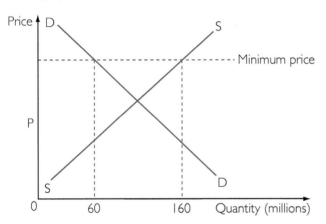

Figure 3.02

There will be costs involved in buying up the surplus to maintain the price and in storing the surplus. The higher price will make it less accessible to the poor.

Remember that to have any impact, a maximum price must be set below the market equilibrium price and a minimum price must be set above the market price.

3.02 Price stabilisation

A government may operate a buffer stock to stabilise the price of a metal, mineral or an agricultural product that is non-perishable. A buffer stock is a store of a commodity.

Buffer stock managers buy the commodity when market prices are threatening to push the price below the lower limit and sell it when market prices are threatening to raise the price above the upper limit. To ensure that buffer stock managers do not have to spend large amounts on storing the product, or run out of money buying the product, the price limits have to be set close to the long run equilibrium price.

Price stabilisation can encourage producers to plan ahead and invest in new production methods.

Progress check A

Operators of buffer stocks buy a commodity more often than they sell it. What does this indicate about where the intervention upper and lower price limits are set?

3.03 Taxes

Types of taxes

Taxes may be categorised in a number of ways:

- Direct and indirect taxes. Direct taxes are paid directly by the tax payers to the tax authorities. Direct taxes are taxes on income and wealth e.g. corporation tax, income tax and inheritance tax. Governments impose direct taxes to raise revenue, influence total demand and affect the distribution of income. Indirect taxes are paid to the tax authorities, not directly by consumers but by the firms and sellers of the products. They are taxes on spending such as VAT (value added tax) and GST (goods and services tax or general sales tax) and excise duty. Governments impose indirect taxes to raise revenue and to influence the products consumed and produced. A tax may be used to reduce consumption of a demerit good.

- Progressive, proportional and regressive tax. A progressive tax takes a higher percentage of the income of the rich, a proportional tax takes the same percentage and a regressive tax takes a smaller percentage.

TERMS

Direct tax: a tax on income and wealth e.g. income tax.

Indirect tax: taxes added onto the cost of goods and paid by sellers of the product, e.g. fuel, alcohol and cigarettes.

Progressive tax: a tax which takes a larger percentage of the income of the rich.

Proportional tax: taxes the same percentage of income as tax for all individuals.

Regressive tax: a tax which takes a larger percentage of the income of the poor.

Taxes: money paid by individuals to governments through spending (VAT, GST) and income (corporation tax, income tax, inheritance tax).

TIP

In assessing whether a tax is progressive, proportional or regressive – remember it is not the amount of the tax paid but the percentage of income paid in tax that is the determinant.

Average and marginal rates of tax

- The average tax rate is the percentage of a person's income paid in tax. It is tax paid/income: T/Y.
- The marginal tax rate is the percentage of extra income paid in tax. It is $\Delta T/\Delta Y$.
- In the case of a progressive tax, the marginal rate of tax is lower than the average tax rate when the tax is regressive. The marginal and average tax rates are the same in the case of a proportional tax.

Revision activity A

A country's income tax system allows a person to earn $8,000 free of tax. Her income between $8,000 and $20,000 is taxed at 15%, her income between $20,000 and $40,000 is taxed at 30% and her income above $40,000 is taxed at 50%. The woman earns $54,000.

a How much taxable income does the woman have?

b How much tax does the woman pay?

c What is her average tax rate?

d What is her marginal tax rate?

e Is this tax system progressive, proportional or regressive?

The impact and incidence of taxes

The impact of a tax is concerned with how a tax affects a market and/or the economy. The imposition of an indirect tax on a product will add an additional cost to producers. Higher cost of production will cause a shift of the supply curve to the left. The decrease in supply will cause a rise in price and a contraction in demand. An increase in income tax may reduce consumer expenditure and output.

The incidence of a tax is concerned with who bears the burden of the tax. Some or all of an indirect tax may be passed from the producers on to the consumers. Consumers bear most of the tax the more price inelastic demand is and the more price elastic supply is. In this case, producers can pass most of the tax on in the form of a higher price, knowing that demand will not contract significantly. Producers bear more of the tax the more price elastic demand is and the more price inelastic supply is.

Specific and ad valorem taxes

A specific tax is the same charge whatever the price of the product. The imposition of a specific tax will cause a parallel shift of the supply curve to the left as shown in Figure 3.03.

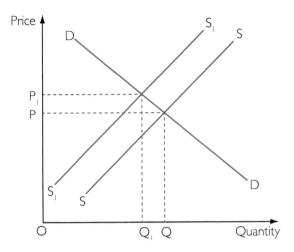

Figure 3.03

An ad valorem, that is percentage tax, will mean that the higher the total amount charged in tax the higher the price. An ad valorem tax will cause a non-parallel shift in the supply curve as shown in Figure 3.04.

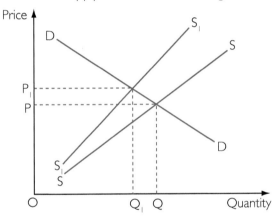

Figure 3.04

A tax may be placed on demerit goods which governments consider are over-consumed and over-produced. Taxing such products will raise the price and so reduce the quantity traded. This change in market activity may increase welfare. A tax will raise revenue and it works with the market, allowing the market to clear.

As it is difficult to measure the harmful effects of demerit goods, a tax may be set too high or too low. Among the other possible disadvantages of a tax are that it may make a domestic industry less competitive, may fall more heavily on the poor, may be politically unpopular, will be less effective when demand is inelastic, there is cost involved in collecting taxes and they may be inflationary.

Progress check B

In what way is the shift in the supply curve caused by the imposition of a specific tax and one caused by the imposition of an ad valorem tax the same and in what way is it different?

TIP

It is useful to give examples of taxes in your own country in assessing the effects of taxation.

Canons of taxation

The canons of taxation are the characteristics of a good tax. Adam Smith identified four qualities (certainty, convenience, economy and equity) and more have been added since his time. Among the qualities are:

- certainty – This means that taxpayers should know how much they have to pay and when, how and where they have to pay the tax.

- convenience – The tax should be easy and straightforward to pay and collect.

- economy – The tax should be cheap to administer and collect.

- equity – This is the idea that the tax should be fair. Economists have developed this criterion by distinguishing between horizontal and vertical equity. Horizontal equity involves people in the same circumstances paying the same amount of tax. Vertical equity involves the greatest burden being placed on those who are most able to pay the tax. Some economists also refer to equity based on the benefit principle. This is the idea that the amount of tax people should pay should be based on the benefits they receive from government spending.

- difficult to evade and avoid – It should be hard for people and firms to reduce their tax burdens by not declaring their taxable income or by other ways of tax avoidance.

- flexibility – The tax should be simple to change and should be adaptable to changing economic circumstances.

- avoidance or minimisation of disincentive effects – In practice, it is difficult to determine if increases in income tax will reduce the incentive to work. This is because whilst some workers may cut back their hours, others may work longer to maintain their net pay and a relatively high number may not be able to change the hours they work.

Subsidies

A subsidy is a payment by the government to consumers or producers to encourage the consumption and production of a product. A subsidy to consumers would be expected to increase demand, shifting the demand curve to the right. Subsidies to producers are more common than subsidies to consumers.

A subsidy to producers will shift the supply curve to the right, lower price and cause supply to extend. A specific subsidy will cause a parallel shift of the supply curve to the right whereas an ad valorem subsidy will cause a non-parallel shift. Figure 3.05 shows the effect of a specific subsidy.

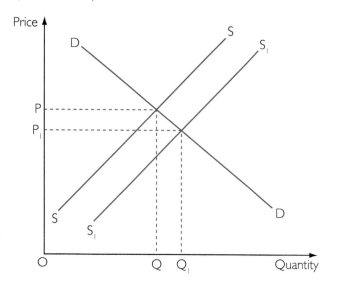

Figure 3.05

A subsidy may result in the quantity traded moving towards a level which benefits society more. For example, it may increase the amount of a merit good which is bought and sold. A subsidy works with the market and should lead to market clearing.

There is a risk that a subsidy may be set too low or too high. There is also a chance that not much of the subsidy may be passed on to consumers in the form of a lower price. The subsidy will be less effective if demand is inelastic, there may be a time lag involved before producers can alter supply and it will involve an opportunity cost as the government spending could have been used for another purpose.

TERM

Subsidies: payments by the government to consumers or producers to encourage production and consumption.

TIP

Demand and supply diagrams are a very useful tool in assessing and evaluating the impact of taxes and subsidies. They can enable you to explore the impact on price, quantity traded and how consumers, producers and the government are affected.

Transfer payments

Transfer payments are payments made by one person or group to another person or group not in return for a good or service. The most common form of transfer payments is money transferred by the government from taxpayers to the recipients of state benefits such as retirement pensions and unemployment benefits.

Transfer payments are, in effect, negative taxes. They add to some people's income without them producing goods or services in return.

Transfer payments redistribute purchasing power usually from the rich to the poor. Some state benefits increase the ability of the poor to buy basic necessities.

Revision activity B

Categorise the following into those that are transfer payments and those that are not transfer payments:

1 State scholarships
2 Pay of teachers
3 Pay of public sector workers
4 Child benefit
5 Housing benefit
6 Charitable donations
7 Pay of actors
8 Dividend payments.

Direct provision of goods and services

A government may provide both public and merit goods. In the case of public goods, a government has to finance their production. It may produce them through state owned enterprises, also called nationalised industries. It may also pay private sector firms to produce them. Merit goods may be provided free or at low prices to consumers to encourage their consumption and to make them accessible to all.

The quantity of goods and services which a government provides is influenced by two key factors. One is the extent to which it considers that free market forces will fail to produce an outcome that will benefit society. The other is its ability to raise tax revenue.

Progress check D

Explain three reasons why a government may provide free primary school education.

TERMS

Transfer payments: payments made by one person/group to another person/group which isn't in return for a good or service, e.g. benefits.

Direct provision: the government supplying a product to consumers.

Privatisation

Privatisation involves the transfer of assets and activities from the public sector to the private sector. It may take the form of denationalising an industry, the sale of government shares in private sector firms and contracting out services.

If a government is concerned that there is a risk that privatising an industry may not increase efficiency or may cause inequity, it may decide to regulate the industry. This may involve placing restrictions on price rises. For instance, a government may pass a law which limits price rises to a figure equivalent to a rise in the price level minus one or two percentage points. It may also seek to stop the firm or firms from using their market power to prevent the entry of new firms.

Arguments in favour of privatisation include increasing efficiency by reducing bureaucracy, increasing the profit motive and possibly increasing competition. Other arguments are to raise government revenue in the short term, to widen share ownership and to reduce government expenditure in the case of loss making state owned enterprises.

Arguments against privatisation include long term loss of government revenue in the case of profitable state owned enterprises, the possibility of abuse of market power if the industry becomes a private sector monopoly, private sector firms not taking into account costs and benefits to third parties and a general loss of government control over the economy.

TERM

Privatisation: transferring assets and activities from the public sector to the private sector.

Progress check E

What is the connection between privatisation and different economic systems?

Nationalisation

Nationalisation involves a government taking firms and industries into public ownership.

A government may operate the industry in the public interest with the aim being to maximise welfare rather than profits and with decisions being based on the full effects of consumption and production on society. It may, for instance, charge low prices for essential products.

Some industries may be more efficient with one producer (a natural monopoly). If such industries are in the private sector, the producers may exploit their market power by charging high prices.

Operating some industries may make it easier for a government to achieve its macroeconomic objectives, such as full employment and price stability.

A government may operate what are called strategic industries. These are industries that the government considers to be essential for the development and survival of the country, for example, the defence industry.

There are a number of arguments against nationalisation. The lack of a profit motive and lack of competition may result in a state owned enterprise becoming complacent. This, in turn, may lead to lower quality and a slower response to changes in consumer demand. State officials may lack business expertise and political interference may reduce efficiency.

TERM

Nationalisation: transferring assets and activities from the private sector to the public sector and placing them under government control.

TIP

It is useful to give examples of privatised and nationalised industries from your own country, and the extent and effect privatisation has had in your country, when assessing and evaluating privatisation and nationalisation.

Revision activity C

Identify, in each case, a government policy measure that could be used to correct the following examples of market failure.

a   Price instability in the rice market

b   The smoking of cigarettes causing health problems for non-smokers

c   Old people not being able to afford a healthy diet

d   A lack of provision of street lighting

e   Under-consumption of dental treatment

Mind maps

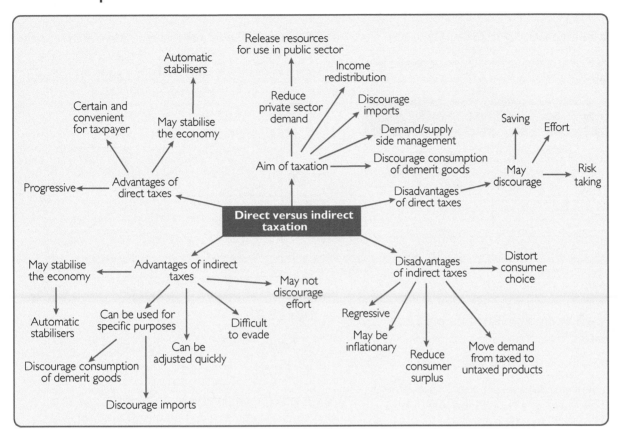

Mind map 3.01: Direct versus indirect taxes

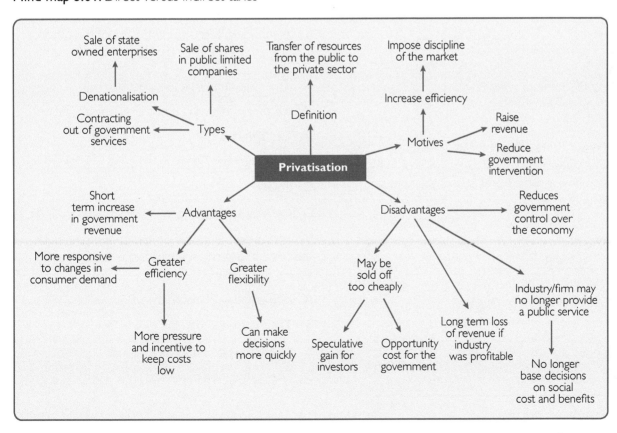

Mind map 3.02: Privatisation

Exam-style Questions

Multiple Choice Questions

1 The demand and supply schedule for a product is shown below.

Price ($)	Quantity demanded per week	Quantity supplied per week
1	3,000	1,800
2	2,800	2,100
3	2,500	2,500
4	2,100	3,200
5	1,500	4,000
6	700	5,000

The government sets a maximum price of $4 per unit. What will be the shortage of the product after four weeks?

A 0   B 1,100   C 2,500   D 4,400

2 A government decides that product X is a demerit good and product Y is a public good. Which policy measures is it likely to adopt in relation to the two products?

	Product X	Product Y
A	Tax	Directly provides
B	Subsidise	Impose a maximum price
C	Directly provides	Subsidise
D	Impose a maximum price	Tax

3 Figure 3.06 shows the market for an agricultural product. The government maintains a price of P_F by intervention buying. Which area shows the amount that government spends?

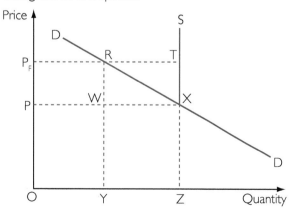

Figure 3.06

A RTX   C OPFRY

B YRTZ   D PPFTX

4 Figure 3.07 shows that the imposition of an indirect tax shifts the supply curve to the left. What is the total tax revenue received by the government?

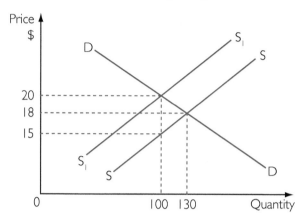

Figure 3.07

A $200   C $500

B $300   D $650

5 A government intervenes in a market and as a result the demand curve shifts to the right. Which government measure could cause this effect?

A A subsidy granted to consumers of the product

B A subsidy granted to producers of the product

C The imposition of a direct tax

D The imposition of an indirect tax

6 Which of the following is not a canon of taxation?

A Certainty

B Convenience

C Equity

D General acceptability

7 Which government policy measure would reduce the price of a product and increase the quantity traded in the market?

A The granting of a subsidy

B The imposition of a tax

C The setting of a maximum price

D The setting of a minimum price

8 A government replaces progressive taxes with regressive taxes. What is the likely outcome?

	Distribution of income	Marginal rate of tax
A	More even	Decrease
B	More even	Increase
C	More uneven	Decrease
D	More uneven	Increase

9 Which change would cause a decrease in price and a decrease in the quantity sold?

A The granting of a subsidy to consumers of the product

B The granting of a subsidy to producers of the product

C The removal of a price ceiling on the product maintained by government legislation and government purchases of surpluses

D The removal of a price floor on the product maintained by government legislation and rationing

10 In Figure 3.08, SS is the original supply curve of a firm. If an ad valorem subsidy is granted to producers of the product what will be the new supply curve?

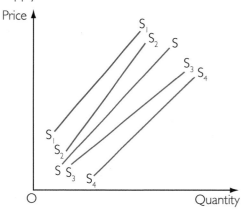

Figure 3.08

A S_1S_1 B S_2S_2 C S_3S_3 D S_4S_4

Data Response Questions

1 Changing prices in Cuba

In recent years the Cuban government has been removing its subsidies on a number of products and the maximum prices which had been imposed on them. Among the subsidies which have been removed are subsidies on cigarettes, salt, toothpaste, peas and potatoes. Before the subsidies were removed many Cubans were buying a number of these products including soap and toothpaste on illegal markets.

The removal of the subsidies caused the price of a bar of soap to rise from $0.03 to $0.21 and the price of toothpaste to increase from $0.08 to $0.32.

The removal of both the subsidies and maximum prices has had a significant effect on the poor. Cuban consumers, in general, are not happy with the measures but the government has stated that the measures were necessary because of the shortage of government revenue.

a   Using a demand and supply diagram, analyse the effect of removing a subsidy on cigarettes.   [6]

b   Compare the change in the price of soap and in the price of toothpaste.   [2]

c   Does the information suggest that the subsidy given to soap and toothpaste was sufficient to achieve the price the government wanted?   [4]

d   Discuss whether it is more justifiable to subsidise soap than to subsidise potatoes.   [8]

2 India's tax reforms

In 2015 the Indian government was seeking to reform the country's tax system. It was planning to introduce a goods and service tax to replace a range of indirect taxes imposed by individual states.

The government made a number of changes in its 2015 budget. It raised the services tax to 14%. This tax is imposed on a number of services including those produced by restaurants, theatres and theme parks. The government also incorporated the education cess (tax) into the service tax. The education cess was introduced in 2004 as an addition to income tax. People and firms paid 3% of their income tax as an education cess to fund a number of educational projects.

Wealth tax was abolished but the surcharge on rich individuals and firms earning a high income was increased. The government mentioned that the cost of collecting the wealth tax had been high and that the forms which people and firms had been required to fill out were too complex.

The government announced that it was planning to cut corporation tax from 30% to 25% in a bid to increase job creation. Corporation tax was the single greatest source of tax between 2005 and 2015. Figure 3.09 shows how the Indian government's tax revenue changed over the period 2006–2012.

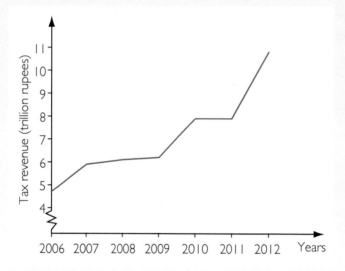

Figure 3.09

The government also mentioned that it was considering replacing subsidies on basic foods with cash payments for the poor.

a   Explain whether a goods and services tax is an indirect tax or a direct tax.   [2]

b   Explain how incorporating the education cess into the services tax may have affected the poor.   [5]

c   Would India's wealth tax have been classified as a good tax?   [3]

d   Using Figure 3.09, comment on whether it can be concluded that tax rates increased over the
period shown.   [4]

e   Discuss whether the poor would benefit more from subsidies on basic foods or from cash payments. [6]

Essay Questions

1 a Explain the difference between a maximum price and a minimum price. [8]

  b Discuss whether the introduction of an effective minimum price will benefit producers. [12]

2 a Explain the characteristics of a good tax. [8]

  b Discuss the effectiveness of government policy measures to correct market failure in the case of merit goods and demerit goods. [12]

REVISION TIP

Avoid ineffective revision. One of the most common ways that students try to revise is also one of the least effective. This way is just to re-read through class notes. Students who do this are trying to remember a mass of information which may have little meaning for them. You must also not leave your revision to the last minute. If you do this, you will feel very pressurised and you are unlikely to do well. In addition, it is important that you do not revise for long periods of time or when you are tired. Diminishing returns can set in relatively quickly.

Engage in active revision. This means to process the information you have learned, in order to develop your understanding, not only of the topics but also the links between topics. It also means developing your skills of application, analysis and evaluation. Undertaking a variety of revision methods will be both more rewarding and interesting.

Chapter 4

The macro economy

Learning summary

After you have studied this chapter, you should be able to:

- describe the shape and determinants of AD and AS curves, AD = C + I + G + (X − M)

- distinguish between a movement along and a shift in AD and AS

- analyse the interaction of AD and AS and the determination of the level of output, prices and employment

- define inflation

- describe degrees of inflation

- explain how inflation is measured

- distinguish between deflation and disinflation

- explain the distinction between money values and real data

- analyse the causes of inflation (cost-push and demand-pull inflation)

- describe the components of the balance of payments (using the IMF/OECD definition): current account, capital account, capital and financial account, balancing item

- explain the meaning of balance of payments equilibrium and disequilibrium

- explain the meaning of balance of payments disequilibrium in each component of the accounts

- discuss the consequences of balance of payments disequilibrium on the domestic and external economy

- define nominal, real and trade weighted exchange rates

- explain how the real and trade weighted exchange rates are measured

- explain how floating, fixed and a managed exchange rate are determined

- analyse the factors underlying changes in exchange rates

- explore the effects of changing exchange rates on the domestic and external economy using aggregate demand, Marshall-Lerner and J-curve analysis

- distinguish between depreciation and appreciation; and devaluation and depreciation

- describe how the terms of trade are measured

- analyse the causes of changes in the terms of trade

- discuss the impact of changes in the terms of trade

- distinguish between absolute advantage and comparative advantage

- describe free trade area, customs union, monetary union and full economic union

- explain trade creation and trade diversion

- explore the benefits of free trade, including the trading possibility curve

- explain the meaning of protectionism in the context of international trade

- describe the different methods of protection and their impact, for example, tariffs, import duties and quotas, export subsidies, embargoes, voluntary export restraints (VERs) and excessive administrative burdens ('red tape')

- evaluate the arguments in favour of protectionism

4.01 Aggregate demand and aggregate supply

Aggregate demand

Aggregate demand (AD) is the total demand for a country's output at a given price level. Aggregate demand is composed of consumer expenditure, investment, government spending and net exports (AD = C + I + G + X − M).

The aggregate demand curve slopes down from left to right. A movement along the AD curve is caused by a change in the price level. This is for three main reasons. One is that as the price level falls, the country's products become more internationally competitive. This is sometimes called the international trade effect. A lower price level also means that the savings people have enables them to buy more – the wealth effect. In addition, a decline in the price level is usually accompanied by a fall in the rate of interest which is likely to increase consumer expenditure and investment – the interest rate effect.

The aggregate demand curve will change its position if any of the components of AD changes for a reason other than a change in the price level. An increase in one or more of the components will cause a rightward shift whereas a decrease will cause a leftward shift (as shown in Figure 4.01)

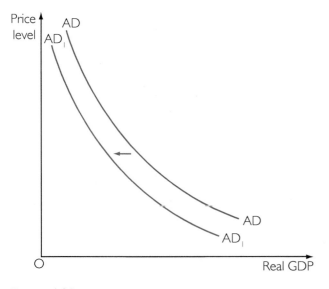

Figure 4.01

Components of aggregate demand

Consumer expenditure is spending by households on consumer goods and services. It is the largest component of the aggregate demand of most countries. Among the determinants of consumer expenditure are disposable income, confidence, the rate of interest, wealth, population size and the distribution of income.

Investment is spending on capital goods. It is the most unstable component of AD – it may rise significantly one year and fall by a noticeable amount the next year. The determinants of investment include disposable income, confidence, the rate of interest, advances in technology, corporation tax and government investment subsidies.

Government spending is spending by the government on goods and services. It is influenced by a range of factors. One is the level of economic activity. A government may spend more during a recession in order to stimulate economic activity. Other influences include the amount of tax revenue that can be raised, the dependency ratio and whether the country is at war or peace.

Net exports (export revenue minus import expenditure) are determined by income levels at home and abroad, the exchange rate and import restrictions.

> ## Progress check A
>
> Explain two reasons why a fall in profit levels may reduce investment.

Aggregate supply

Aggregate supply (AS) is the total supply that domestic producers are willing and able to sell at a given price level.

The elasticity of the aggregate supply curve can change over its length. When there is considerable spare capacity in the economy, the curve may be perfectly elastic. This is because it will be possible for firms to employ more resources without raising average costs. As real GDP approaches the full employment level, aggregate supply becomes more inelastic. This is because firms start to experience shortages of resources which increase their price. When the economy reaches full capacity, aggregate supply becomes perfectly inelastic.

A movement along the aggregate supply curve is caused by a change in the price level. A change in any influence other than a change in the price level will cause a shift in the AS curve. The causes of a shift in the supply curve are changes in costs of production and changes in the quantity or quality of resources. Specific reasons include rises in wage rates, subsidies, immigration of workers, net investment, improved education and training, and advances in technology. Figure 4.02 shows an increase in AS.

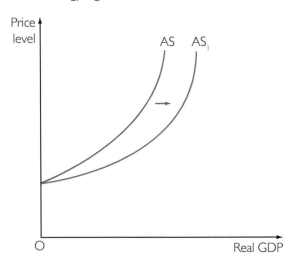

Figure 4.02

Progress check B

What effect would a widespread flood have on a country's aggregate supply?

TERMS

Consumer expenditure: money spent by households on consumer goods and services.

Investment: money spent on capital goods.

Government spending: money spent by government on goods and services.

Net exports: export revenue minus import expenditure.

Aggregate demand (AD): total demand for a country's output at a given price level.

Aggregate supply (AS): total supply that domestic producers are willing and able to sell at a given price level.

TERM

Exchange rate: price of a country's currency compared to other currencies.

Interaction of aggregate demand and aggregate supply

Macroeconomic equilibrium occurs where AD = AS. When this situation is met there is no pressure on the price level or the country's output (real Gross Domestic Product (GDP)).

An increase in AD occurring when there is considerable spare capacity may have no effect on the price level but will increase the country's output and employment. This is illustrated in Figure 4.03.

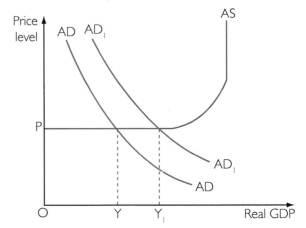

Figure 4.03

An increase in AD which takes place when the economy is beginning to experience shortages of resources will result in a rise in output, price level and employment. This is shown in Figure 4.04.

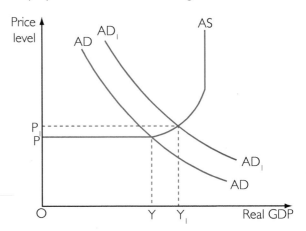

Figure 4.04

When an economy is operating at full capacity, an increase in AD will be purely inflationary. It will increase the price level but have no effect on output and employment as illustrated in Figure 4.05.

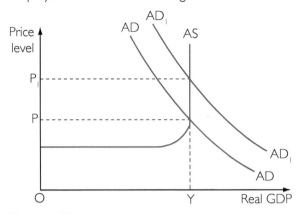

Figure 4.05

An increase in AS when an economy is initially producing at or close to full capacity would increase output and would put downward pressure on the price level. This is illustrated in Figure 4.06.

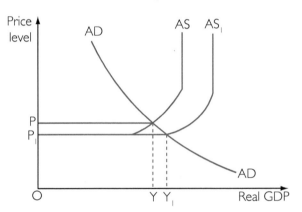

Figure 4.06

If an economy has considerable spare capacity, an increase in AS will increase productive capacity but will have no impact on output or the price level. This situation is shown in Figure 4.07.

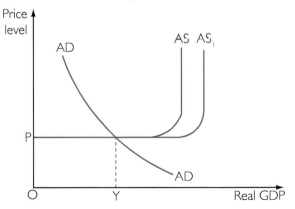

Figure 4.07

Governments aim for sustained economic growth which requires AD and AS to increase in line with each other (as shown in Figure 4.08).

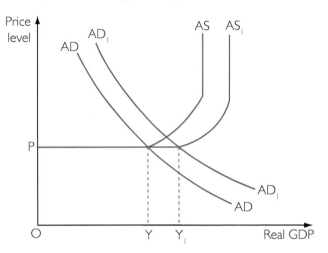

Figure 4.08

TERM

Sustained economic growth: where aggregate demand and aggregate supply increase in line with each other.

Revision activity A

Decide whether the following changes in Brazil's economy would have increased the country's aggregate demand, increased the country's aggregate supply, increased both the country's aggregate demand and aggregate supply, decreased the country's aggregate demand, decreased the country's aggregate supply, or decreased both the country's aggregate demand and aggregate supply.

a A rise in government spending on education

b An increase in net exports

c An increase in the money supply

d Net immigration

e A rise in unemployment

4.02 Inflation

The nature of inflation

Inflation is a sustained rise in the general price level, and so a fall in the value of money. Higher prices mean that each unit of the currency will buy less.

An increase in a country's general price level would mean that, on average, prices are rising. Some prices may be falling but overall the cost of living is rising with people having to pay more in total for the products they buy.

A creeping inflation rate is a low and steady rate of inflation. In contrast, hyperinflation is a very high rate of inflation. It is often taken to mean an inflation rate above 50%. It may be much higher. Zimbabwe, for example, experienced a monthly inflation rate of 3.5 million % in 2008. In 2015, the Zimbabwean Government phased out the local currency in favour of the US dollar. It exchanged Zimbabwean dollars for US dollars at the rate of 35 quadrillion (35,000,000,000,000,000) Zimbabwean dollars for US$1.

Accelerating inflation means that the general price level is increasing at a more rapid rate. Non-accelerating inflation is steady rate of inflation.

Stagflation is high inflation accompanied by high unemployment and low economic growth. Slumpflation is high inflation, high unemployment and a decrease in national output.

Unanticipated inflation arises when the inflation rate is not what people expected. It can make it difficult for firms and households to plan.

TERM

Inflation: a sustained rise in the general price level which causes a fall in the value of money.

Measuring inflation

One way governments assess what is happening to the general price level, is to calculate a consumer price index. This is a measure of the average change in the prices of a representative basket of goods and services purchased by households.

To calculate a consumer price index, a base year is selected. This should be a relatively standard year in which there were no unusual events. The base year is given an index figure of 100 and other years are compared to it. A survey is undertaken of household spending to find out people's spending patterns. The information gathered is used to decide which items to include in the representative basket and what weights to attach to them. Weights reflect the proportion spent on the products. The more people spend on an item, the more significant is a change in its price. Information on price changes of the products is collected from a range of retail outlets and suppliers. The price change is multiplied by its weight and then all are totalled to give the index figure. For example, if the consumer price index was 100 in 2012 and 108 in 2013, the inflation rate would be 8%.

Most economies measure a consumer price index. The UK government also measures the Retail Prices Index (RPI). This is a form of consumer price index but differs from most countries' consumer price indices in the sense that it includes mortgage payments and local taxation.

TERM

Consumer price index: measure of the average change in price of a representative basket of goods and services purchased by households.

Progress check C

What happens to the weight attached to food over time in most countries?

Deflation and disinflation

Deflation is a fall in the general price level. A fall in the price level caused by advances in technology can benefit an economy as it can make the country's products more internationally competitive. In contrast, a fall in the price level caused by a decrease in aggregate demand may be harmful as it may set in process a deflationary spiral with demand continuing to fall and unemployment rising.

Disinflation is a fall in the inflation rate. It means that the price level has risen more slowly than in the previous year.

TERMS

Deflation: fall in general price level which causes a rise in the value of money..

Disinflation: fall in the inflation rate.

The distinction between money values and real data

Money data is data measured in current prices, also referred to as nominal value. This means that the data has not been adjusted for inflation. If a person's wages are increased by 12%, this is a nominal increase.

Real data is data measured in constant prices. This means it has been adjusted for inflation. In the above example, if rate of inflation is 5% whilst the person's money wages have been increased by 12%, their real wages have increased by 12% − 5% = 7%.

Progress check D

What is meant by 'a fall in the real price of laptops'?

Causes of inflation

Cost-push inflation is caused by a decrease in aggregate supply. Such a decrease is, in turn, caused by increases in the costs of production. For instance, increases in the cost of oil or increases in wages, not matched by increases in productivity, may raise costs which firms pass on to consumers in the form of higher prices. The initial rise in prices can then set off a sustained increase in prices.

Demand-pull inflation occurs when aggregate demand grows at a more rapid rate than aggregate supply. It may, for instance, be the result of a consumer boom. It may also arise if the money supply grows faster than increases in the country's output.

TERMS

Cost-push inflation: a rise in the price level caused by a decrease in aggregate supply resulting from an increase in the costs of production.

Demand-pull inflation: a rise in the general price level caused by aggregate demand growing by more than aggregate supply.

Money values: data measured at current prices.

Real data: data measured in constant prices.

Progress check E

Explain what type of inflation a consumer boom may cause.

Consequences of inflation

The effects of inflation are influenced by its rate, whether the rate is stable or fluctuating, whether the inflation was correctly anticipated or not, its cause and how the rate compares with other countries.

The costs of inflation include a random redistribution of income, menu costs, shoe leather costs, inflationary noise, fiscal drag, a loss of international competitiveness and discouragement of investment. Borrowers may gain and lenders may lose if the inflation rate exceeds the interest rate. Firms may experience higher costs due to having to change price labels and having to move money around financial institutions in search of the highest interest rate. Inflation may make it difficult to determine if relative prices have changed. People and firms may also find that their incomes are dragged into higher tax brackets if they are not adjusted by inflation. If the country's inflation rate is higher than rival countries, it may experience a decrease in demand for its exports and an increase in demand for its imports. The uncertainty created by inflation may also discourage investment.

The possible benefits of inflation include a stimulus to investment. This may occur if the inflation rate is low, stable and caused by demand-pull factors. Inflation can also reduce debt in real terms and can enable firms to continue in production and maintain employment in difficult times by cutting real wages while maintaining money wages.

Progress check F

In what circumstance would a rise in wages not result in cost–push inflation?

TIP

In interpreting the impact of inflation, it is important to compare how the country's inflation rate compares to that of other countries, particularly the country's main trading partners.

4.03 Components of the balance of payments

The balance of payments is a record of the economic transactions between a country's residents and residents in other countries over the period of a year. Flows of money into the country are given a positive sign and are referred to as credit items. In contrast, flows of money out of the country are given a negative sign and are called debit items.

The main sections of the balance of payments are the current account, the capital account, the financial account and net errors and omissions.

The current account is probably the section of the balance of payments which receives the most media attention. It consists of trade in goods (exports and imports of visible goods), trade in services (exports and imports of invisible items), primary income (investment income in the form of profits, interest and dividends) and secondary income (includes government contributions to international organisations, bilateral aid and workers' remittances). If credit items exceed debit items, the country has a current account surplus whereas if debit items are greater than credit items, there is a current account deficit.

The capital account is relatively small. It includes sales of embassy buildings and land and debt forgiveness.

The financial account can cover very significant sums of money. It records transactions in assets and liabilities. It includes direct investment, portfolio investment, loans and changes in reserves.

The sum of debit items and the sum of credit items should be equal and the balance of payments should balance. In practice, however, there are so many transactions and there can be a time delay in reporting these transactions. To ensure that debit and credit are equal, a net errors and omissions item is included. If, for instance, debit items exceed credit items by $10 billion, it means that there has either been a mistake or some credit items have been left out. A net errors and omissions figure of plus $10 billion would be added to balance the balance of payments. Compilers of the balance of payments continue to find where the discrepancy lies.

TERM

Balance of payments: yearly record of economic transactions between a country's residents and residents in other countries.

Revision activity B

The following are items which appear in the Nigerian balance of payments. Decide, in each case, whether they:

i   would appear in trade in goods, trade in services, primary income, secondary income or the financial account.

ii are debit or credit items.

    a Sales of Nigerian crude oil to Spain

    b Purchases of chemicals by Nigerian firms from the Netherlands

    c Purchase of insurance by Nigerians from Italian firms

    d Travel by Nigerian business people on South African airlines

    e Sales of shares in Nigerian firms to citizens living in Kenya

    f A UK firm based in Nigeria sending its profits back to the UK

    g Ghanaians working in Nigeria sending money home to Ghana

TIP

Terms used about items in the balance of payments change over time – e.g. income became primary income and current transfers became secondary income in the balance of payments of most countries in October 2014. Keep up to date by looking online at the balance of payments data for your own country and other major countries.

Meaning of balance of payments equilibrium and disequilibrium

The balance of payments, in theory, should always balance as credit items (money coming into the country) must be matched by debit items (money going out of the country). In practice, because of the large number of transactions involved and the delay in reporting them, a balancing item known as net errors and omissions is added to ensure that the balance of payments balances.

A large debit item on net errors and omissions would indicate that more money has left the country than has currently been accounted for.

Balance of payments equilibrium and balance of payments disequilibrium usually refer to equilibrium or disequilibrium on the accounts within the overall balance.

The current account will be in deficit if earnings from the exports of goods and services, receipts of primary income and secondary income are less than expenditure on imports of goods and services and primary income and secondary income sent abroad.

If net transfers in the financial account are in surplus, it means that direct, portfolio and other investment into the country (transactions in liabilities) is greater than direct, portfolio and other investment going out of the country (transactions in assets).

Progress check G

What would have to be true for a country to have a balance of trade deficit and a current account surplus?

Causes of balance of payments disequilibrium

A trade in goods and services deficit may be structural and/or cyclical. A structural deficit arises due to a lack of international competitiveness. A cyclical deficit occurs as a result of incomes abroad falling and/or incomes at home rising. A lack of international competitiveness may arise due to an overvalued exchange rate, a relatively high inflation rate, relatively low productivity and a lack of innovation.

There are a number of reasons why the financial account may be in deficit. A rise in interest rates abroad and expectation that foreign share prices and foreign government bond prices will increase may result in a net outflow of portfolio investment. A fall in corporate taxes abroad, a rise in economic prospects in foreign countries are among the reasons why there may be a net outflow of direct investment.

A deficit or surplus on the financial account will have implications for the current account balance in the future. Debit items in the financial account will result in an inflow of income in the form of profit, interest and dividends into the current account in the longer term.

Consequences of balance of payments disequilibrium on domestic and external economy

A current account surplus makes a positive contribution to a country's aggregate demand but involves an opportunity cost in the form of forgone consumption of imports and may put upward pressure on the price level by adding to the money supply whilst involving a net outflow of products.

A current account deficit makes a negative contribution to a country's aggregate demand. It means a country is 'living beyond its means' – consuming more products than it is producing.

A current account surplus will, ceteris paribus, put upward pressure on the price of a country's currency while a current account deficit will put downward pressure on the price of the currency.

A current account deficit can be financed by a net inflow of direct or portfolio investment, borrowing or drawing on the country's reserves of foreign currency.

How significant a current account disequilibrium is, depends on its size, duration and cause.

Revision activity C

Decide whether the following statements about the balance of payments are correct or incorrect and explain why.

a The current account always balances

b Transactions in assets appear as a credit item in the balance of payments

c Debit items are balanced by credit items

d A government will always seek to avoid a current account disequilibrium

e The merchandise balance is the difference between the volume of exports of goods and the volume of imports of goods

f Devaluation need not reduce a trade deficit

4.04 Foreign exchange rates

Definitions and measurement of exchange rates

The nominal exchange rate is the market price of one currency in terms of another or group of currencies. It is the rate quoted on the foreign exchange markets and in the media.

The real exchange rate is a currency's value in terms of its real purchasing power. It is the nominal exchange rate adjusted by prices at home and abroad. It is, in effect, a measure of international price competitiveness.

A rise in the real exchange rate means a country's products have become more expensive relative to foreign products either because the nominal exchange rate has risen and/or because its inflation rate is higher than its trading partners.

If a comparison is made of different countries' GDP figures at the current exchange rate, it may give a misleading indicator of the purchasing power of the currency at home. To overcome this problem, GDP can be converted into a common currency at a purchasing power parity rate. This is a rate at which two currencies would be able to purchase the same quantity of products in the two economies.

The trade weighted exchange rate is also known as the effective exchange rate. It is a weighted average exchange rate which reflects the relative importance of different currencies in terms of their shares in the country's international trade. For example, in the US's trade weighted exchange rate in 2015, the euro had a weighting of 16.6%, the Canadian dollar 12.6%, the Japanese yen 6.4% and the UK pound 3.3%.

TERMS

Nominal exchange rates: market price of one currency in terms of other currencies.

Real exchange rate: currency's value in terms of purchasing power.

Effective exchange rate or trade weighted exchange rate: reflects the importance of different currencies in terms of their shares in international trade.

Floating exchange rate: determined by the market forces of demand and supply.

Fixed exchange rate: set and maintained at a particular level by government or central bank acting on behalf of the government.

Determination of exchange rates – floating, fixed, managed float

A floating exchange rate is one determined by the market forces of demand and supply. A rise in the price of a currency brought about by a rise in demand for the currency and/or a fall in the supply is known as appreciation. A fall in the price of a currency caused by a fall in demand for the currency and/or a rise in its supply is referred to as depreciation.

A fixed exchange rate is one that is set at a particular level and maintained at that level by a government or central bank acting on behalf of the government. A change from a fixed rate to a higher fixed rate is called a revaluation. In contrast, a devaluation is a reduction in a fixed rate.

A managed float is an exchange rate system where the price of the currency is largely determined by market forces but one in which the government will intervene to avoid large fluctuation in price.

A central bank, acting on behalf of the government, may maintain a fixed exchange rate, or seek to influence a managed float directly by buying and selling the currency or indirectly by raising or lowering the interest rate.

To offset downward pressure on a fixed exchange rate or a managed float, a central bank may buy the currency, using reserves of foreign currency, or raise the interest rate.

TIP

Keep a record of what is happening to your country's exchange rate, noting the causes of any changes or, in the case of a fixed exchange rate, causes of upward or downward pressure on the exchange rate.

Factors underlying fluctuations in exchange rates

A country's currency is demanded by traders wishing to buy the country's exports, tourists wishing to visit the country, financial investors wishing to place money in the country's banks and to buy shares in the country's firms and the government's bonds, foreign firms wishing to set up in the country or purchase domestic firms and speculators who anticipate a rise in the value of the currency.

A country's currency is supplied by those wishing to purchase foreign currency in order to buy imports, go on foreign holidays, place money in foreign banks, purchase foreign shares and government bonds, to set up firms or buy firms in foreign countries and to speculate that the price of the currency will fall relative to foreign currencies.

The major causes of fluctuations in exchange rates are changes in international competitiveness, changes in income at home and abroad, changes in the economic performance of the economy, changes in the rate of interest at home and abroad and speculation. A floating exchange rate will appreciate if net exports increase, hot money flows are attracted into the country by a rise in the rate of interest, foreign direct investment increases or there is speculation that the price of the currency will rise in the future.

Progress check H

Identify two reasons why someone may sell US dollars to buy the UAE's dirham.

Effects of changing exchange rates on the economy

A fall in the price of a currency will reduce export prices, in terms of foreign currency, and will raise import prices, in terms of the domestic currency.

A rise in the price of a currency will raise export prices, in terms of foreign currency, and will reduce import prices, in terms of the domestic currency.

The Marshall-Lerner condition states that the value of the price elasticity of demand for exports plus the price elasticity of demand for imports must be greater than one for a devaluation/depreciation to result in an improvement in the trade balance.

The J-curve shows a trade deficit initially increasing following a devaluation/depreciation and then reducing. This is because, at first, demand for exports and imports is inelastic as there is no time for buyers to notice and respond to the change in prices. As buyers adjust to the price changes, demand may become elastic.

The reverse J-curve shows an appreciation/, revaluation, at first increasing a trade surplus as demand is inelastic and then reducing a trade surplus as demand becomes more elastic over time.

If demand for exports is inelastic, producers may seek to benefit from a fall in the price of the currency by maintaining their price in terms of foreign currency. This will raise revenue when converted back into the domestic currency.

A fall in the price of a currency which results in an increase in net exports will raise aggregate demand and, if there is spare capacity in the economy, will increase the country's output and employment.

A rise in the price of a currency will tend to reduce inflationary pressure as it will lower import prices and may reduce aggregate demand.

TERMS

Marshall-Lerner condition: the value of the price elasticity of demand for exports plus the price elasticity of demand for imports must be greater than one for a devaluation/depreciation to result in an improvement in the trade balance.

J-Curve: shows a trade deficit initially increasing following a devaluation/depreciation and then reducing.

Reverse J-Curve: shows an appreciation/ revaluation, at first increasing a trade surplus as demand is inelastic and then reducing a trade surplus as demand becomes more elastic over time.

Revision activity D

A country's exchange rate against the US dollar is initially, 10 pesos = $1. The country's firms sell 20 million products at an average price of 20 pesos. The country imports 25 million products at an average price of $2.

The value of the pesos then falls to 15 pesos = US$1. The country's exports rise to 30 million selling at 20 pesos and its imports fall to 15 million bought at an average price of $2.

a Calculate the initial trade balance.

b Calculate the trade balance after the depreciation of the pesos.

c What does the change in the trade balance indicate about the combined price elasticities of demand for the country's exports and imports?

4.05 Terms of trade

Measurement of the terms of trade

The terms of trade can refer to the ratio of products exchanged between countries. For example, Country A may exchange 1 unit of tin for 8 units of wheat from Country B. The terms of trade can also refer to the ratio of the index of average export prices to the index of average import prices. The formula for the terms of trade is:

$$\text{Terms of trade} = \frac{\text{index of average price of exports}}{\text{index of average import prices}}$$

An improvement or favourable movement in the terms of trade occurs when the ratio gets larger – export prices rise relative to import prices. It means that the country can gain more imports in exchange for a given volume of exports.

TERM

Terms of trade: the ratio of the price of exports and imports.

The causes and consequences of changes in the terms of trade

Whether an improvement in the terms of trade will have a beneficial effect on the current account of the balance of payments will depend on its cause. Higher export prices due to higher demand will increase export revenue. In contrast, higher export prices due to a rise in the costs of production may lower export revenue.

Deterioration or an unfavourable movement in the terms of trade takes place when the ratio declines – export prices fall relative to import prices. Again, the effect deterioration in the terms of trade has on the current account of the balance of payments will depend on its cause. A fall in the exchange rate, for instance, will cause deterioration in the terms of trade but its effect on the current account position will depend on the price elasticity of demand for exports and imports.

Countries which export mainly agricultural products may experience significant changes in their terms of trade. A bumper harvest of a country's main crop, for instance, may reduce the price of the crop which will lower the terms of trade. In contrast, a rise in global economic activity may increase demand for oil which, in turn, may raise the price of oil and improve the terms of trade of oil producing countries.

4.06 Absolute and comparative advantage

Absolute advantage is the ability of a country to produce a product using fewer resources than another country. Comparative advantage is the ability of a country to produce a product at a lower opportunity than another country.

In theory, trade should benefit two countries if there is a difference in their opportunity cost ratios and if the exchange rate lies between the opportunity cost ratios. International trade enables countries to specialise and enjoy higher output.

A trading possibility curve shows an economy's post trade consumption possibilities. Figure 4.09 shows that before trade, for instance, an economy can produce any combination on the line joining 500 cars and

2,000 computers. In this case, the opportunity cost of one car is four computers. When international trade is considered, one car can be exchanged for six computers. The economy has a comparative advantage in producing cars. The economy can increase its consumption from X to Y by concentrating on car production and exporting cars in return for computers.

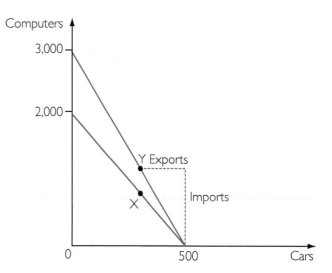

Figure 4.09

In practice, specialisation and trade may not be as straightforward and beneficial as the law of comparative advantage suggests. With so many countries and products, it can be difficult for economies to determine where their comparative advantage lies. Advances in technology, discoveries of minerals and changes in labour productivity, for instance, can change comparative advantage over time. When economies change their output, their opportunity cost ratios may change as resources are unlikely to be equally efficient in different uses. So, for example, if an economy can produce 5,000 chairs with half of its resources, it does not necessarily mean that devoting all its resources to their production will increase output to 10,000. It may increase by more if advantage can be taken of the economies of scale, and by less if diseconomies of scale are experienced. The benefits from trade may be offset by high transport costs or import restrictions. In addition, the government may be concerned about depending on a narrow range of products. Overspecialisation can make an economy vulnerable to changes in costs of production and demand.

TERMS

Absolute advantage: where a country can produce a product using fewer resources than another country.

Comparative advantage: ability of a country to produce a product at a lower opportunity than another country.

Revision activity E

The Table 4.01 shows the production possibilities in two countries.

Country X		Country Y	
Product A	Product B	Product A	Product B
0	128	0	48
16	96	2	36
32	64	4	24
48	32	6	12
64	0	8	0

Table 4.01: The production possibilities of Country X and Country Y

a Which country has the absolute advantage in producing both products?

b What is the opportunity cost of producing product A in each country?

c Which country has the comparative advantage in producing product B?

d Would an exchange rate of 7 units of product B for 1 unit of product A benefit both countries? Explain your answer.

Progress check I

How do factor endowments influence comparative advantage?

TIP

In explaining comparative advantage, it is useful to give a numerical example or to illustrate the concept on a diagram.

Other explanations/ determinant of trade flows

Trade flows may be influenced by factors other than comparative advantage. If transport costs are high, a country may trade mainly with countries nearby. The existence of trading blocs may also influence trade flows. Whilst members are more likely to trade with each other, non-members may find it more difficult to export to member countries. A country may have a comparative advantage in a product but may still import it because demand for the product is so high.

TERM

Trading bloc: group of countries that have agreed to reduce or remove some trade restrictions between them.

Progress check J

Identify three reasons why a supermarket may buy food from abroad.

4.07 Economic integration

A trading bloc is a group of countries that have agreed to reduce or remove some trade restrictions between themselves. Some also have other economic links. Trading blocs have different levels of economic integration. A free trade area has the lowest degree of economic integration whilst an economic union has the highest degree. The more integrated a trade bloc is, the more the member countries act as one economy.

A free trade area is a group of countries that agree to remove barriers to the movement of products between each country. One of the most well-known examples of a free trade area is the North American Free Trade Area (NAFTA) which consists of the US, Canada and Mexico.

A customs union goes further in terms of economic integration. As well as removing trade barriers between each other, member countries have to agree to impose a common external tariff that is the same tariff on non-members. An example of a customs union is Mercosur. This has Argentina, Brazil, Paraguay and Uruguay as full members and Venezuela about to become a full member.

Full economic union involves the member countries operating as one economy. It has a number of features. In addition to removing trade restrictions between each other and imposing a common external tariff, members operate a common market. This involves free movement between member countries not only of products but also of labour, capital and enterprise. Another feature is the operation of common economic policies, for example, a common competition policy and a common agricultural policy. There are the same tax rates. A full economic union also involves monetary union, with member states operating the same currency and the central bank of the trading bloc setting the rate of interest for the member countries. The Caricom Single Market and Economy (CSME) is getting close to full economic union. It has a common market, common policies in agriculture and tourism, co-ordination of national indirect taxes and budget deficits. Eight of the members of this trading bloc operate the same currency, the Eastern Caribbean dollar, and have their interest rate set by the Eastern Caribbean Central Bank.

Progress check K

How does geography influence the composition of trade blocs?

TERMS

Free trade area: group of countries that agree to remove barriers to the movement of products between each country.

Customs union: group of countries that agree to remove barriers to the movement of products between each country and to impose a common external tariff on non-members.

Full economic union: group of countries operate as one country with a single market and the same economic policies.

TERMS

Tariff: a tax on imported or exported goods.

Monetary union: group of countries that operate a single market, common external tariff with non-members, the same currency with a central bank setting the rate of interest for the member countries.

Trade creation and trade diversion

Trade creation and trade diversion are the possible effects on a country's pattern of trade that may occur when it joins a trade bloc.

Membership of a trading bloc which involves free trade between members and a common external tariff, can involve both trade creation and trade diversion. Trade creation, in this case, occurs when a country moves from buying products from higher cost non-members to lower costs member countries. Consumers gain from trade creation as they can now buy more of the product at a cheaper price. Figure 4.10 shows how welfare can be increased as a result of trade creation.

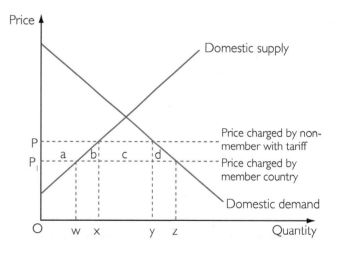

Figure 4.10

Figure 4.10 shows by switching purchases from a non-member country (with a tariff) to a member country (without a tariff), consumer surplus rises by the area a + b + c + d. Producer surplus falls by a and tariff revenue by c. This gives a net gain of b + d.

Domestic producers of the product may initially lose out but in the longer term they may gain. They may switch from making products that other countries have a comparative advantage in to producing products that the country is more efficient at.

Trade diversion takes place when trade is diverted away from more efficient non-members towards less efficient member countries. The effect of trade diversion is somewhat uncertain. Figure 4.11 shows that a country initially buys a product from a non-member country with a tariff imposed on it. The country then buys from a member country which would charge a higher price than the non-member in the absence of a tariff.

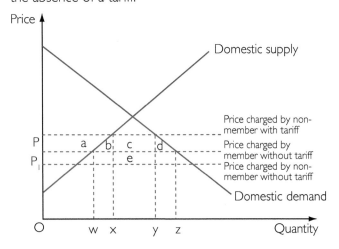

Figure 4.11

The switch in importing from the non-member to the member causes consumer surplus to rise by a + b + c + d. Producer surplus falls by a and tariff revenue by c + e. The a + c effects cancel each other out. Welfare will rise if b + d > e but will fall if b + d < e.

Progress check L

Why may a recession in one country result in a fall in aggregate demand in another country?

4.08 The benefits of free trade

Free trade is the exchange of products between countries without any restrictions. Free trade allows countries to exploit their comparative advantages and so increase output. By specialising and trading, countries can both produce and consume more as shown in the trading possibility curve diagram in Figure 4.09.

Consumers can benefit from free trade as the increased competition created by free trade can lower prices and raise the quality of products available for consumers. It can also enable consumers to have access a greater range of products.

Firms will have a wider choice of raw materials which may reduce their costs of production. In addition, they will have a larger market which will enable them to take greater advantage of economies of scale.

New ideas and advances in technology can be spread more widely and more quickly with free trade. Both consumers and firms may benefit from the dispersion of new ideas, new methods of production and new capital equipment.

Revision activity F

Figure 4.12 shows the domestic market for copper and the world price.

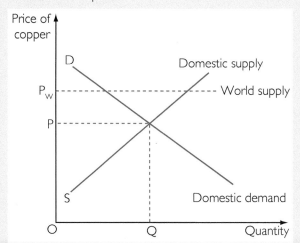

Figure 4.12

An economy initially does not engage in international trade. If it then becomes an open economy, explain the effect on the following.

a   Domestic consumers

b   Domestic producers

c   Foreign producers

4.09 Protectionism

Methods of protection

Protection involves protecting domestic industries from foreign competition by placing restrictions on international trade.

Methods of protection include a tariff (a tax on imports), a quota (a limit on the quantity of imports), an embargo (a ban on imports of particular products or from particular countries), administrative burden ('red tape'), exchange control (a limit on the amount of foreign currency that can be bought) and a voluntary export restraint (an agreement between two countries to limit imports). A government may also seek to give domestic producers a competitive advantage by subsidising their output.

A tariff is sometimes also called an import duty. It will, in effect, increase costs of production for importers. As a result, it may raise price and cause demand to contract. The effect a tariff will have will depend on its size, how much of the tax is passed on to consumers and the price elasticity of demand.

A quota will restrict supply, push up price and, again, reduce the quantity demanded. Whilst a tariff will generate government revenue, a quota will not unless a government enforces the quota by selling licenses. A quota increases the price foreign producers receive, whereas a tariff may force foreign producers to lower the price in a bid to remain competitive. By restricting the availability of foreign currency, demand for imports may fall.

An embargo is, in effect, the most extreme form of a quota. It prevents any of the product being imported or stops trade with a particular country.

A greater administrative burden may be imposed on importers by requiring them to fill out an excessive amount of paperwork.

Exchange control reduces demand for imports by limiting the amount of foreign currency that importers can buy.

Voluntary export restraints create shortages of imports which can push up their price and reduce the quantity demanded. Excessive paper work, 'red tape', will raise importers' costs of production, raise price and lower the quantity demanded.

A subsidy given to domestic producers will encourage domestic firms to increase their output and lower price. This may encourage domestic consumers and foreigners to buy more of the country's products. A subsidy may be given to firms that compete with imports and/or it may be given to firms that export.

Progress check M

What is the difference between a tariff and a quota?

Arguments in favour of protectionism

Arguments in favour of protectionism include – to protect infant industries, to protect declining industries, to protect strategic industries, to prevent dumping, to improve the balance of payments position, to protect domestic employment and to protect industries against cheap foreign labour.

Infant industries are also known as sunrise industries. The infant industry argument is that a new industry in a country, which may go on to develop a comparative advantage, may initially need help to compete with well-established industries. This is because, before it has grown to a certain size, its unit costs may be higher as it cannot take full advantage of economies of scale. There is a chance that the social benefit of developing a new industry may outweigh the private cost of higher priced imports. It is, however, difficult to identify which industries will be successful and there is a risk that an industry may become dependent on protection.

Declining industries are also known as sunset industries. A government may seek to protect sunset industries to allow them to decline gradually and so avoid a rise in unemployment. The intention would be to remove the protection gradually, but industries may try to resist the protection being removed. It can also be argued that any subsidies used to protect sunset industries might be better used to protect sunrise industries.

Strategic industries are considered to be key industries that a government wants to ensure remain in domestic ownership. Some governments seek to protect agriculture in order to achieve food security. Governments may also want to ensure that it has its own supplies of weapons and may want to see other important industries to be under national control. Such action may, however, result in retaliation.

Taking action against dumping is generally regarded as a valid reason for imposing import restrictions. Dumping involves selling products in a foreign market at below cost price. A firm may engage in dumping to get rid of surplus stock to prevent driving down price in the home market. It may also seek to drive out domestic firms by selling at low prices. If it is trying to gain a monopoly share of the market, consumers may lose out in the long run. In practice, however, it can be difficult to determine whether foreign firms are engaging in dumping.

Import restrictions may reduce a current account deficit in the short run. If they lead to retaliation, however, lower imports may be matched by lower exports. Import restrictions also do not tackle the causes of balance of payments' problems.

A government may think that import restrictions will increase employment or at least prevent unemployment in declining industries. Again there is a risk of retaliation. In addition, if industries that are protected produce raw materials and components, other domestic industries will be disadvantaged. For instance, if steel is protected, domestic car firms will have higher costs of production. This will reduce their international competitiveness and so may lower employment. Protecting domestic industries that produce finished products can also create disadvantages for other domestic industries. This is because if consumers have to pay higher prices for the protected products, they will have less to spend on other products.

Some argue that domestic industries should be protected from competition from low wage countries. They claim that such competition may drive down wages at home. This argument, however, confuses low wages with low costs of production. A country may have low wages but if it also has low productivity, its unit costs will be high. The US has high wages but relatively low unit costs in many industries because its labour force is well educated and trained and works with advanced technology.

Progress check N

Producers in a country employ child and slave labour. Would it be justifiable for the government of another country to impose trade restrictions on the offending country?

TERMS

Embargo: a ban on the trade of a particular product or trade with a particular country.

Import quota: limit on number of imported goods, restricting goods.

Protectionism: protecting domestic industries from foreign competition.

TIP

In answering a question on the arguments for and against protectionism, do not devote too much attention to describing the methods of protection – concentrate on the arguments.

Mind maps

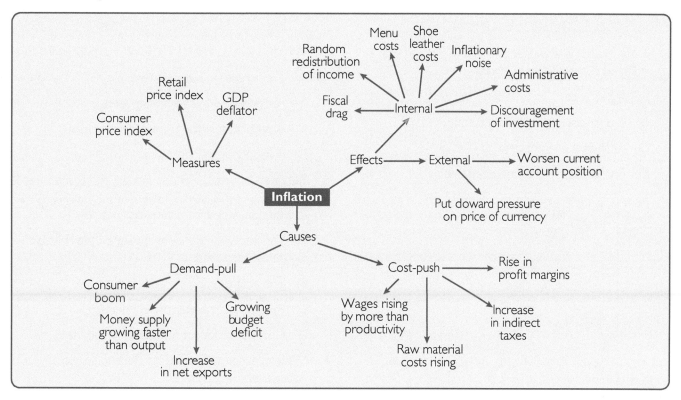

Mind map 4.01: Inflation

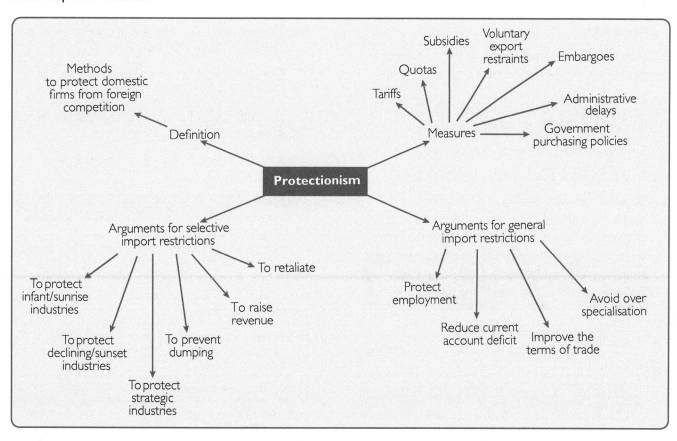

Mind map 4.02: Protectionism

Exam-style Questions

Multiple Choice Questions

1   What could have caused the shift in the aggregate demand curve shown in Figure 4.13?

A   A decrease in income tax

B   A decrease in the money supply

C   An increase in imports

D   An increase in the rate of interest

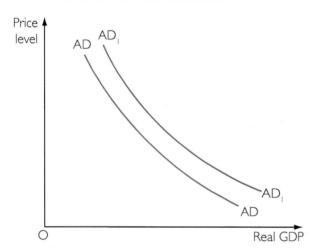

Figure 4.13

2   Why are changes made regularly to the weights used in a consumer price index?

A   Rates of taxation alter

B   Spending patterns change

C   The quality of products increases

D   There are seasonal fluctuations in prices

3   Table 4.02 shows the amount consumers of a country spend on five items and the percentage change in the price of the products in the same year.

Product	Percentage of consumers' expenditure	Percentage price change
Food	20	15
Electricity	5	10
Transport	10	20
Entertainment	5	−10
Clothing	10	30

Table 4.02: Consumer expenditure pattern and price changes

What was the overall rise in the weighted cost of living index?

A   0%   B   15%   C   16%   D   17%

4   Which one is a possible cause of cost-push inflation?

A   An increase in bank lending

B   An increase in government spending

C   A reduction in the price of the currency

D   A reduction in income tax

5   Between January 2009 and January 2010, the rate of inflation in Pakistan fell from 25% to 10.5%. What can be concluded from this information?

A   The internal purchasing power of the Pakistani rupee increased.

B   The cost of living in Pakistan increased.

C   Pakistan's consumer price index fell.

D   Costs of production declined in Pakistan.

6   Which change will affect the trade in services balance of the Maldives?

A   The payment of interest on a loan by a firm in the Maldives to an Indian bank.

B   The purchase of fish caught by fishermen in the Maldives by a Sri Lankan firm.

C   The sale of insurance by a bank based in Hong Kong to a hotel chain in the Maldives.

D   The setting up of a factory in the Maldives by an Australian firm.

7   Table 4.03 shows the balance of payments account for a country.

Balance of payments	$bn
Exports of goods and services	150
Imports of goods and service	130
Primary income	−20
Secondary income	30
Net direct investment	−10
Net portfolio investment	−20
Net other investment	−20
Drawing on reserves	10

Table 4.03: The balance of payments

Which combination describes the country's balance of payments position?

	Current account balance	Financial account balance
A	Deficit	Deficit
B	Deficit	Surplus
C	Surplus	Surplus
D	Surplus	Deficit

8 The trade weighted exchange rate for the New Zealand dollar is the rate of exchange between the New Zealand dollar and:

A the currencies of countries it has trading agreements with.

B the currencies of countries operating floating exchange rates.

C the currencies of its main trading partners.

D the currencies of its neighbouring countries.

9 What could cause an increase in the supply of Argentine pesos on the foreign exchange market?

A An increase in the value of Argentine imports

B An increase in foreign direct investment in Argentina

C A decrease in portfolio investment in Argentina

D A decrease in the value of Argentine exports

10 What is the most likely cause of a depreciation in the value of Bangladesh's currency, the taka?

A A decrease in foreign direct investment in Bangladesh

B A decrease in Bangladesh's inflation rate

C An increase in Bangladesh's interest rate

D An increase in the number of tourists visiting Bangladesh

11 Which circumstance would increase the likelihood of a fall in the price of a country's currency, improving its trade balance?

A Demand for its exports is income elastic and incomes in its trading partners are falling.

B Demand for its imports is income elastic and incomes at home are rising.

C The combined price elasticities of demand for its exports and imports is less than one.

D The price elasticity of supply of its exports is greater than one.

12 Figure 4.14 shows the foreign exchange market for the Egyptian pound.

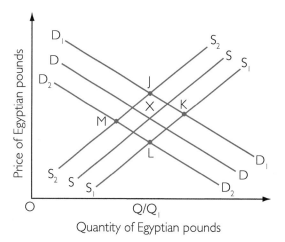

Figure 4.14

The initial position is X. Egyptians then take more holidays abroad and Egyptian firms sell fewer exports. What is the new equilibrium position?

A J   B K   C L   D M

13 Table 4.04 below shows the ability of two countries to produce TVs and chairs in a given time period.

	Production of TVs per worker	Production of chairs per worker
Country X	10	20
Country Y	20	80

Table 4.04: Production possibilities of Country X and Country Y

What can be concluded from the information?

A Country X has an absolute advantage in TVs and Country Y has a comparative advantage in chairs.

B Country X has an absolute advantage in TVs and Country Y has an absolute advantage in chairs.

C Country X has a comparative advantage in TVs and Country Y has an absolute advantage in chairs.

D Country X has a comparative advantage in chairs and Country Y has an absolute advantage in TVs.

14 Country X has a comparative advantage in producing paper and Country Y has a comparative advantage in producing watches. The two countries, however, decide not to specialise and trade. What could explain this decision?

  A The exchange rate lies within the countries' opportunity cost ratios.

  B There is perfect mobility of factors of production between the countries.

  C Trade is based on absolute rather than comparative advantage.

  D Transport costs are low relative to the opportunity cost differences between the countries.

15 Figure 4.15 shows the production possibility curves of two countries X and Y.

As a result of advances in technology in country Y, its production possibility curve shifts from Y to Y1. According to the law of comparative advantage, what should country X do following the change?

  A Cease trading with country Y.

  B Continue to export agricultural goods to country Y.

  C Import both agricultural goods and manufactured goods from country Y.

  D Switch to exporting manufactured goods to country Y.

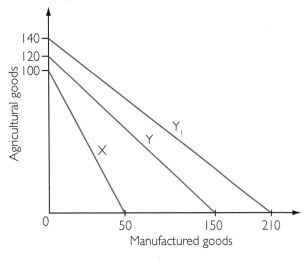

Figure 4.15

16 In Figure 4.16, DD represents domestic demand, DS domestic supply and WS the world supply. The product is imported at a price of PW. If a tariff is imposed which shifts the world supply curve to WS1, what will be the government's tariff revenue?

  A TUV   C UVXY

  B UWY   D YVZ

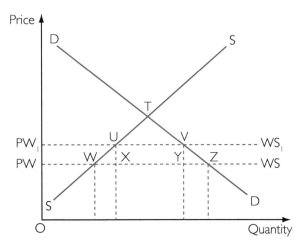

Figure 4.16

17 Which feature is found in a customs union but not a free trade area?

  A A common currency

  B A common external tariff

  C Uniform direct tax rates

  D Uniform indirect tax rates

18 What would cause a favourable movement in the terms of trade of a country?

  A Export volume falling more slowly than import volume

  B Import prices falling more than export prices

  C An improvement in the trade in goods balance

  D An improvement in the current account balance

19 Table 4.05 shows details about the exports and imports of goods of a country.

	Exports		Imports	
	Price per unit	Number of units	Price per unit	Number of units
Year 1	$400	10,000	$500	14,000
Year 2	$560	10,000	$600	14,000

Table 4.05: Price and quantity of exports and imports

What happened to the balance of trade and the terms of trade from year 1 to year 2?

	Balance of trade	Terms of trade
A	Deteriorated	Deteriorated
B	Deteriorated	Improved
C	Improved	Improved
D	Improved	Deteriorated

20 Which of the following would be classified as a credit item on the current account of the balance of payments of Pakistan?

A   Money spent in Pakistan by Egyptian tourists

B   Payments made to a French airline by Pakistani business people travelling from Pakistan to France

C   Purchase of vaccinations from Cuba by Pakistani hospitals

D   Reinvestment in Pakistan of profits by Pakistani owners of clothes companies in Sri Lanka

Data Response Questions

1 Measuring inflation

Many countries use consumer price indices to measure inflation. These are weighted price indices which reflect both changes in prices and changes in household spending patterns. There are a number of reasons why household spending patterns alter over time. These include changes in tastes and relative prices. As these factors vary from country to country, weights also vary. Table 4.06 compares some of the weights in the consumer price indices of India and Pakistan.

	India	Pakistan
Category	Weight (%)	Weight (%)
Food and beverages	45.86	34.83
Alcohol and tobacco	2.38	1.41
Clothing and footwear	6.53	7.57
Housing, fuel and light	16.91	29.41
Health	5.89	2.19
Transport and communications	8.59	7.20
Education	4.46	3.94
Recreation and culture	1.68	2.02
Miscellaneous	7.7	11.43

Table 4.06: Selected weights in the consumer price indices of India and Pakistan 2015 (base year 2010).

The selection of products is revised regularly to ensure that they are representative of the pattern of expenditure by households. Each time they are revised, some new items are added to the 'basket' of consumer products and some are removed. It is interesting to note that some economists claim that consumer price indices do not always provide an accurate measure of inflation.

a What is meant by a base year? [2]

b What can be concluded about the amount spent on clothing and footwear in India and Pakistan from the information given? [3]

c What would be expected to happen to the weighting given to recreation and culture in India over time? [3]

d Would India or Pakistan have been more affected by a 10% rise in the price of health in 2015? [2]

e i   What is meant by changes in relative prices? [2]

   ii What effect would there be on India's and the Pakistan's inflation rates if there was a 10% rise in the price of housing and household utilities in each country. [2]

f Discuss whether consumer price indices provide an accurate measure of inflation. [6]

2 The Chinese renminbi and UK pound sterling

For some time, many economists argued that both the Chinese renminbi (yuan) has been undervalued. On a number of occasions, the Chinese government has intervened in the foreign exchange market to prevent the yuan from rising in value against the US dollar.

The pound sterling fluctuated against the US dollar but was relatively stable between 2012 and 2015 (see Table 4.07). Changes in the exchange rate can affect both the current account position on the balance of payments and the inflation rate.

Year	Changes in the value of the pound sterling 2012–2015	Current account balance	
	Exchange rate Currency units per US$	$bn	% of GDP
2012	0.63	−46.3	−1.6
2013	0.64	−91.5	−2.9
2014	0.61	−117.7	−4.0
2015	0.65	−149.2	−4.5

Table 4.07: The dollar/pound exchange rate and the UK current account position 2012–2015

a i   Identify two ways the Chinese government could intervene in the foreign exchange market to prevent the yuan rising in value against the US dollar. [2]

   ii Explain what is meant by a currency being 'undervalued'. [4]

b i   Does Table 4.07 support the statement that the value of the pound was relatively stable between 2012 and 2015? [2]

   ii Comment on the relationship between the exchange rate and the current account balance shown in Table 4.07. [4]

c Discuss whether a depreciation in the exchange rate will increase the rate of inflation. [8]

Essay Questions

1   a   Distinguish between absolute advantage and comparative advantage.   [8]

     b   Discuss whether a government should always pursue a policy of free trade.   [12]

2   a   Explain what may cause a deterioration in the terms of trade.   [8]

     b   Discuss whether the formation of regional trading blocs promotes competition.   [12]

REVISION TIPS

Adding to your notes

As you progress through the course and check through your notes, you should get used to adding to them. You should do this for a number of reasons including:

✓ to fill in any gaps.

✓ to provide relevant examples.

✓ to show links to other topics.

✓ to take into account recent developments.

Government macro intervention

Learning summary

After you have studied this chapter, you should be able to:

- ■ explain the measures of fiscal policy, monetary policy and supply side policy

- ■ discuss the effectiveness of fiscal, monetary and supply side policies to correct balance of payments disequilibrium

- ■ analyse expenditure-reducing and expenditure-switching

- ■ discuss the effectiveness of fiscal, monetary and supply side policies to correct inflation and deflation

5.01 Types of policy

Fiscal policy

Fiscal policy covers government decisions on taxation and government spending. It aims to influence aggregate demand. Reflationary/expansionary fiscal policy seeks to increase the aggregate demand whereas deflationary/contractionary fiscal policy seeks to reduce the aggregate demand.

A government imposes taxes for a variety of reasons. As well as seeking to influence economic activity, taxes are levied to raise revenue, to discourage the consumption of demerit goods, to reduce income and wealth inequalities and to dissuade people from buying imports.

There are various upward pressures on government spending. These include an ageing population, advances in medical technology, military conflicts and increases in the number of students going to university.

Discretionary fiscal policy covers government decisions to change government spending and taxes rates and/or tax coverage. Automatic stabilisers are changes in government spending and tax revenue that occur as a result of changes in real GDP and which reduce economic fluctuations.

Fiscal policy is also sometimes known as budgetary policy. A government's budget position is the relationship between tax revenue and government expenditure. A government has a budget surplus when tax revenue exceeds government expenditure and it has a budget deficit when government expenditure exceeds tax revenue. A cyclical deficit and a cyclical surplus arise due to changes in the economic cycle. When there is a low level of economic activity, tax revenue is likely to be low whilst government spending on benefits and, possibly spending to increase economic activity, is likely to be high. In contrast, tax revenue is likely to be high and government spending may be relatively low during a period of high economic activity. A structural deficit and a structural surplus occur when there is an imbalance between tax revenue and government spending. A structural deficit and a structural surplus will not be self-correcting. A budget deficit or surplus may have both a cyclical and a structural element.

Progress check A

A government decides to use deflationary fiscal policy rather than devaluation to reduce the country's current account deficit. What does this suggest about its objectives for the internal and external value of the currency?

TIP

AD and AS analysis is very useful in explaining and evaluating government macroeconomic policy.

Monetary policy

Monetary policy covers government and/or central bank decisions on money supply and the rate of interest.

The central bank implements monetary policy on behalf of the government. It sets the rate of interest, controls the money supply and may set or influence the exchange rate.

Monetary policy aims to influence aggregate demand. Reflationary/expansionary monetary policy seeks to increase aggregate demand whilst deflationary/contractionary monetary policy seeks to reduce aggregate demand.

The manipulation of exchange rates is sometimes included in monetary policy but is sometimes treated as a separate policy.

Revision activity A

Explain whether the following changes would be likely to result in an appreciation or a depreciation in the value of the Australian dollar.

a   A rise in the US rate of interest

b   A rise in incomes in the European Union

c   A fall in the quality of Australian products

d   The introduction of successful expenditure reducing policies in the USA

e   The hosting of a global sporting event in Australia

f   An increase in multinational companies setting up branches in Australia

Progress check B

Explain why measures adopted by a central bank to reduce a current deficit may cause demand-pull inflation.

Supply side policy

Supply side policy seeks to increase aggregate supply by increasing the quantity and quality of resources. Among supply side measures (also called instruments or tools) are education, training, cuts in income tax, cuts in unemployment benefit, cuts in corporation tax, privatisation, deregulation and a reduction in trade union power.

Supply side policy has the potential to improve all the government's macroeconomic objectives in the long run.

TERMS

Fiscal policy: government decisions on taxation and government spending.

Monetary policy: government or central bank decisions on supply of money and rate of interest.

Supply side policy: measures to increase aggregate supply by raising the quality and/or the quantity of resources.

TIP

To determine whether a policy measure such as a cut in income tax is a supply side policy measure or a fiscal policy measure, consider what was the government's intention in introducing the measure. If it was to increase aggregate supply, it is a supply side policy measure. In contrast, if it was to increase aggregate demand, it is a fiscal policy measure.

5.02 Fiscal, monetary and supply side policies to correct balance of payments disequilibrium

Among the fiscal policy measures a government could use to reduce a current account deficit are an increase in income tax and a cut in government spending on benefits. An increase in income tax and lower benefits would reduce disposable income. Lower disposable income may reduce consumer expenditure. This may reduce demand for imports and, with a smaller domestic market, may put more pressure on domestic firms to increase their exports.

To reduce a financial account deficit, a government may seek to attract foreign direct and portfolio investment by providing fiscal stability, that is not making frequent changes to taxes and government spending and achieving budget balance over the economic cycle.

Among the monetary policy measures a government could use to reduce a current account deficit are to lower the value of the currency and to raise the rate of interest. Devaluing the currency will make export prices lower, in terms of other currencies, and will make import prices higher, in terms of the domestic economy. Lower export prices and higher import prices may result in a rise in export revenue and a fall in import expenditure if the combined price elasticity of demand (PED) for exports and imports is greater than one. A higher interest rate may reduce spending including spending on imports and put pressure on domestic firms to increase exports by encouraging saving in the domestic economy at the expense of spending.

To reduce a financial account deficit, a government through its central bank may lower the rate of interest. This may increase foreign direct investment as multinational companies may expect that there will be a higher level of aggregate demand in the country and may welcome lower borrowing costs to finance their capital expenditure.

Supply side policy measures may improve the current account position as they may reduce costs of production, and so prices, of domestic products and may raise their quality. For example, improved education and training may improve labour productivity and so increase international price and quality competitiveness.

Supply side policy measures may reduce a financial account deficit by making it more attractive for foreign firms to set up in the country, for foreign banks to lend to domestic firms and citizens and for foreigners to buy shares in domestic firms. For example, foreign firms may welcome a well-trained labour force and a low corporation tax rate.

A government may also use trade policy measures such as tariffs, quotas and export subsidies.

Progress check C

Explain why the effect of a rise in the rate of interest on import expenditure is uncertain.

5.03 The effectiveness of fiscal, monetary and supply side policies to correct balance of payments disequilibrium

Fiscal policy measures may influence the balance of payments position through affecting aggregate demand. Some work automatically to offset fluctuations in economic activity.

Fiscal policy measures to reduce a current account deficit may not be effective if households and firms do not react in the way expected. For instance, an increase in income tax may not reduce consumer expenditure if households are optimistic about the future – they may just reduce their saving.

Some fiscal policy measures may also have effects which may reduce export revenue and increase import expenditure. For example, a rise in income tax may encourage workers to press for wage rises which, if they lead to higher wages, may reduce international competitiveness.

A number of fiscal policy measures can experience a time lag and some may have adverse side effects.

The rate of interest can be changed more quickly than some taxes and the increased mobility of financial capital means it may have a significant impact on hot money flows. The change in the interest rate can, nevertheless, take approximately 18 months to work through the economy and affect aggregate demand. By the time it has had its full impact, economic conditions may have changed.

A lower interest rate may reduce a current account deficit by lowering the exchange rate but the effect may be offset by stimulating a rise in spending which may increase import expenditure. Similarly, a rise in the rate of interest may reduce spending on imports but it may also lead to a rise in spending on imports if it results in a rise in the exchange rate.

A change in the exchange rate can offset changes in the domestic price level and influence aggregate demand. Attempts to influence the exchange rate, however, can be offset by movements in other countries' exchange rates and by speculation.

A lower exchange rate may reduce a deficit on the current account of the balance of payments but it may also increase the inflation rate by increasing aggregate demand and raising the price of imported products.

Supply side policy measures have the potential to increase both the price and quality competitiveness of domestic products. They may, however, take a long time to have an effect, are expensive and some may not work.

5.04 Expenditure-reducing and expenditure-switching

Policies designed to correct a current account deficit may be described as expenditure-reducing or expenditure-switching.

Expenditure-reducing policy, which can also be called expenditure-dampening policy, is designed to reduce a current account deficit by reducing household spending. The policy does not discriminate between imports and domestically produced products. Lower household spending would result in spending on imports falling and the reduction in spending on domestically produced products may encourage domestic firms to make greater efforts to export their products.

Expenditure-reducing policy measures include raising income tax, cutting government spending and increasing the rate of interest.

Expenditure-reducing policy may improve the current account position but may have an adverse effect on employment and economic growth as it will reduce household spending. This may be offset in the longer term by an increase in net exports.

Expenditure-switching policy is designed to reduce a current account deficit by encouraging domestic consumers to switch their spending from imports to domestically produced products and foreign consumers to switch their spending from foreign made products to the country's exports. For example, expenditure switching policy measures introduced by the Bangladeshi government would be intended for people, both domestic consumers and foreigners, to buy more Bangladeshi produced products and fewer products made by other countries.

Expenditure-switching policy measures may involve a trade-off. For instance, devaluation may improve the current account position but at the cost of an increase in the inflation rate.

Expenditure-switching policy measures include trade restrictions, government subsidies, devaluation and trade fairs.

Revision activity B

Complete the following flow chart:

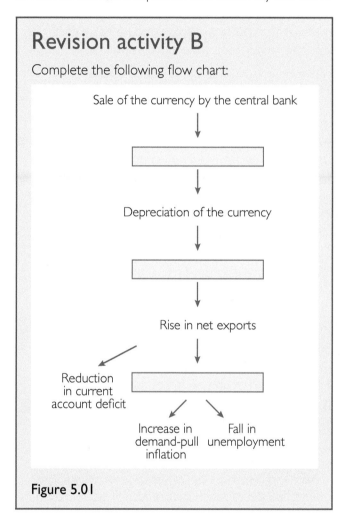

Figure 5.01

Progress check D

Why might moving from a current account deficit to a current account surplus create inflationary pressure?

Progress check E

Are exchange controls an expenditure-reducing or an expenditure-switching policy measure?

Revision activity C

Decide whether the following are likely to decrease or increase the ability of a government to reduce a current account deficit by using expenditure-switching policy measures.

a An increase in global incomes

b An increase in trade restrictions abroad

c A high domestic income elasticity of demand for imports

d The adoption of expenditure-reducing policies by foreign governments

e The existence of spare capacity in the economy

TERMS

Expenditure-reducing policy: designed to reduce current account deficit by reducing household spending.

Expenditure-switching: designed to reduce a current account deficit by encouraging domestic consumers to switch their spending from imports to domestically produced products and foreign consumers to switch their spending from foreign made products to the country's exports.

5.05 Fiscal, monetary and supply side policies to correct inflation and deflation

To correct demand-pull inflation, a government may implement deflationary fiscal policy by reducing government spending and/or increasing taxes. Government spending is a component of AD, so reducing government spending will directly reduce AD. Higher taxes may lower consumer expenditure and so AD.

A government may also use deflationary monetary policy to correct demand-pull inflation. It may seek to do this by increasing the rate of interest, reducing the growth of the money supply or raising the exchange rate. A higher interest rate may encourage saving and reduce borrowing. A reduction in the growth of the money supply may enable the growth of aggregate supply to keep pace with the growth of aggregate demand. A higher exchange rate may reduce AD, or at least the growth of AD, by lowering net exports.

To correct deflation caused by falling AD, a government is likely to use reflationary fiscal and or monetary policy. For instance, a government may cut indirect taxes to encourage people to spend more and may seek to encourage commercial banks to lend more.

To correct cost-push inflation a government may increase the exchange rate. This will reduce the cost of imported raw materials. It may also put pressure on domestic firms to keep their costs low in order to compete both at home and abroad.

Supply side policy is usually the main policy used to correct cost-push inflation. Increasing the efficiency of markets and resources can lower costs of production. For instance, deregulation may reduce firms' administrative costs and trade union reform may reduce upward pressure on wages.

Progress check F

Why might the imposition of import restrictions increase the inflation rate?

5.06 The effectiveness of fiscal, monetary and supply side policies to correct inflation and deflation

Inflation can be difficult to correct. Indeed, inflation can cause inflation. Workers may demand higher wages, households may increase their spending and firms may raise their prices in expectation that inflation will continue. Their actions will cause what they were expecting.

In the case of trying to correct demand-pull inflation, there is no guarantee that raising taxes and/or the rate of interest will reduce consumer expenditure. People may cut back on saving rather than spending.

Supply side policy measures used to correct cost-push inflation may take time to work. There is also no guarantee that they will work. For instance, privatisation may increase prices if the privatised firms have significant market power. Rising costs may also be generated from outside the country, for instance, a restriction in the supply of oil by OPEC may increase the price of fuel.

There are a number of reasons why it may be difficult to stop a deflationary spiral. People and firms may be so pessimistic about the future, that any cut in income tax or the rate of interest may fail to encourage a rise in consumer expenditure and investment. In this case, higher government spending is likely to be the preferred policy measure. Tax revenue, however, may be low during a deflationary spiral and a government may be concerned about increasing the size of a budget deficit. A central bank may also have cut the rate of interest so low that it may not be possible to cut it much further. If this is the position, a central bank may resort to increasing the money supply.

Increasing incentives for firms and workers may result in a more uneven distribution of income.

TIP In evaluating the effectiveness of a policy measure, first analyse how the policy measure should work, then explore its strengths and weaknesses and the unintended consequences it may have.

Progress check G

Identify one expenditure-reducing measure and one expenditure-switching measure which are not available to a country which is a member of an economic union.

Revision activity D

Match the following policy measures with the following pairs of government objectives in Table 5.01 they could solve.

Policy measure	Pairs of government macroeconomic objectives
A cut in the rate of interest	Reduce a current account surplus Reduce cost-push inflation
An increase in government spending on education	Reduce demand-pull inflation Reduce income inequality
A rise in income tax	Increase economic growth Increase net exports
The removal of tariffs	Reduce cost-push inflation Reduce unemployment

Table 5.01: Government policy measures and macroeconomic objectives

Mind maps

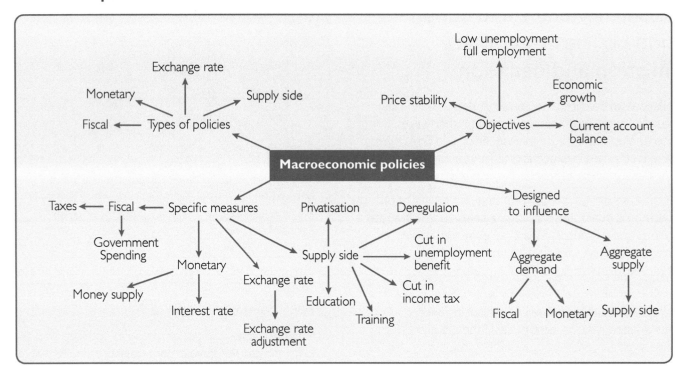

Mind map 5.01: Macroeconomic policies

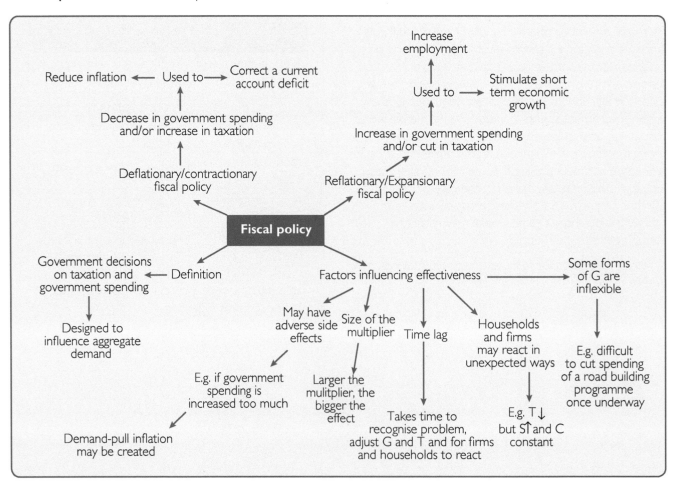

Mind map 5.02: Fiscal policy

Exam-style Questions

Multiple Choice Questions

1   Which policy measure is most likely to be effective in reducing a balance of trade deficit?

   A   Devaluation of the currency

   B   An increase in government spending on state benefits

   C   A reduction in the rate of interest .

   D   A reduction in income tax

2   A country's current account position moves from a surplus to a deficit. What will be the result?

   A   A decrease in the money supply

   B   A decrease in unemployment

   C   An increase in the exchange rate

   D   An increase in real GDP

3   A government decides to introduce an expenditure-switching measure to reduce a balance of trade deficit. Which of the following is an expenditure-switching measure?

   A   A decrease in state benefits

   B   A government subsidy to domestic producers

   C   An increase in income tax

   D   An increase in the rate of interest

4   What change must be caused by a devaluation?

   A   A fall in employment

   B   A fall in the budget surplus

   C   A fall in the rate of interest

   D   A fall in the terms of trade

5   A government uses an expenditure-reducing measure to correct a balance of payments current account deficit. In the short term, what effect would such a measure have on consumer expenditure and net exports?

	Consumer expenditure	Net exports
A	Decrease	Decrease
B	Decrease	Increase
C	Increase	Increase
D	Increase	Decrease

6   A government wants to reduce both the country's inflation rate and its current account surplus. What could be an appropriate government measure to achieve these objectives?

   A   Devalue the currency

   B   Decrease tariffs on imports

   C   Increase the exchange rate

   D   Increase income tax

7   Which government policy measure would be most likely to reduce a current account deficit and unemployment?

   A   Devaluation

   B   Decrease in income tax

   C   Increase in the rate of interest

   D   Increase in corporation tax

8   Which of the following is not an automatic stabiliser?

   A   Income tax

   B   Sales tax

   C   State retirement pension

   D   Unemployment benefit

9   Which measure is a deflationary monetary policy measure?

   A   A deliberate reduction by the central bank in the rate of interest

   B   A deliberate reduction by the government of its budget deficit

   C   A sale of government securities by the central bank

   D   A sale of state owned enterprises to the private sector

10 Which policy measure may reduce demand-pull inflation but increase cost-push inflation?

   A   A rise in the rate of interest

   B   A rise in government spending on training

   C   A decrease in corporation tax

   D   A decrease in import tariffs

Data Response Questions

I The rise of the BRICS

The original term 'BRICs' referred to Brazil, Russia, India and China. It was first used by Jim O'Neill, an investment analyst working for the investment bank, Goldman Sachs. In 2010 the original four countries were joined by South Africa and became the BRICS. The BRICS are forecast to be the dominant economies by 2050 and are already the four largest economies outside the OECD (Organisation for Economic Co-operation and Development).

The reasons why the BRICS are expected to overtake the USA and other developed economies in a few decades is the relatively rapid economic growth rates of some of their members. The BRICS avoided going into recession towards the end of the first decade of the twenty first century but all experienced a cyclical budget deficit and in more recent years some have experienced negative economic growth.

When Jim O'Neill coined the term BRICS he was not thinking of them as a trading bloc but they are beginning to think of themselves as a group and they held their first official summit meeting in June 2009.

The BRICS initially had high economic growth rates and increasing values of exports and imports. In more recent years, the macroeconomic performance of the countries has varied. Brazil, India and South Africa have recently experienced current account deficits whilst China, and Russia have continued to experience current account surpluses. All the countries impose a range of trade restrictions. Exports account for approximately a third of the gross domestic product (GDP) of Russia and South Africa, a quarter of the GDP of China and India but less than a fifth of the GDP of Brazil. Table 5.02 shows a range of economic data on the BRICS.

	Economic growth Rate (%)	Inflation rate (%)	Unemployment rate (%)	Income per head (US$)
Brazil	-3.7	9.5	6.9	15,800
Russia	-3.8	15.4	5.8	23,700
India	7.2	4.9	4.9	6,300
China	6.9	1.5	4.1	14,300
South Africa	1.3	4.6	25.5	13,400

Table 5.02: Selected economic data 2015

a   Explain what is meant by a cyclical budget deficit.   [4]

b   Analyse how economic growth may affect the value of a country's imports.   [4]

c   How far does the extract suggest the BRICS are open economies?   [6]

d   Discuss the extent to which the extract supports the view that the BRICS have a similar
    macroeconomic performance.   [6]

2 Venezuela facing runaway inflation

In 2016 the International Monetary Fund (IMF) forecast that inflation in Venezuela might reach 750% in a couple of years. Figure 5.02 shows how Venezuela's inflation rate and interest rate have changed in recent years.

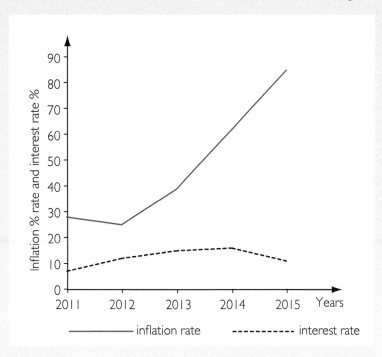

Figure 5.02

The price of Venezuela's currency, the bolivar, has fallen on foreign exchange markets. This has recently been due to the decrease in the price of oil. In the case of Venezuela, oil accounts for nearly 95% of the country's exports. At the end of 2015 the official exchange rate was 6.3 bolivars to the dollar but on illegal markets, 630 bolivars had to be exchanged for one dollar.

One of the main causes of Venezuela's very high inflation rate has been the central government printing more and more money to finance a large and growing budget deficit.

The government has used a range of policy measures to reduce the inflation rate. It has imposed price ceilings on a number of products, provided subsidies to farmers and nationalised some food processing firms and some farmland.

a   What is meant by a budget deficit?   [2]

b   Explain what type of inflation might be caused by an increase in the money supply.   [4]

c   Assess whether Figure 5.02 shows the expected relationship between changes in Venezuela's
     interest rate and inflation rate.   [4]

d   Analyse how a fall in the price of oil could cause a fall in Venezuela's exchange rate.   [4]

e   Discuss whether subsidies given to farmers will reduce inflation.   [6]

Essay Questions

1 a Explain the causes of a fall in a country's exchange rate. [8]

   b Discuss whether a fall in a country's exchange rate will reduce a deficit on the current account of the balance of payments of the country. [12]

2 a Explain the effects of an appreciation of its currency on an economy's inflation rate. [8]

   b Discuss whether a rise in an economy's inflation rate will cause the value of its currency to fall. [12]

REVISION TIPS

Tables

It is useful to draw up tables as these can enable you to process information and make comparisons. For example, you might find it useful to compare demand-pull and cost-push inflation.

Try filling in Table 5.03 in Activity 5.01.

Activity 5.01

	Demand-pull inflation	Cost-push inflation
Definition		
Illustrated by		
Examples of causes		
Impact on real GDP		
Policy to reduce		

Table 5.03: A comparison between demand-pull inflation and cost-push inflation

Section 2:
A LEVEL

Basic economic ideas and resource allocation

6.01 An efficient allocation of resources

The efficient allocation of resources is also called the socially optimum allocation. It is the best use of resources. It occurs when the highest quantity of wants is being met with the scarce resources available. The right goods are being produced in the right quantities at the lowest possible cost and economic welfare is maximised. An efficient allocation of resources is achieved when marginal social benefit (MSB) equals marginal social cost (MSC).

TERMS

Marginal Social Benefit (MSB): the change in social benefit from consuming one more unit.

Marginal Social Cost (MSC): the change in social cost from producing one more unit.

When there is an efficient allocation of resources, economic welfare is maximised. The value that society places on the products being produced will equal the cost of producing those products.

To achieve an efficient allocation of resources, it is necessary for there to be economic efficiency.

6.02 Productive and allocative efficiency

Economic efficiency occurs when both productive efficiency and allocative efficiency are achieved.

Productive efficiency is concerned with how resources are used. To attain productive efficiency, both technical efficiency and cost efficiency have to be achieved. Productive efficiency occurs when products are made with the least possible quantity of resources (technical efficiency) and the lowest cost methods (cost efficiency). In micro terms, productive efficiency is often measured in terms of long run average costs. A firm may be described as productively efficient if it is producing at the lowest point on the long run average cost curve. In this case, a firm would have the lowest unit cost possible and would not be wasting resources. It would be producing where average cost (AC) equals marginal cost (MC).

In macro terms, productive efficiency is achieved when an economy is making full use of resources. When an economy is producing on its production possibility curve, it cannot produce more of one type of product without producing less of another type of product.

Allocative efficiency is concerned with what resources are used to produce. It is achieved when resources are allocated to produce the right products in the right quantities. This means that what is produced reflects consumers' demand. More precisely, allocative efficiency is achieved when price equals marginal cost. Price reflects the value that consumers place on the product and marginal cost is effectively the cost of the last unit.

A firm is allocatively efficient when it produces where the price (the value placed on the product by consumers) equals the marginal cost (the cost of producing the last unit produced). An economy is allocatively efficient when it uses the economy's resources to make those products which will provide the greatest satisfaction for consumers.

TERMS

Productive efficiency: when products are made with the least possible quantity of resources and the lowest cost methods.

Allocative efficiency: when resources are allocated to produce the right products in the right quantities.

Revision activity A

Decide whether the following would affect allocative or productive efficiency and whether they would increase or reduce efficiency.

a A reduction in unemployment

b A shift of resources from producing demerit goods to producing merit goods

c A reduction in surpluses

d A reduction in labour productivity

e A switch from producing less popular to more popular products

f A reduction in organisational slack

Progress check A

What does the existence of unemployment indicate about the efficiency of an economy?

TIP

Remember it cannot be assumed that because an economy is producing on its production possibility curve, that it is allocatively efficient. To decide whether allocative efficiency is being achieved, it would also be necessary to know the preferences of people in the economy.

6.03 Pareto optimality

Pareto optimality occurs when it is not possible to make someone better off without making someone else worse off. It is also sometimes referred to as Pareto efficiency or social efficiency. It does not take into account the distribution of income.

A Pareto improvement occurs when a reallocation of resources makes at least one person better off while making no-one worse off.

Progress check B

In what circumstance would a reallocation of resources increase economic welfare?

6.04 Dynamic efficiency

Dynamic efficiency relates to efficiency over time. A firm is said to be more dynamically efficient when it improves its production processes and becomes more responsive to changes in consumer demand as a result of investment and innovation.

In the short term, spending more money on research and development and new capital equipment may increase average costs of production. In the longer term, however, by increasing output per unit, average costs of production should fall.

When a firm becomes more dynamically efficient, it will be producing at a lower average cost, producing better quality products and responding more quickly and fully to changes in market conditions.

An economy is said to be more dynamically efficient when, again, its rate of investment and innovation increases and when it is moving resources more quickly from declining to expanding industries.

Progress check C

How may increased government spending on education affect dynamic efficiency?

TERMS

Pareto optimality: occurs when it is not possible to make someone better off without making someone else worse off.

Dynamic efficiency: when rate of investment and innovation increases and when resources are moved more quickly from declining to expanding industries.

6.05 Market failure

Market failure occurs when the free market forces of demand and supply do not achieve an efficient allocation of resources. There are a number of causes of market failure including:

- a lack of markets. There are no markets for public goods. People do not reveal their demand and so private sector firms have no incentive to produce public goods.

- the existence of externalities. Consumption and production decisions are not likely to take into account all the effects on society. Not all costs and benefits are reflected in market prices. As a result, the level of consumption and production may not maximise economic welfare.

- a lack of competition in markets (market power). Competition may promote efficiency by providing an incentive (in the form of profit) to the producers who make what consumers want at the lowest average cost and a punishment (in the form of going out of business) for those which do not keep the cost low and do not respond to changes in consumer demand. Firms that have market power may restrict output in order to raise price. This may result in them producing where price exceeds marginal cost and so may result in them being allocatively inefficient. The lack of competition may also mean that they do not produce at the lowest possible average cost and so are productively inefficient.

- information failure. Consumers and/or producers may lack information, may have inaccurate information or may have different amounts or quality of information. For example, a person may be persuaded by an unscrupulous roofer that more extensive work has to be done on his roof than is necessary because he lacks the knowledge of the state of his roof to challenge the roofer's advice. Governments consider that information failure occurs in the case of merit and demerit goods. In the case of these goods, there is a divergence between the value the government places on them and the value that consumers place on them. The government considers that they will not be consumed or produced in the quantities that will maximise economic welfare if left to market forces. In practice, merit and demerit goods also generate externalities. Merit goods also have an element of equity, in the sense that the government may think that everyone, whatever their income, should have access to them.

- a failure of markets to clear. In the case of some markets, surpluses or shortages may be long lasting. For instance, a labour market may not clear. Coal miners, for instance, may remain unemployed for a long period of time, if they are occupationally and/or geographically immobile.

Progress check D

Why is it difficult to achieve allocative efficiency in the case of public goods?

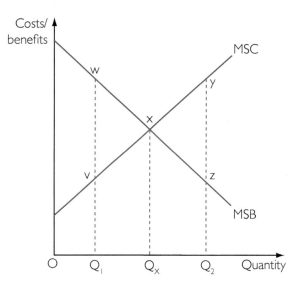

Figure 6.01

TERM

Market failure: when the free market forces of demand and supply do not achieve an efficient allocation of resources.

6.06 An inefficient allocation of resources

An inefficient allocation of resources occurs when society is not maximising its economic welfare. Marginal social cost is not equal to marginal social benefit.

Figure 6.01 shows that the allocatively efficient quantity is Q. At this point the value society places on the product (reflected in MSB) is equal to the cost of producing that quantity (reflected in MSC). If the quantity traded was Q_1, there would be a welfare loss of vwx. In this case, the product is being under-consumed and under-produced. The value that society places on the product is greater than the cost of producing it. Increasing output from Q_1 to Q_x would benefit society. There is also a welfare loss, xyz, if the quantity traded is Q_2. This time the product is overconsumed and over-produced. It costs more to produce the product than the value society gains from consuming it. Economic welfare would be increased by reducing the output of the product and switching resources to making products more highly valued by society.

Revision activity B

Explain whether the following statements about allocative and productive efficiency are true or false.

a   A shift to the right of a production possibility curve indicates an increase in productive efficiency

b   If average revenue is above marginal cost, resources are being used inefficiently

c   When allocative efficiency is achieved there is no welfare loss

d   For economic efficiency to be achieved marginal social cost has to be at a minimum for all products

e   Information failure can result in allocative inefficiency

---

6.07 Social costs and benefits

Social costs are the total costs of an economic activity. They consist of both private costs and external costs. Private costs are the costs incurred by consumers and producers of the product. External costs are the costs to third parties (see below). Social costs minus private costs equal external costs.

Social benefits are the total benefits of an economic activity. They consist of both private benefits and external benefits. External benefits are the benefit received by third parties (see below). Social benefits minus private benefits equal external benefits.

Progress Check E

What would it mean if social costs equal private costs?

TIP

Be careful not to confuse social costs and external costs. Many students write about social costs when they mean external costs. Social costs is a wider term than external costs. Social costs cover all the costs to society arising from an economic activity – the costs to the consumers, producers, anyone indirectly affected and the cost to the environment.

6.08 Externalities

Externalities are effects on third parties, that is people who are not directly involved in the production or consumption of a product. First and second parties are the producers and consumers of the product.

TERM

Externalities: the effects on third parties who are not directly involved in the production or consumption of a product.

These effects are sometimes called spill-over effects. When making their consumption and production decisions, consumers and producers do not usually take into account externalities.

Positive externalities (also referred to as external benefits) are beneficial effects that third parties receive without paying for them. There are positive externalities of both consumption and production.

Figure 6.02(a) shows that when there are positive externalities of consumption, the marginal social benefit (MSB) will exceed the marginal private benefit (MPB), the quantity is below the allocatively efficient level and there is a welfare loss of vwx.

Figure 6.02(b) shows that when there are positive externalities of production, the marginal private cost (MPC) will exceed the marginal social cost (MSC). This is because the output of the firm or firms lowers the cost experienced by third parties. Again, the quantity

Positive externalities

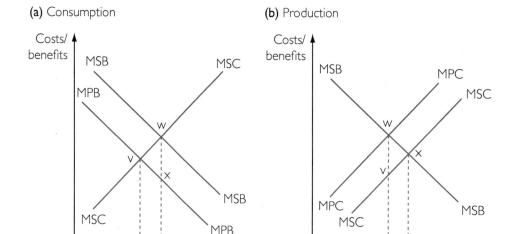

Figure 6.02

is below the allocatively efficient level and there is a welfare loss of vwx.

Negative externalities (also called external costs) are harmful effects imposed on third parties who do not receive financial compensation.

Figure 6.03(a) shows that when there are negative externalities of consumption, the marginal private benefit will exceed the marginal social benefit. This is because the consumption of the product is reducing the welfare on third parties. The quantity is above the allocatively efficient level and there is a welfare loss of xyz.

Figure 6.03(b) shows that when there are negative externalities of production, the marginal social cost will exceed the marginal private cost. The output of the firm or firms is imposing costs on third parties. The quantity is above the allocatively efficient level and there is a welfare loss of xyz.

Progress check F

Identify a first party, a second party and a third party involved in the production and consumption of air travel.

6.09 Decision making using cost-benefit analysis

Cost-benefit analysis (CBA) is a method of appraising a major investment project such as a railway line, airport and a main road. A CBA takes into account social costs and benefits whereas a private investment appraisal considers private costs and private benefits. So, whereas a CBA includes external costs and benefits, a private investment appraisal does not.

The first stage of a CBA is to identify the costs and benefits involved. Decisions will have to be made on the depth and width of the scope of the CBA. Monetary values are assigned to the present and future costs and benefits. In some cases, shadow prices are used. These are estimated prices. Calculating monetary values is easier in the case of private costs and benefits than in the case of external costs and benefits. In calculating private benefits, an estimate has to be made of consumer surplus.

TERM

Cost-benefit analysis (CBA): analysis of the social costs and social benefits of a project.

Negative externalities

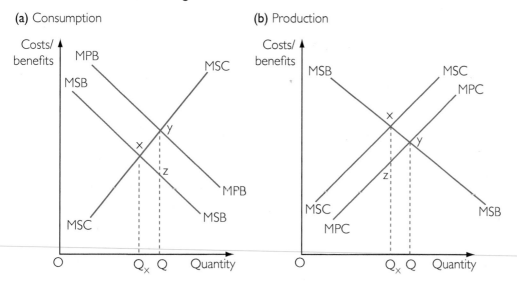

Figure 6.03

Externalities may be estimated by using questionnaires, considering how much those who suffer would have to be compensated and how much people would be prepared to pay for the benefits, valuing time saved when, for example, a new road is built by using the average wage and examining the effects of similar projects.

Future costs and benefits are discounted (given a lower value). This is because money paid out in the future is less of a sacrifice than money paid out now, and money received now is more valuable than money received in the future as it can be put to use or can earn interest.

The costs may be weighted to take into account how they are distributed and the income of those incurring the costs. For example, a few people experiencing very high costs may be thought to be more significant than many people being only slightly affected. In addition, loss of income incurred by the poor might be considered to have more of an impact than the equivalent loss for the rich.

Calculations have to be adjusted for risk and uncertainty. When all the costs and benefits have been added up and compared, the net present value is calculated. Then a decision is made. The project will not be recommended if social costs exceed social benefits. Even if there is a positive net value (also referred to as a net social benefit), the project may not be approved if the net social benefit is less than that of a rival project or if it will be politically unpopular.

According to what is known as the Pareto criterion, a project is desirable only if there are gainers and no one is worse off. According to this view, a project would be approved only if the gainers fully compensate the losers, with the gainers still being better off after doing so. The Hicks-Kaldor criterion is more lenient. It suggests a project should be approved if the gainers could, in principle, compensate those who lose and still enjoy a net increase in welfare.

A CBA has the advantage that it seeks to make a decision based on the full costs and benefits of a project. This should make it more likely that an allocatively efficient decision will be made.

A CBA has a number of possible limitations. It may be narrow in its scope and may not include all those likely to be affected by the project. In practice, it is difficult to place a monetary value on external costs and external benefits. For instance, how should the loss of wildlife habitats be valued? People likely to be affected by the investment project tend to exaggerate costs (in the hope that they may be compensated) and underestimate benefits (for fear they may have to pay for them). It can be very expensive and time consuming to carry out a CBA. Political pressure may influence the recommendation of a CBA. Pressure groups may try to influence the outcome and a government may reject the recommendation of a CBA if it thinks it will lose votes.

Progress check G

What is the difference between a cost-benefit analysis and a private sector investment project?

Revision activity C

a Categorise the following effects of building and operating a new airport into private benefits, private costs, external benefits and external costs.

1 Air and noise pollution generated by flights to and from the airport

2 Air fares collected by the airlines that use the airport

3 A fall in the price of houses close to the airport

4 Destruction of wildlife habitats

5 Increased custom for local taxi choice

6 Insurance paid by the airport operators

7 Revenue for airport operators

8 Traffic congestion near the airport

9 Wages paid to workers building the airport

b Using the information in Table 6.01, calculate the marginal social benefit and the marginal social cost. What is the allocatively efficient output?

Output	Social benefit	Marginal social benefit	Social cost	Marginal social cost
20	100		90	
21	120		100	
22	150		120	
23	200		150	
24	240		190	
25	260		220	

Table 6.01

TIP

In analysing CBA, it is useful to give a local example of a large investment project, for instance, the proposed building of a new road or a new hospital.

Mind maps

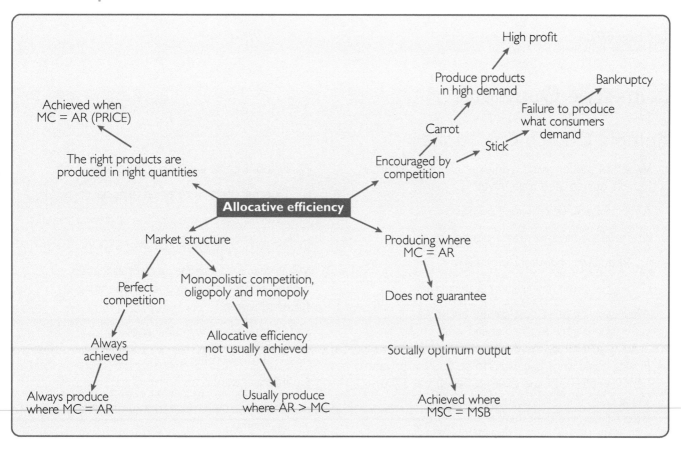

Mind map 6.01: Allocative efficiency

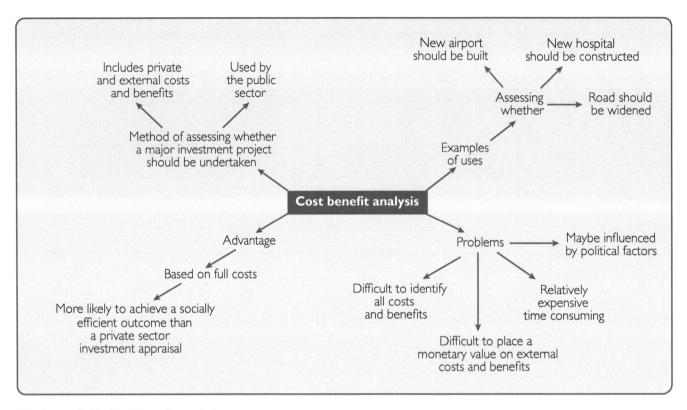

Mind map 6.02: Cost benefit analysis

Exam-style Questions

Multiple Choice Questions

1 Which of the following is an example of an external benefit of increased train travel?

  A Increased overcrowding on trains

  B Reduced fares for train passengers

  C Reduced congestion on roads

  D Higher profits for train operating firms

2 After carrying out a cost-benefit analysis, a government decides to go ahead with a hospital building scheme as there is a net social benefit. Private costs were calculated to be $500 m, private benefits at $600 m and external benefits at $700 m. What does this information indicate about the external costs of the scheme?

  A External costs were equal to private costs.

  B External costs were equal to social costs.

  C External costs were less than external benefits.

  D External costs were less than $800 m.

3 What effect will a more efficient allocation of resources have on an economy operating at full employment?

  A Output will remain unchanged.

  B Output will rise.

  C Inflation will occur.

  D There will be a more even distribution of income.

4 Figure 6.04 shows a change in the output of an economy from production point X to production point Y.

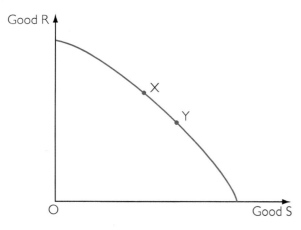

Figure 6.04

What effect will this movement have on allocative and productive efficiency?

	Allocative efficiency	Productive efficiency
A	Remain unchanged	Remain unchanged
B	Remain unchanged	Uncertain
C	Uncertain	Remain unchanged
D	Uncertain	Uncertain

5 Figure 6.05 shows that the allocation of resources is initially at X. Which reallocation of resources would lead to a Pareto improvement?

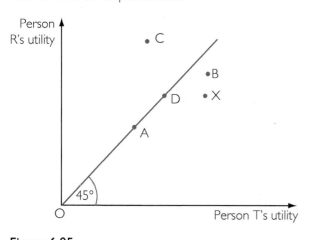

Figure 6.05

A   A   B   B   C   C   D   D

6 In which circumstance might the imposition of a tax on a product result in an efficiency gain?

A The price of the product is initially equal to marginal cost.

B The price of the product rises to where average revenue exceeds average cost.

C There is already a tax on a complementary good.

D There is already a tax on a substitute good.

7 Figure 6.06 shows a market in equilibrium at a price of P. A government then sets a minimum price of PX and maintains this price by purchasing any surplus supply. What is the net loss to society of this policy?

A Area PP_XUV	**C** Area YTUZ
B Area NP_XU	**D** Area YTVUZ

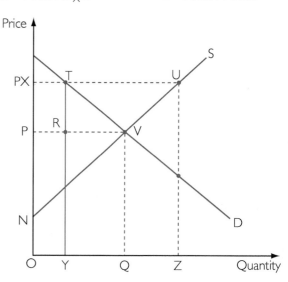

Figure 6.06

8 An economy, where most of the population are vegetarians, experiences a change in its production from point X to point Y on Figure 6.07.

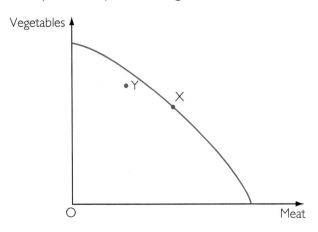

Figure 6.07

What effect does the change in production have on allocative efficiency and productive efficiency?

	Allocative efficiency	Productive efficiency
A	Decrease	Decrease
B	Decrease	Increase
C	Increase	Decrease
D	Increase	Increase

9 A government is producing a product. Its objective is to maximise economic welfare. To achieve this objective, it should produce up to the point where:

A the benefit from consuming the last unit equals the cost of producing the last unit.

B the cost of producing the last unit is zero.

C the gap between social benefit and social cost is greatest.

D the total benefit of consuming the product is maximised.

10 An oil tanker ran aground on a beach. Oil leaked from the tanker on to the beach. The government spent $60,000 to clean up the beach. The loss to the local tourist industry was $85,000. The firm which owns the oil tanker spent $90,000 on repairing the oil tanker. What was the social cost of the accident?

A $60,000   C $175,000

B $90,000   D $235,000

Data Response Questions

1 Challenges facing Latin American firms

A number of Latin American countries are seeking to increase the efficiency of their firms. There are thought to be a number of reasons why manufacturing and services are relatively inefficient in the region.

One is poor infrastructure. Overcrowded seaports and airports and badly maintained roads and railways increase transport costs. Indeed, it costs more to transport some products from Latin America to the United States than it costs to send the same products from China to the United States. Higher transport costs can contribute to inflation and unemployment – see Table 6.02.

Country	Inflation %	Unemployment %
Argentina	16.8	5.9
Brazil	9.5	6.9
Chile	3.9	5.8
Colombia	4.2	8.6
Venezuela	85.0	6.0

Table 6.02: Inflation and unemployment rates in selected Latin American countries in 2015

A lack of competition in a number of industries in Latin America reduces the pressure on firms to keep their costs low and to respond quickly and fully to changes in consumer demand.

Another major cause of inefficiency in the region is thought to be a lack of bank loans available to firms wanting to expand and innovate.

a   What is meant by firms being efficient? [3]

b   Explain what evidence there is in the information provided that some Latin American firms are allocatively inefficient. [3]

c   Analyse two policy measures Latin American governments could introduce to increase efficiency. [6]

d   i   Using Table 6.02, comment on whether high inflation rates are associated with high unemployment rates. [2]

ii   Discuss whether inefficiency is indicated by:

• a high unemployment rate

• a high inflation rate. [6]

2 Popular sports

Cricket is the world's second most popular team sport. It was estimated that football had 3.5 billion fans and cricket 2.5 billion fans in 2016. Cricket is particularly popular in India. This is reflected in the salaries paid to cricketers playing in the Indian Premier League (IPL) Twenty20 cricket league (see Table 6.03).

League	Country	Sport	Average player salary US$ millions
NBA	N. America	Basketball	4.58
IPL	India	Cricket	4.33
MLB	N. America	Baseball	4.17
EPL	UK	Football	3.82
NHL	N. America	Ice Hockey	2.62
Bundesliga	Germany	Football	2.29
NFL	USA	Gridiron Football	2.11
La Liga	Spain	Football	1.86
Serie A	Italy	Football	1.74
Ligue 1	France	Football	1.49
NPB	Japan	Baseball	0.66
CSL	China	Football	0.39

Table 6.03: Highest paid sports leagues 2014–2015 season

Firms involved with cricket teams and selling coverage of their matches to TV companies are seeking to increase the number of global spectators. They are doing this by improving the experience that spectators gain and catering for different groups of spectators. For instance, the Twenty20 format has proved to be very popular with television viewers.

Despite its global popularity, not many people watch or play cricket in the USA, the world's biggest sports market and where sport has a high income elasticity of demand. A number of firms are seeking to change this situation. One of these is the Times of India Group, an Indian Media firm. It has put on high profile cricket matches in the USA with world stars. To date, the firm has hired baseball stadiums to play the matches but is considering building cricket stadiums in the USA. The building of such stadiums would have a number of effects on local communities.

If cricket becomes a more popular spectator sport in the USA it may encourage more US citizens to play cricket. More people playing sport can increase the health of the population so may raise their productivity and earning potential.

a   Explain what is meant by high income elasticity of demand. [2]

b   Using Table 6.03, analyse the extent to which football accounts for the highest paid sport stars. [3]

c   What evidence is there in the information provided that the US cricket market is becoming more dynamically efficient? [3]

d   Explain one private benefit and one external benefit that may arise from people playing sport. [4]

e   Discuss the extent to which the use of cost-benefit analysis could help in deciding whether to build a cricket stadium. [8]

Essay Questions

1   Discuss whether market forces will ensure an efficient allocation of resources. [25]

2   a   Explain what is meant by an efficient use of resources. [12]

    b   Discuss the extent to which merit goods are evidence of market failure. [13]

REVISION TIPS

Mind maps

Mind maps can also be called spider diagrams. You can put a topic in the centre and then move out to show connected points. You may find it useful to draw up mind maps with fellow students and you may want to put some up on your wall.

Try completing the following mind map on Cambridge Economics A Level in Activity 6.01.

Activity 6.01

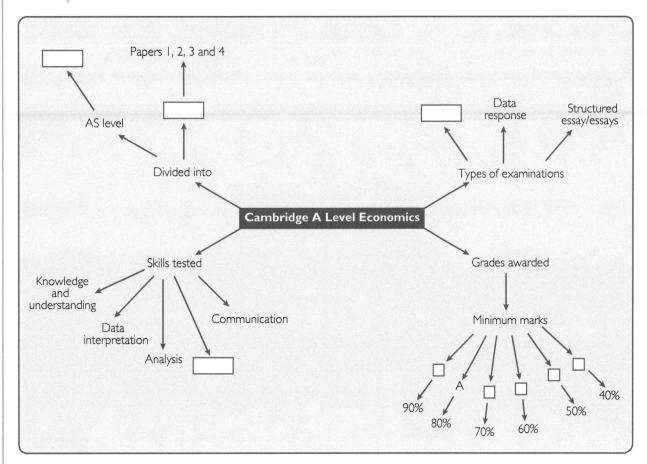

Mind map 6.03

Chapter 7

The price system and the micro economy

Learning summary

After you have studied this chapter, you should be able to:

- explain the law of diminishing marginal utility

- outline the relationship between the law of diminishing marginal utility and an individual demand schedule and curve

- use figures to illustrate the equi-marginal principle

- assess the limitations of marginal utility theory

- compare rational behaviour model and behavioural economic models

- draw budget lines to explain the income and substitution effects of a price change

- apply indifference curve analysis

- describe the short run production function

- distinguish between fixed and variable factors of production

- calculate total, average and marginal product

- explain the law of diminishing returns

- calculate marginal cost and average cost

- distinguish between fixed costs and variable costs

- describe the long run production function

- explain the shape of the short run and long run average cost curve

- analyse the relationship between economies of scale and decreasing costs

- describe internal and external economies of scale and diseconomies of scale.

- explain total, average and marginal revenue

- distinguish between normal and abnormal profit

- assess the characteristics of different market structures of perfect competition, monopoly, monopolistic competition and oligopoly

- compare the performance of firms in different market structures in terms of revenue, output, profits, efficiency, X-inefficiency, barriers to entry and exit, price competition, non-price competition and collusion

- analyse contestable markets and their implications

- explain how the concentration ratio varies between different market structures

- analyse the reasons for small firms

- explain integration, diversification, mergers and cartels

- explain the traditional profit maximising objective of firms

- describe the relationship between elasticity and revenue

- discuss other objectives of firms including survival, strategic and sales maximisation

- explain the principal agent problem (for example, the divorce of ownership from control)

- analyse behavioural approach to the decision making of a firm, the prisoner's dilemma, two player pay-off matrix, kinked demand curve

- explain pricing policy including price discrimination, limit pricing, price leadership and mutual interdependence in the case of oligopoly (including game theory)

7.01 Law of diminishing marginal utility and its relationship to the derivation of an individual demand schedule and curve

Utility is the satisfaction a person gains from consuming a product. Marginal utility is the change in total utility a person experiences as a result of consuming the last unit. Consumers tend to experience less satisfaction for each additional unit of a product consumed – the law of diminishing marginal utility.

Total utility rises when marginal utility is positive, reaches its peak when marginal utility is zero and falls when marginal utility is negative. These relationships are shown in Figure 7.01.

TERMS

Utility: satisfaction from consumption of a product.

Marginal utility: the change in total utility a person experiences as a result of consuming the last unit of a product.

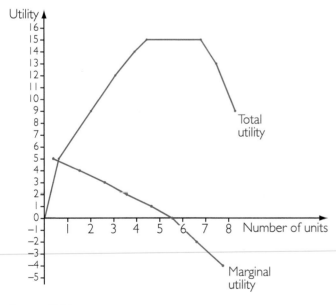

Figure 7.01

An individual demand schedule and curve is based on the marginal utility curve. If, for instance, a person gains

a marginal utility of $9 from the fifth unit and $7 from the sixth unit, this will represent the price they would be prepared to pay for the different quantities. This information can be used to draw up a demand schedule and draw a demand curve. For instance, in this case a fall in price from 9 to 7 would result in an extension in demand from 5 to 6.

Progress check A

Why would a person be unlikely to consume a quantity of product where total utility is falling?

Equi-marginal product

The equi-marginal principle states that consumers will gain the highest total utility from their income by consuming the combination of products which ensures that the utility from the last $ spent on each product is equal. The formula for this is:

$$\frac{\text{Marginal utility (MU) of product A}}{\text{Price (P) of product A}} = \frac{\text{MU of product B}}{\text{P of product B}}$$

$$= \frac{\text{MU of product C}}{\text{P of product C}}$$

TERM

Equi-marginal principle: states that consumers will gain the highest total utility from their income by consuming the combination of products which ensures that the utility from the last dollar spent on each product is equal.

Limitations of marginal utility theory

In practice, people do not always behave in the way marginal utility theory suggests. There are a number of reasons for this. One is that not all products can be divided into small units. While a person can decide whether to buy eight or nine apples, a number of the products they buy are indivisible such as a car. People also often buy on habit and impulse rather than carefully weighing up the marginal utilities of everything they purchase. In addition, for some products marginal utility may increase, the more a person has. For instance, a collector of first edition books may gain more satisfaction from the twentieth book than from the nineteenth book.

Although there are limitations to marginal utility theory, it does help to explain the inverse relationship between price and demand that occurs in the case of most products.

> ## Progress check B
>
> What should a consumer do if she is getting more satisfaction per dollar spent on apples than on oranges?

7.02 Rational behaviour model and behavioural economic models

The rational behaviour model assumes that people act logically, rationally and in a self-interested way. For instance, it is assumed that consumers seek to maximise utility and compare the satisfaction they would gain from different combinations of products.

Behavioural economics is a mixture of economics and psychology which recognises that people can behave in ways that may seem irrational. Behavioural economic models explore how and why people make some decisions that might not seem to be best for them. An early behavioural model, developed by Daniel Kahneman and Amos Tversky in 1979 is prospect theory. This is the view that people dislike losses more than they like gains. A more recent behavioural model is nudge theory developed by Richard Thaler and Cass Sunstein. This is the idea that people can be helped to make better choices by the way choices are presented to them. For instance, in the UK a workplace pension scheme which automatically enrols people but gives them the right to opt out has had a greater take-up than one requiring people to opt in.

> **TIP**
>
> Observe and read about changes in consumer and producer behaviour. See if you can use economic theory to explain these changes.

7.03 Budget lines

A budget line shows the various combinations of two products that a consumer can buy with a given income and given prices.

If there is a rise in income, the budget line will shift out parallel to the right. A fall in the price of one product will cause the budget line to pivot outwards. Figure 7.02 illustrates the effect of a fall in the price of apples, with income and the price of oranges remaining unchanged.

> **TERM**
>
> Budget line: illustrates the various combinations of two products a consumer can buy with a given income at a given price.

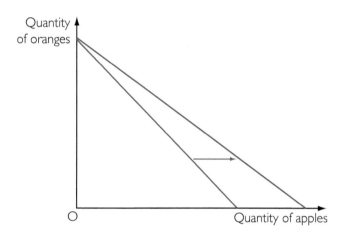

Figure 7.02

> ## Progress check C
>
> How does a budget line reflect relative price changes?

Income and substitution effects of a price change

The income and substitution effects explain why the quantity demanded of a product changes when price changes. A higher price will cause the demand for most products to fall for two reasons. One is that people's purchasing power will decrease. They will be able to buy less of all products, including this one – the income effect. The other reason is that people will switch from buying the product to buying a substitute – the substitution effect.

Some products have exceptional demand with the income and substitution effects working in opposite directions. One example is a Giffen good. This is a low quality product which has a direct relationship between price and demand. In this case, a rise in price will cause a rise in the quantity demanded. A Giffen good has the usual substitution effect with the higher price encouraging consumers to switch to a substitute. The substitution effect, however, is more than offset by a negative income effect. With lower purchasing power, people will not be able to afford higher quality products and so will have to buy more of the Giffen good.

Veblen goods have both increasing marginal utility and income and substitution effects which work in opposite directions. A Veblen good is an expensive product which people buy to show how rich they are. A rise in the price of a Veblen good reduces people's purchasing power but people switch from substitutes to buying the product as it now becomes a more impressive purchase.

7.04 Indifference curve analysis

A budget line shows the various combinations of two products that a consumer can buy with a given income and given prices.

An indifference curve is a graph showing the different combinations of two products which are assumed to give equal satisfaction. One curve joins all the points which give the same satisfaction.

An indifference curve is based on an indifference schedule. For instance, 23 oranges and seven apples may give a consumer the same satisfaction as 20 oranges and eight apples and six oranges and 21 apples.

As the person has more or less of one product, its marginal utility changes. The more apples a person has, the less he will value each extra apple. For instance, when he has 20 oranges and 8 apples, he may be prepared to give up one apple only if he gets 3 oranges in return. When he has 18 apples, he will value them less highly and swapping 2 apples for one orange may give him the same satisfaction.

A number of indifference curves can be drawn. People would prefer more of both products and so will prefer a position on a curve further from the origin. This will give them more satisfaction. A collection of indifference curves is called an indifference map.

People's choice of combinations of products is limited by their income. Maximum satisfaction is on the indifference curve furthest from the origin and which touches the budget line. On Figure 7.03 point T is where the indifference curve CC just touches the budget line WW. The combination of R quantity of product X and S quantity of product Y will give maximum satisfaction.

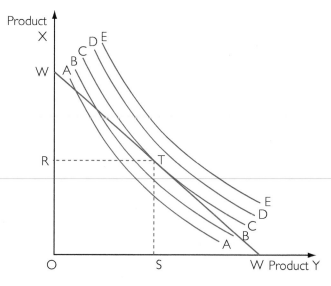

Figure 7.03

If people's income increases or the prices of both products they purchase decrease, their budget lines will move out to the right and so they are able to enjoy more of both products. Figure 7.04 shows that an increase in income moves the combination of products on to a higher curve BB.

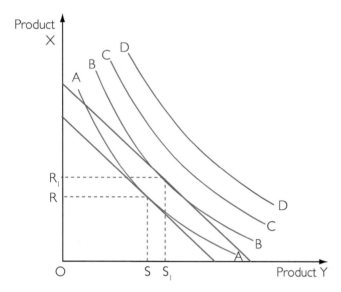

Figure 7.04

If the price of only one of the products increases, the budget line will pivot inwards and will touch a lower indifference curve and so less satisfaction will be gained.

> ## Progress check D
>
> What would a straight downward sloping indifference curve indicate?

7.05 Short-run production function

Nature of the short-run production function

The short run is defined as the period of time when a firm has at least one fixed factor of production.

The short-run production function shows the relationship between the factors of production a firm uses, at least one of which is in fixed supply, and the output it produces:

TP (total product): capital (f), enterprise (v), labour (v) and land (f).

Total product is the total output of a good or service produced by a firm. In this example, capital and land are in fixed supply and enterprise and labour in variable supply.

Fixed and variable factors of production

A fixed factor of production is one which is not changing in quantity. In most cases the fixed factor of production is capital. In the short run, most firms' factory or office size will be unchanged.

A variable factor of production is one which changes in quantity. For instance, a firm may use more raw materials to increase its output.

Law of diminishing returns

The law of diminishing returns (also known as the law of variable proportions) states that as more of a variable factor of production is employed with a fixed factor of production, a point will be reached where marginal product will decline. This will cause total output to rise by a diminishing amount.

A firm may be producing a higher output as a result of employing more labour. At first as more workers are employed, marginal product usually increases (increasing returns) but afterwards it declines. Diminishing returns set in because less efficient combinations of factors of production are used. The proportion of the labour employed is too high relative to the capital or land employed.

Table 7.01 shows that diminishing returns set in after three workers are employed. Average product is total output divided by the number of workers or other input employed. Marginal product is the change in output which results from employing one more worker or other input. Average product is below marginal product when marginal product is rising. It is a rise in marginal product which is pushing up average product.

When marginal product is falling, average product is dragging down average product and marginal product is below average product.

No. of workers	Total product	Average product	Marginal product
0	0	-	
			20
1	20	20	
			30
2	50	25	
			40
3	90	30	
			30
4	120	30	
			20
5	140	28	
			16
6	156	26	

Table 7.01: Diminishing returns

Progress check E

Why have diminishing returns been less of a problem in agriculture than was originally forecast by economists including Malthus?

TERM

Law of diminishing returns: states that as more of a variable factor of production is employed with a fixed factor of production, a point will be reached where marginal product will decline.

7.06 Short-run costs of production

Marginal cost and average cost

Marginal cost (MC) is the change in total cost when output is changed by one unit. Average cost (AC), which is also called average total cost or unit cost, is total cost divided by output.

Short-run cost function – fixed costs versus variable costs

In the short run, total cost is made up of fixed costs and variable costs. Total cost (TC) equals total fixed cost (TFC) plus total variable cost (TVC).

Fixed costs (FC) are costs which do not alter when output changes. These costs are incurred even when output is zero and are the costs associated with fixed factors of production. They are also referred to as overheads and indirect costs. Examples include building insurance and rent. Variable costs (VC) are costs which are directly related to output. If output increases, variable costs rise. They are also called direct costs or prime costs and include raw material costs.

Average fixed cost (AFC) is total fixed cost divided by output. As total fixed cost does not change as output rises, average fixed cost falls as output rises. Overheads are spread over a larger output. Average variable cost (AVC) is total variable cost divided by output. As output increases, AVC usually falls at first as increasing returns are experienced and then rises when diminishing returns are encountered.

Marginal fixed cost is zero as fixed costs do not change. As a result, marginal cost is equal to marginal variable cost.

TERMS

Marginal cost (MC): the change in total cost if output is changed by one unit.

Average cost (AC): total cost divided by output.

Total cost (TC): total fixed cost (TFC) plus total variable cost (TVC).

Fixed cost (FC): a cost that does not alter when output changes.

Variable cost (VC): a cost that does alter when output changes.

Average fixed cost (AFC): total fixed cost divided by output.

Average variable cost (AVC): total variable cost divided by output.

Revision activity A

Complete Table 7.02.

Output	Total cost	Fixed cost	Variable cost	Average cost	Average variable cost	Average fixed cost	Marginal cost	Marginal variable cost
0	100							
1		100						
2				90				
3	201							
4								19
5			180					
6							80	

Table 7.02: Costs of production

TIP

Students sometimes suggest that total cost will fall as output rises. In the short run AFC will fall and it is possible, in both the short and long run, that AC will fall. Total cost, however, rises with output.

Explanation of shape of short-run average cost

The short-run average cost (SRAC) curve falls at first because both AFC and AVC decline. After it reaches its minimum point, the SRAC curve rises. The increase in AVC outweighs the fall in AFC. Figure 7.05 illustrates AC, AVC and AFC.

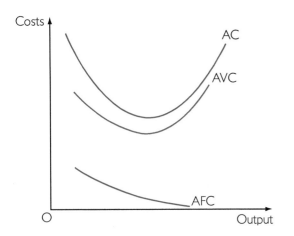

Figure 7.05

The shape of the AVC curve, and so the short-run AC curve, is influenced by increasing and diminishing returns.

The marginal cost curve cuts the average cost curve at its lowest point. When the average cost curve is falling, marginal cost is below average cost whereas when average cost is rising, marginal cost is above average cost as illustrated in Figure 7.06.

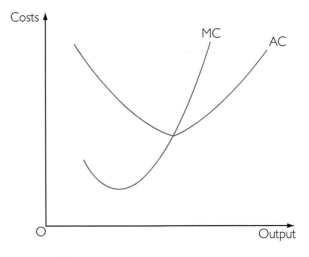

Figure 7.06

Progress check F

What is the connection between diminishing returns and costs of production?

7.07 Long-run production function

The long run is the period of time when a firm can adjust all its factors of production and so all inputs are variable.

The long-run production function shows the relationship between the factors of production a firm uses, all of which are variable, and the output it produces.

In the long run, when all the factors of production can be changed, the most efficient combination of inputs are as following:

$$\frac{\text{Marginal product of factor A}}{\text{Price of factor A}} = \frac{\text{MP of factor B}}{\text{P of factor B}}$$
$$= \frac{\text{MP of factor C}}{\text{P of factor C}}$$

Returns to scale are the changes in output which occurs when a firm changes its scale of operation by altering all its factors of production. Increasing returns to scale are experienced when output increases at a greater rate than inputs. Constant returns to scale are when output and input increases at the same rate. Decreasing returns to scale occur when output increases at a slower rate than inputs.

7.08 Long-run costs of production

In the long run, all costs are variable as there is time to alter all the factors of production employed.

In the long run, a firm can change the size of its factory, farm or offices. Every scale of production can be represented by a SRAC curve. On the assumption that a firm will always seek to minimise the cost of producing any given output, the long-run average cost curve is found by linking the lowest point on a series of SRAC curves. This is shown in Figure 7.07. The long-run average curve (LRAC) is sometimes called the envelope curve of all SRAC curves.

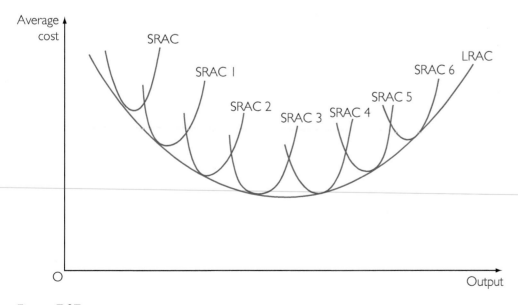

Figure 7.07

Relationship between economies of scale and decreasing costs

A U-shaped LRAC curve shows that a firm first experiences economies of scale with average costs falling. It then reaches its optimum output which is the lowest average cost. Past this point, the firm experiences diseconomies of scale. Figure 7.08 shows the U-shaped LRAC curve.

It is also possible that a LRAC curve may be downward sloping over a large range of output if economies are very significant. It may also be L-shaped if average costs fall at first and then constant returns to scale are experienced over a large range of output. The minimum efficient scale (MES) is the lowest level of output where all economies of scale have been fully exploited.

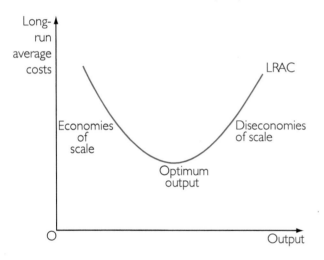

Figure 7.08

Internal and external economies and diseconomies of scale

Internal economies of scale are the benefits, in the form of lower long-run average costs, a firm experiences as a result of increasing its output.

There is a range of different types of internal economies of scale including buying economies (discounts for bulk buying), financial (cheaper to and easier to borrow), managerial (employing specialists), marketing (advertising and transporting products more cheaply), research and development (ability to set up a R & D department), risk bearing (diversifying to reduce the risks of changes in market conditions), technical (making use of large, cost efficient equipment) and staff facilities (such as canteens and healthcare treatment).

External economies of scale are the benefits, in the form of lower long-run average costs, available to all the firms in the industry as the result of the industry growing larger. Examples of external economies of scale include the availability of skilled labour, the development of ancillary industries, specialist markets, specialist courses at colleges and universities, disintegration (allowing firms to specialise) and shared research facilities.

Internal diseconomies of scale are the disadvantages, in the form of higher long-run average costs, which result from a firm growing too large. They include management problems of control, co-ordination and communication along with poor industrial relations.

External diseconomies of scale occur when the industry grows too large and as a result firms in the industry experience higher long-run average costs. Examples of external diseconomies include competition over factors of production driving up their price and traffic congestion if firms are located close together increasing transport costs.

Whilst internal economies and diseconomies of scale include movements along the LRAC curve, external economies of scale and external diseconomies of scale involve shifts in the LRAC curve. External economies of scale cause the LRAC curve to move downwards and external diseconomies of scale involve an upward shift of the LRAC curve.

Progress check G

Identify four economies of scale open to a firm that produces a wide range of products.

TERMS

Internal economies of scale: the benefits a firm experiences as a result of increasing its output.

External economies of scale: the benefits a firm experiences as a result of the industry growing in size.

Internal diseconomies of scale: the disadvantages which result from a firm growing too large.

External diseconomies of scale: when the industry grows too large and as a result firms in the industry experience higher long run average costs.

7.09 Total, average and marginal revenue

Total revenue is the total amount earned from selling a product and is price multiplied by the quantity sold.

Average revenue (equivalent to price) is total revenue divided by the quantity sold.

Marginal revenue is the change in total revenue resulting from the sale of one more unit.

7.10 Normal and abnormal (supernormal) profit

Normal profit is the minimum level of profit needed to keep the firm producing the product in the long run. It is sometimes referred to as the opportunity cost of supplying capital to the industry. Economists include normal profit in costs of production whereas accountants do not. So in economics, normal profit is earned where average revenue equals average cost. The level of normal profit varies from industry to industry because there are different levels of risks and stress involved.

Abnormal profit, also called supernormal profit, is any profit earned in excess of normal profit and is earned where average revenue is greater than average cost.

7.11 Different market structures

Market structure describes the main features of a market particularly in terms of the level of competition in the market. The four main market structures which economists assess are perfect competition, monopolistic competition, oligopoly and monopoly.

Moving from perfect competition to monopoly, the level of competition is usually thought to decrease. Economists examine the characteristics, behaviour and performance of market structures.

In perfect competition, there are many buyers and sellers, the product is homogeneous, there is free entry into and exit from the market and buyers and sellers have perfect information.

Monopolistic competition has features of both monopoly and perfect competition. In conditions of monopolistic competition, there is a large number of

buyers and sellers, the product is differentiated and there are no or very low barriers to entry into and exit from the market.

In conditions of oligopoly, the market is dominated by a few large firms, the product is differentiated or identical, there are barriers to entry into and exit from the market and firms are interdependent.

In a pure monopoly, there is only one seller, the product is unique, there are very high barriers to entry into and exit from the market and firms outside the market will lack perfect information. For purposes of government regulation, a monopoly is sometimes defined as a firm which has a market share of 25% or more and a dominant monopoly as a firm which has a market share of 40% or more.

TERMS

Perfect competition: a market structure where there are many buyers and sellers, the product is homogeneous, there is free entry into and exit from the market and buyers and sellers have perfect information.

Oligopoly: a market which is dominated by a few large firms, the product is differentiated or identical, there are barriers to entry into and exit from the market and firms are interdependent.

Monopoly: sometimes defined as a firm which has a market share of 25% or more.

Pure monopoly: a market structure where there is a single seller.

Revision activity B

Decide which of the following statements are true and which are false and briefly explain why.

a   The income effect of a price change relates to the ability to buy a product and the substitute effect relates to the willingness to buy it.

b   Average fixed cost and average variable cost always fall as output increases.

c   Demand for skilled labour is more inelastic than demand for unskilled labour.

d   If the supply of labour is perfectly elastic, all of the workers' earnings will be economic rent.

e Trade unions always seek to increase members' wage rates.

f Small firms may continue to survive if they provide for a niche market.

g If a firm is a price maker, total revenue will be maximised when marginal revenue is zero and price elasticity of demand is unitary.

h A perfectly competitive firm can sell any quantity at the market price whereas a monopolist can only sell more by lowering price.

i A perfectively competitive market is a contestable market and so a contestable market is a perfectly competitive market.

TIP

Very few real world markets fit all the characteristics of one market structure. If you are asked to decide, from given data, which market structure a particular market is operating in, you should base your decision on the main features and mention which features do not exactly fit. For example, in most cities restaurants might be considered to be an example of a monopolistically competitive market. There is usually a relatively high number of restaurants, their menus are differentiated, they are relatively easy to set up, there are few barriers to entry and exit, market concentration is low and normal profits are earned in the long run. Some restaurants, however, may be part of a larger chain and may have more market power.

Progress check H

Explain two possible barriers to exit from an industry.

7.12 Contestable markets

The idea of contestable markets focuses on potential rather than actual competition. A contestable market may contain any number of firms but to be a perfectly contestable market it must have no barriers to entry and exit. In the long run, only normal profits will be earned. A monopoly in a contestable market may be forced to act efficiently due to the threat of competition.

Hit and run competition is a feature of a contestable market with abnormal profits attracting firms to enter the market. They may then leave when the profit level falls back to normal in search of higher profits in another industry.

Progress check I

What implication does the theory of contestable market have for privatisation?

7.13 The concentration ratio

The concentration ratio shows the market power of the largest firms in the market. A concentration ratio may show the percentage of output, assets or employment of, for instance, the largest five firms. It is, however, most commonly the percentage share of sales of the largest firms. For example, a three firm concentration ratio of 70% would mean that the three largest firms account for 70% of sales.

In perfect competition, the market concentration ratio will be very low. It will be low in monopolistic competition and very high in monopoly. Indeed, in a pure monopoly there is a one firm market concentration ratio of 100%.

A concentration ratio can be particularly revealing in markets which contain a relatively high number of firms. In such if, for instance, the four largest firms account for 90% of all sales, the market would be operating under conditions of oligopoly rather than perfect competition or monopolistic competition.

TIP

Concentration ratios are a key indicator of the type of market structure firms are operating in.

TERM

Concentration ratio: shows the market power of the largest firms in the market.

7.14 Survival of small firms

Despite the advantages of large firms, most firms in most countries are small. There are a number of reasons why small firms survive including:

- the scope for economies of scale may be limited in some industries
- consumers may like the personal service small firms can provide
- entrepreneurs may not want to expand
- demand for the product may be relatively low
- there may be co-operation between small firms
- large firms may contract out work to small firms
- high transport costs may restrict the size of the market
- advances in technology may reduce the cost advantages of large firms
- there may be government assistance for small firms

Progress check J

A firm wishes to grow. What may stop it from expanding?

7.15 Integration, diversification, mergers and cartels

Growth of firms

Firms may seek to increase their size in order to take greater advantage of economies of scale, to gain a larger market share, to prevent other firms taking them over and to achieve greater security by diversifying.

Firms can grow internally and externally. Internal growth involves a firm increasing its output by increasing the resources it employs. This is sometimes referred to as organic growth. A firm may seek to grow by opening branches in foreign countries. A multinational company has its headquarters in one country but producers in more than one country. External growth involves increasing the size of the firm by taking over or merging with another firm.

Mergers

There are three main types of mergers. One is a horizontal merger – also called horizontal integration.

This involves firms merging which are at the same stage of production and producing the same product. A vertical merger (vertical integration) takes place when two firms at different stages of production in the same industry combine. A conglomerate merger (conglomerate integration) involves the combination of two firms which produce different products.

A horizontal merger will result in the new firm having a larger market share. It may also be able to take greater advantage of economies of scale. There is a risk, however, that diseconomies of scale may be experienced.

Vertical integration forwards enables a firm to take greater control over the marketing of its products and vertical integration backwards helps to ensure supplies. There is no guarantee, however, that the sizes of the two firms will match.

A conglomerate merger enables a firm to diversify but it can be difficult to manage the output of different products.

Diversification

Diversification can take a number of different forms. A firm may diversify in terms of the products it produces, the markets it operates in and where it produces.

Diversification may involve developing products. For instance, a firm may start producing a more expensive range of perfume.

A firm may diversify into a related market by engaging in vertical integration or into new markets by engaging in a conglomerate merger.

Producing a range of products in a range of markets can reduce the impact on a firm of a sudden and sharp fall in demand for one of its products or in one of its markets. It involves spreading risks. It may, however, be difficult to manage a very diversified firm and such a firm may not be able to exploit some economies of scale, such as buying economies, to the same extent as more specialised firms.

Cartels

Firms may seek to gain the advantages of monopoly power by forming cartels. A cartel is a group of firms that produce separately but sell as one firm. A cartel will seek to maximise joint profits by fixing the output produced by members or the price charged. In most countries cartels are illegal. This, however, does not stop some firms illegally forming cartels and cartels being formed across national borders. Probably the best known cartel is the international organisation OPEC (the Organisation for Petroleum Exporting Countries).

Cartels often break down because of the strong incentive for members to break any output quotas needed to enforce a monopoly price. It will also be difficult to maintain the price if it is not possible to stop the entry pf new producers.

TERMS

Merger: where two or more firms join together to form a larger firm.

Integration: the merging together of two firms.

Diversification: a firm may diversify in terms of the products it produces, the markets it operates in and where it produces.

Cartels: a group of firms that produce separately but sell as one firm.

7.16 The traditional profit maximising objective of firms

The traditional objective of firms is profit maximisation, that is making as much profit as possible. Profit is maximised where marginal revenue equals marginal cost.

In practice, it can be difficult for firms to calculate the profit maximisation level of output because it requires precise measurement and market conditions are always changing. Firms may instead add a profit margin to their long-run average cost.

7.17 Relationship between elasticity, marginal, average and total revenue for a downward sloping demand curve

When a firm is a price maker, it has to lower price in order to sell more of the product. A fall in price will cause total revenue to rise when marginal revenue is positive and price elasticity of demand is greater than one. Total revenue will reach its peak when marginal revenue is zero and PED is unitary. Total revenue falls when marginal revenue is negative and PED is less than one. Figure 7.09 shows these relationships.

A firm will seek to produce at a point on the demand curve where demand is elastic. An increase in the quantity sold when demand is inelastic will lower price.

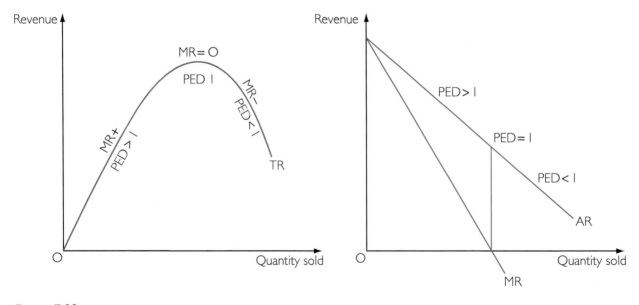

Figure 7.09

TIP

In a diagram, the marginal revenue curve should cut the horizontal axis half way along from where the average revenue curve would cut it if it were to be drawn down to the axis.

7.18 Other objectives of firms

There is a range of other objectives a firm may pursue including sales maximisation, survival, sales revenue maximisation, acting strategically (including driving out rivals, keeping out potential rivals and colluding) and profit satisficing.

Sales maximisation involves a firm producing as much as possible up to the point where it is still making normal profit (average revenue equals average cost). There are a number of advantages in aiming for growth. In the short term, aiming for growth may involve some sacrifice of profit but in the longer term, a larger firm may gain higher profit. This is because the firm is able to take greater advantage of economies of scale and gain greater market power. Managers are particularly keen to aim for growth. This is because managers' salaries and status are often more closely connected with the size of the firm rather than its profitability. An increase in size also makes it more difficult for a firm to be taken over, increasing the chance of survival and managers' chances of retaining their jobs. In addition, higher output may enable a firm to take greater advantage of economies of scale.

Survival may become a firm's main objective due to adverse market conditions. A rise in costs of production or a fall in demand may mean that a firm experiences a loss. In such a situation, a firm may strive to stay in the market if it can cover its variable costs and believes that market conditions will improve in the future.

Sales revenue maximisation occurs when a firm produces where marginal revenue is zero. The level of output which ensures the highest total revenue may be higher than maximum profit revenue. Managers' salaries may be linked to sales figures as well as the size of the firm and high total revenue may make it easier for firms to sell shares and to borrow.

Driving out rivals may be a short term objective of a firm. If a firm has market power, it may sacrifice some profit for a while by engaging in predatory pricing. This involves the firm setting a price which it considers will be low enough to drive out a rival firm which has higher costs of production or more reserves of retained profits. If it is successful, it is likely to raise price once its rivals have left the market.

Keeping out rival firms by engaging in limit pricing may become a firm's main objective if it feels threatened by the possible entry of rivals into the market. If it sets price at a relatively low level, potential entrants which are likely to have high costs, at least initially, may be discouraged from joining the market.

Colluding may increase firms' profits but the practice may be illegal and may be difficult to sustain (see below).

Profit satisficing involves aiming for a satisfactory rather than a maximum profit level. Pursuing such an objective may allow a firm to pursue other objectives to satisfy not only the firm's shareholders but also other stakeholders in the firm including managers and workers. Profit satisficing also recognises that it may be difficult and possibly risky to aim for maximum profit.

In the long term, the other objectives mentioned may not conflict with profit maximisation. Increasing in size, maximising sales revenue and reducing the number of its rivals may enable a firm to charge higher prices and lower its costs. Profit satisficing may increase the motivation of managers and workers and so raise productivity and reduce costs of production.

7.19 The principal agent problem

The principal agent problem relates to the difficulty people (principals) may experience ensuring that those who are acting on their behalf (agents) are pursuing their best interests. The problem arises because the agents are likely to have more specialised knowledge than the principals. Indeed, this is why they are employed. For example, a family selling their home may employ an estate agent. The estate agent may recommend that the family accepts a relatively low price in order to make a quick sale, convincing them that a higher price is not attainable. This might not be in the best interest of the family.

The principal agent problem can occur in firms where the ownership and control are separated between shareholders and managers. The self-interest of managers may mean that they follow objectives that are not always in the best interest of the shareholders. As indicated above, for example, managers may pursue sales maximisation. They may do this even if it means, at least, in the short run, that profits and dividend payments are reduced.

Managers are likely to have more expertise and more information about the firm than shareholders. There are, however, ways that shareholders can encourage managers to act in their best interests. They can link managers' pay to profits and they can give managers shares to give them a vested interest in maximising profits.

7.20 Behavioural approach to the decision-making of a firm

Mutual interdependence is a feature of oligopoly. In deciding its market strategy, a firm takes into account what rival firms are doing and how they might react, for instance, to a change in its price, output or spending on advertising.

An example of thinking strategically is the prisoner's dilemma. This is based on two people being arrested and held separately. If neither confess, they may get, for instance, two years' imprisonment. If only one confesses and implicates the other, the non-confessor might get ten years' imprisonment and if both confess they may get a four-year sentence. In deciding what to do, they are not allowed to collude but each has to consider how the other would react. The best strategy, in the absence of collusion, is to confess.

TERMS

The Prisoner's dilemma: a two-player matrix that can be used to show how the strategy adopted by one firm is influenced by how it thinks its rival will react.

Principle agent problem: relates to the difficulty people (principals) may experience ensuring that those who are acting on their behalf (agents) are pursuing their best interests.

The prisoners' dilemma is an example used in game theory. Game theory is the study of how people behave in strategic situations which emphasises how the outcome of a decision depends not only on the choices made by one player but also on what other players decide to do. A two-player matrix can be used to show how the strategy adopted by one firm is influenced by how it thinks its rival will react. The example here shows that initially two firms are charging $10 each and making a profit of $50 million each. One firm, Y, is considering whether to lower its price to $6 and suspects that its rival, Firm Z, might be about to do the same. The matrix shows that the effect the price cut will have on its profits will depend on what Firm Z does. If Firm Z does not cut its price, Firm Y's profit will rise but if Firm Z matches the price cut both firms, will experience a fall in profit.

		Firm Y's price	
		$10	$6
Firm Z's price	$10	$50 million profit each	$75 million profit for Firm Y $20 million profit for Firm Z
	$6	$20 million profit for Firm Y $75 million profit for Firm Z	$30 million profit for each

The kinked demand curve illustrates why price may not change much in an oligopolistic market where collusion does not occur. It is based on the idea that oligopolists will be reluctant to raise price in case their rivals do not do the same. They may also be unwilling to lower price but this time because they think their rivals will match their price change. This results in a demand curve that is kinked at the current market price. There are, in effect, two demand curves joined together (see Figure 7.10). Above the current price, demand is elastic and so a rise in price would cause demand to fall by a greater percentage and so would reduce revenue. Below the current price, demand is inelastic. If price is cut below the current price, demand will rise by a smaller percentage and so revenue would fall.

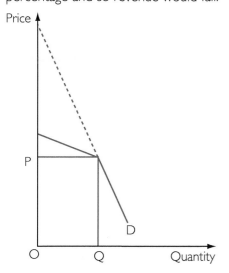

Figure 7.10

Progress check M

What is the relevance of the prisoners' dilemma for the behaviour of oligoplists?

7.21 Conduct of firms: pricing policy and non-price policy

Perfectly competitive firms are price takers. The price is set by the intersection of the market demand and supply curves. An individual firm's output is too small to influence price and its average revenue equals marginal revenue. It cannot charge more than the market price because no-one would buy its product and there is no reason to charge less as it can sell any quantity at the going market price.

Perfectly competitive firms do not advertise as there is perfect knowledge and the products are homogeneous.

Monopolistically competitive firms, oligopolists and monopolists are price makers. Their output influences price and their average revenue exceeds marginal revenue. Advertising is on a small, local scale in the case of monopolistically competitive firms but may be on a large, national scale in the case of oligopolies and monopolists. Such large scale advertising can be used to create and reinforce brand loyalty, attract new customers and act as barriers to entry.

As well as advertising, other forms of non-price competition are a prominent feature of many oligopolistic markets. Non-price competition includes brand names, packaging, free gifts, free delivery and competitions.

Oligopolists may engage in collusion to reduce uncertainty and to drive up price to increase abnormal profit. Collusion is often short term because it is usually illegal, firms have a temptation to cheat by lowering their price to gain extra market share, it is difficult to set a price which will benefit all the firms equally and because not all the major firms may be willing to join the cartel.

Price leadership is a feature of a number of oligopolistic markets. A price leader is a firm which is the first one to change price and which is followed by its competitors. A price leader may be the largest firm, the most profitable firm or the firm which is considered to have the best record in setting the price.

Firms with market power may engage in price discrimination. This involves charging different prices to different groups of consumers for the same product. The aim is to increase profits by capturing more of the consumer surplus by dividing the market into sub markets and charging a higher price in a sub market where demand is less elastic and less in a sub market where demand is more elastic. To be able to charge different prices in different sub markets, a firm has to keep the sub markets separate. Among the ways a market may be segmented is according to location, time of purchase, age of consumers, gender of consumers and wealth of consumers.

TIP

Remember new entrants into an industry may not be small firms. They may be large firms, well established in other industries that have decided to diversify.

7.22 Performance of firms: in terms of output, profits and efficiency

Monopolists and oligopolists may restrict output in order to push up price but they may also seek to increase output in order to take greater advantage of economies of scale.

Monopolists and oligopolists can earn abnormal profit in the short run and long run. This is because barriers to entry and exit will prevent new firms entering the industry to compete away the abnormal profit. Monopolistically competitive and perfectly competitive firms can only earn abnormal profit in the short run. In the long run, they will earn normal profit as, in the absence of barriers to entry and exit, will mean that new firms will come into the industry and drive down price and profit.

Perfectly competitive firms always produce where MC = AR (P) and, if these fully reflect all costs and benefits, will be allocatively efficient. In the long run, perfectly competitive firms are also productively efficient, producing at the lowest point on the average cost curve. Figure 7.11 shows the long-run equilibrium output of a firm producing under conditions of perfect competition.

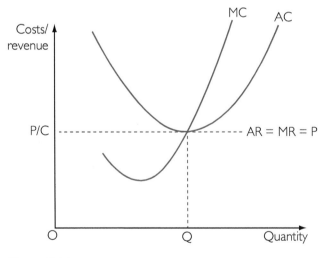

Figure 7.11

Monoplistically competitive firms produce where AR (P) exceeds marginal cost and so are allocatively inefficient. They also produce with excess capacity and are not productively efficient. Oligopolists also fail to be productively efficient and are not allocatively efficient.

Private sector monopolies are both productively and allocatively inefficient. Figure 7.12 shows a monopolist producing where AC > MC and P > MC.

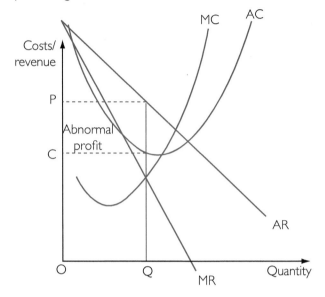

Figure 7.12

A monopolist may also be X-inefficient. The lack of competition may take the pressure off a monopoly to keep costs low and to maximise profits. For instance, it may keep stock levels too high and may not innovate. There is the chance, however, that a monopoly may produce at lower average cost than more competitive firms if economies of scale are significant. A natural monopoly is an industry where having more than one firm in the industry would increase average cost. For example, having more than one firm being responsible for a country's rail network may result in problems of co-ordination and wasteful duplication. State owned enterprises may seek to be allocatively efficient.

Non-price competition is a feature of both monopolistic competition and oligopoly. It is particularly significant in oligopolistic markets where advertising and other forms of non-price competition can be on a large scale.

Perfectly competitive firms and monopolistically competitive firms act independently but oligopolists may collude. A pure monopolist would not have another firm to collude with but a legal or dominant monopolist might.

Progress check N

Is perfect competition perfect?

Revision activity C

Complete Table 7.03.

Feature	Perfect competition	Monopolistic competition	Oligopoly	Pure monopoly
No. of firms in the market	Very many		Dominated by a few large firms	One
Market concentration ratio		Low	High	
Barriers to entry and exit		None or low		
Type of product produced				Unique
Influence on price			Price maker	
Ability to earn supernormal profit in the long run	No			

Table 7.03: Comparison of market structures

Mind maps

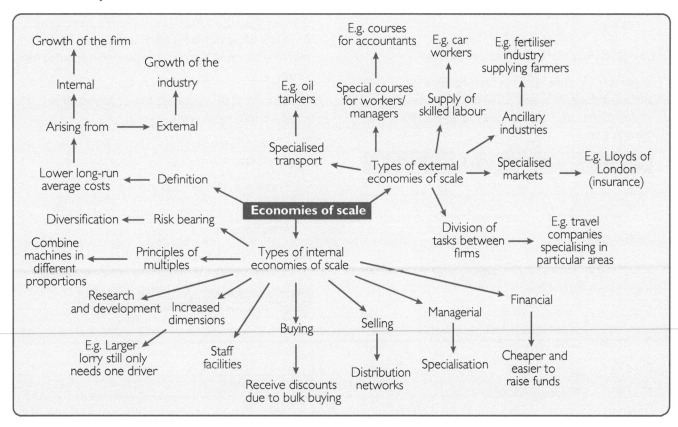

Mind map 7.01: Economies of scale

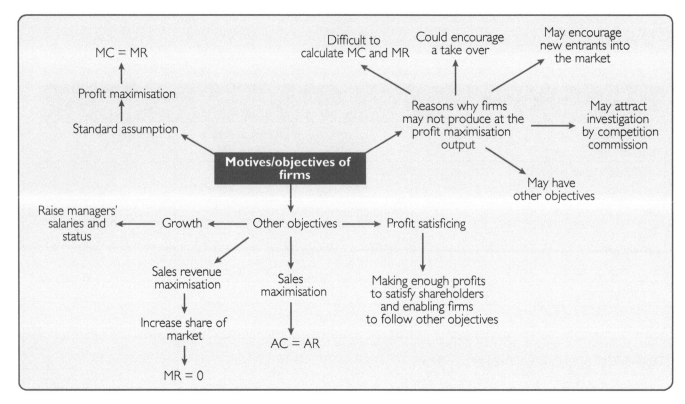

Mind map 7.02: Objectives of firms

Exam-style Questions

Multiple Choice Questions

1 A person allocates her expenditure between three products, X, Y and Z. Table 7.04 shows the prices of the products and the marginal utilities the person gains.

Product	X	Y	Z
Price ($)	10	1	2
Marginal utility (units)	50	8	10

Table 7.04

How should the person's spending alter in order to maximise her utility?

	X	Y	Z
A	More	Less	More
B	More	Less	Less
C	Less	More	More
D	Less	More	Less

2 Basic food products such as rice and bread are cheaper than diamonds. This is despite basic food products being more essential to people's lives than diamonds. What could explain this paradox of value?

A Basic food products are a necessity whereas diamonds are a want.

B Diamonds are in greater supply than basic food products.

C There is a difference in market structures.

D There is a difference between total and marginal utility.

3 Table 7.05 shows the short-run marginal cost of producing product X.

Units of X	Marginal cost ($)
1	40
2	30
3	30
4	60
5	80

Table 7.05: Marginal cost

Total fixed cost is $20. At what level of output is short-run average total cost lowest?

A   2 units   C   4 units

B   3 units   D   5 units

4   A firm's total fixed cost is $8,000. Its average total cost is $10 and its average variable cost is $8. What is the firm's output?

A   800 units   C   4,000 units

B   1,000 units   D   8,000 units

5   When do diminishing returns occur?

A   Adding extra units of a variable factor of production to a fixed factor causes a fall in marginal output.

B   Changing all the factors of production employed results in a less than proportionate increase in output.

C   Increasing demand starts to slow down.

D   Increasing output results in costs rising more rapidly than revenue.

6   Figure 7.13 shows a person's indifference curve, RR, and points that represent different combinations of Product S and Product T.

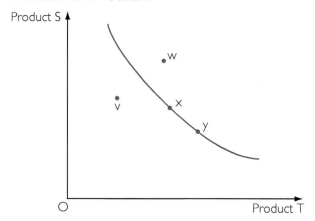

Figure 7.13

What can be concluded from the information?

A   Product S is more expensive than Product T.

B   Product T cost more to produce than Products S.

C   The individual is indifferent between combinations v and z.

D   The individual prefers combination w to combination y.

7   Figure 7.14 shows two lines and two indifference curves of a consumer.

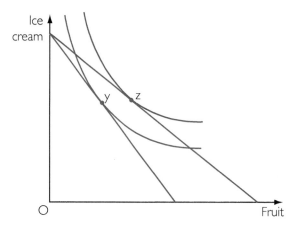

Figure 7.14

Which combination of changes would cause a consumer's equilibrium to move from y to z?

	Price of fruit	Price of ice cream	Income
A	Constant	Constant	Constant
B	Constant	Increase	Increase
C	Increase	Constant	Increase
D	Increase	Increase	Constant

8   Table 7.06 shows how output changes when the inputs of two factors of production, capital and labour alter.

Output	Capital	Labour
200	20	40
400	40	80
600	50	100
800	70	140
1,000	105	210

Table 7.06: Output and factors of production

Over which range of output does the firm experience increasing returns to scale?

A   200–400   C   600–800

B   400–600   D   800–1,000

9 A firm is in long-run equilibrium where its average revenue equals its average cost and its marginal revenue equals its marginal cost. Its average revenue exceeds its marginal revenue and its marginal cost. In which market circumstances is the firm operating?

	Market structure	Level of profit
A	Monopoly	Normal
B	Monopoly	Supernormal
C	Perfect competition	Normal
D	Perfect competition	Supernormal

10 What does the kinked demand curve show?

A Consumers of a product produced by an oligopolist will be more sensitive to price changes in the short run than in the long run.

B Demand for the product of an oligopolist is more inelastic above the market price than below the market price.

C Oligopolists expect rivals to match any reduction in price but not any increase in price.

D Oligopolists at first experience decreasing average revenue then increasing average revenue.

11 The owner of a small private beach decides to charge tourists for its use. There is a fixed cost but no variable cost in allowing people to use the beach. What should the owner do to maximise her profits?

A Attract as many tourists as possible

B Charge the highest price possible

C Minimise total cost

D Maximise total revenue.

12 What is the short-run supply curve of a perfectly competitive firm based on?

A Its marginal cost curve above its average variable cost curve

B Its marginal cost curve above its average total cost curve

C Its average variable cost curve

D Its average total cost curve.

13 Figure 7.15 shows a firm producing under conditions of monopolistic competition in the short run. Which area shows the firm's total cost at the profit maximising output?

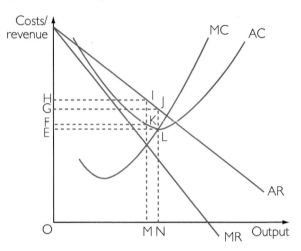

Figure 7.15

A OFKM
C OECN

B FHIK
D EGJL

14 Firms in an industry collude and charge a common price of P. Each firm agrees to restrict its output to a production quota determined by the industry cartel. The firm is given a quota of Q as shown in Figure 7.16.

What is the maximum short-run increase in supernormal profit the firm could receive by cheating on the agreement?

A JKLM
C JKLM + HMNG

B JKLM − HMNG
D HMNG

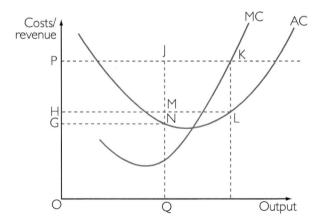

Figure 7.16

15 Figure 7.17 shows the output of a monopolist. If it produces at the profit maximising output, what is the gap between its output and the allocatively efficient output?

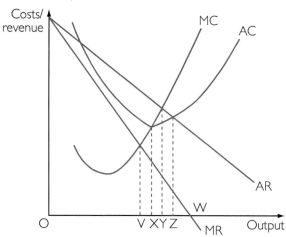

Figure 7.17

A VW   B VY   C XY   D XZ

Data Response Questions

1 The US air travel market

The US air travel market is dominated by a small number of large airlines. Table 7.07 shows the share of the seven largest airlines operating at US airports.

Airline	% share
Southwest	22
American	18
Delta	17
United	11
JetBlue	5
SkyWest	4
European Jet	3.5

Table 7.07: A share of passengers carried at US airports by airlines in 2015

In 2015 the price of aviation fuel, which makes up 30% of airlines' cost of production, fell. In Europe, where barriers to entry and exit are lower, this reduction resulted in lower fares. In the USA, however, the outcome was just higher profits for the airlines. The five largest airlines made record profits in 2015.

The barriers to entry are high in the USA because there is a law banning foreigners from owning more than 25% of voting shares in a US domestic airline. There is also a shortage of take-off and landing slots at the US's busiest airports. One airline operates more than half of the seat capacity at 40% of the country's one hundred largest hubs.

The market has become more concentrated as a result of mergers. In 2013, there was a merger between American and US Airways which created the world's largest carrier. This increased American's share of seating capacity at Philadelphia airport to just over 75% and resulted in fares rising by more than the national average.

In July 2015 the US Department of Justice started an investigation into overpricing and restriction on the growth of capacity in the US airline market. The airlines denied collusion and pointed out that their profits fluctuate with them making losses in some years.

a   Explain whether aviation fuel is a fixed or a variable cost for an airline.   [3]

b   Calculate, and comment on, the four firm concentration ratio for the US air travel market in 2015.   [4]

c   Explain the circumstances which may encourage firms to collude.   [5]

d   Discuss whether high barriers to entry into a market will ensure that the firms in the market will enjoy supernormal profits.   [8]

2 Cola wars

Coca-Cola and Pepsi-Cola dominate the carbonated soft drink (fizzy drink) market in the United States of America. In 2015, Coca-Cola had a 48% share and Pepsi-Cola had 21% of the market. That same year Coca-Cola held the two of the top market share spots for individual drinks. The classic Coca-Cola drink was in top place and Diet Coke in second place. Pepsi-Cola claimed third place.

Both companies have seen the total sales of fizzy drinks decline as US consumers have been switching to healthier drinks including bottled water, juices, sports and energy drinks. In the light of this change in the market, Coca-Cola and Pepsi-Cola have been following rather different strategies. Coca-Cola has and continues to spend more on advertising than its rival. It is also specialising in soft drinks and is increasing its market share of fruit drinks.

Pepsi-Cola tends to change its objectives and market strategy more frequently. In 2010, for instance, it decided not to advertise its drinks at the Super Bowl sporting event and instead launched an online competition for the nomination of good causes that Pepsi-Cola might finance. This approach did result in more money being given to charities but did not generate many more sales. As a result, in 2011 Pepsi-Cola went back to advertising at the Super Bowl. In 2016 it signed a 10-year sponsorship agreement with the NFL. The firm has increased its spending on marketing and advertising but still not to the same level as Coca-Cola.

Whilst Coca-Cola has some diversification in terms of soft drinks, Pepsi-Cola has diversification not only in terms of soft drinks but also in terms of snack foods. In 2012, it launched a new drink, Pepsi Next, which has 60% less sugar content than the classic Pepsi drink. This is in keeping with its long term objective to transform the company into a producer of healthier drinks and snacks.

a   Does the information indicate that Coca-Cola had a monopoly of the fizzy drinks market in 2015? Explain your answer.   [2]

b   In what circumstances may a firm benefit from engaging in a price war?   [4]

c   What evidence is there in the information that Pepsi-Cola is becoming more allocatively efficient?   [4]

d   Comment on whether increasing spending on advertising will increase a firm's profits.   [4]

e   Discuss whether Pepsi-Cola's approach to diversification is more likely to be successful than Coca-Cola's approach.   [6]

Essay Questions

1   Changes in consumer expenditure alter firms' output. A decrease in consumer expenditure may reduce output and costs of production.

   a   Explain why, according to utility theory, consumers would change their spending patterns.   [12]

   b   Discuss whether reducing the scale of production will reduce costs of production.   [13]

2   a   Compare monopoly and monopolistic competition.   [12]

   b   Discuss whether a monopoly always disadvantages consumers.   [13]

REVISION TIP

It would be useful to make a list of the key diagrams you need to know for each section of the syllabus. Practise drawing these diagrams. You may want to put some correct versions on your wall and to include some on your revision cards.

Government microeconomic intervention

- analyse how the use of indirect taxes and subsidies may be used to correct market failure

- explore price and output decisions under nationalisation and privatisation

- explain how prohibition and licences can affect markets

- analyse how the creation of property rights can reduce market failure

- explain how the provision of information can help to achieve an efficient allocation of resources

- discuss the advantages and disadvantages of pollution permits

- explain how behavioural insights and nudge theory can influence the actions of economic agents

- describe why equity may conflict with efficiency

- analyse the impact of price stabilisation, means-tested benefits and other transfer payments

- explain how progressive income taxes, inheritance and capital taxes can influence income and wealth distribution

- describe a negative income tax

- explain poverty trap analysis

- draw and interpret Lorenz curves

- interpret the Gini coefficient

- explain the idea of inter-generational equity

- define demand for labour and describe the factors affecting it

- explain how marginal revenue product theory is related to an individual's demand for labour

- define supply of labour and describe the factors affecting the supply of labour

- explain wage determination under free market forces

- analyse the role of trade unions and government in wage determination

- discuss the causes of wage differentials

- explain the nature and influences on economic rent

- analyse the impact of monopsony in labour markets

- discuss the effectiveness of government microeconomic policy measures

8.01 Indirect taxes and subsidies

An indirect tax may be imposed to correct negative externalities. A tax on any activity that generates negative externalities can be called a Pigovian tax. Figure 8.01 shows that the imposition of an indirect tax converts the external cost into a private cost and moves the quantity traded to the allocatively efficient level.

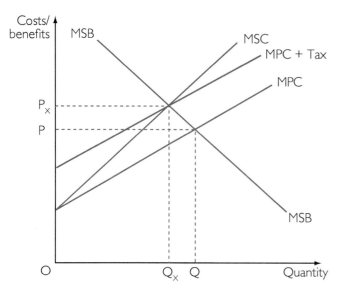

Figure 8.01

A sin tax is a type of Pigovian tax. Such a tax is designed to discourage unhealthy living. Examples include excise duty on alcohol, gambling and tobacco.

To move the market quantity to the allocatively efficient level, an indirect tax would have to equal the marginal external cost as shown in Figure 8.01. In practice, it is difficult to put a monetary value on external costs.

Indirect taxes can result in economic agents basing their decisions on the full costs of their actions and behaving in ways that benefit both themselves and others. They also raise revenue. Although indirect taxes may increase efficiency, they may increase inequality as they tend to be regressive.

Pigovian subsidies are designed to increase the demand or the supply of products that generate positive externalities. Figure 8.02 shows a subsidy given to producers moves the quantity traded to the allocatively efficient level of Q_x.

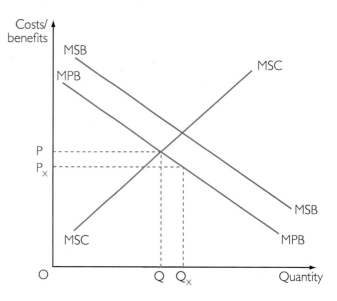

Figure 8.02

There is a risk that subsidies may encourage productive inefficiency as firms may feel less pressure to keep their costs low. Subsidies may also reduce pressure on firms to be dynamically efficient with firms becoming reliant on payments from the government.

TERMS

Pigovian tax: a tax on negative activities, to discourage them.

Pigovian subsidies: subsidies on activities that generate positive externalties.

Progress check A

What may restrict a government's ability to raise the rate of corporation tax?

TIP

To analyse and evaluate the effectiveness of taxes and/or subsidies to correct market failure, you should make use of diagrams.

8.02 Price and output decisions under nationalisation and privatisation

To promote economic welfare, a nationalised industry may seek to be allocatively efficient by producing where price equals marginal cost. In the case of a natural monopoly, with significant economies of scale, the allocatively efficient output may be achieved where the firm makes a loss as shown in Figure 8.03.

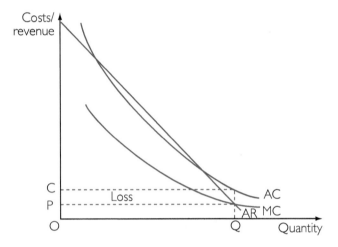

Figure 8.03

In such a situation the government may subsidise a nationalised industry or a private sector monopoly to achieve allocative efficiency.

A nationalised industry is more likely to base its decisions on social costs and social benefits than a private sector industry where the firms or firm are more likely to take into account only private costs and private benefits.

The price and output decisions of a privatised industry will be influenced by whether the industry remains a monopoly. The more competition there is in the privatised industry, the more pressure there will be on the firms to be allocatively and productively efficient.

A privatised monopoly, pursuing the objective of profit maximisation may restrict output to push up price. There may be a deadweight loss created. In general terms, deadweight loss is the loss in economic welfare

caused by an increase in price above the efficient level and a fall in output below the efficient level. Deadweight loss can arise because of taxes, tariffs and monopoly.

The deadweight loss of a monopoly is the loss in consumer surplus which arises because a monopolist restricts output and pushes up price. Consumers would benefit from output increasing to the allocatively efficient level.

Figure 8.04 shows a monopolist producing the profit maximising output of Q. This is below the allocatively efficient level of QX and creates a deadweight loss of Z.

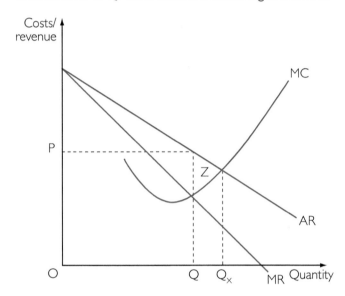

Figure 8.04

> ## TERM
>
> Deadweight loss: the loss in economic welfare caused by an increase in price above the efficient level and a fall in output below the efficient level.

Monopolists may use their market power to convert some consumer surplus into producer surplus. Figure 8.05 shows that an industry moving from perfect competition to monopoly would result in a rise in price from P to P_1 and a fall in output from Q to Q_1. There is a fall in consumer surplus of PP_1CB. Of this PP_1CD is converted from consumer surplus to producer surplus. DCB just disappears – it is a deadweight loss.

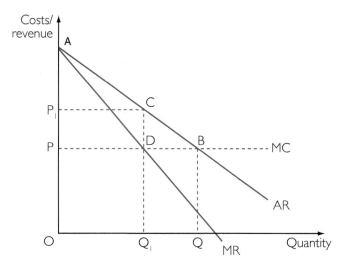

Figure 8.05

consuming and producing certain products will depend, in part, on the level of support for such a measure. If most people do not support it, there is a risk of illegal markets developing.

A government may require firms to have a licence to produce or sell a product. Such licences can help the government to regulate a market. For example, a government may remove the licences from shops that illegally sell cigarettes to children. A government may also use licences to favour domestic firms.

Progress check B

Why is the sale of cigarettes to children banned by many governments whereas the same governments allow cigarettes to be sold to adults?

Revision activity A

Rising incomes in China have increased consumption of foods with a high fat and sugar content. For instance, between 2005 and 2015, Chinese consumption of ice cream increased by 150%, cakes by 30% and chocolate by 120%. This change in the Chinese diet has increased obesity, which in turn has increased the number of people suffering from obesity-related illnesses including diabetes. It has also increased tooth decay. The rise in sugar and high fact food consumption has led to more dental products and diabetes tests being sold.

a What type of income elasticity of demand does the information suggest ice cream has in China?

b Explain one external cost arising from the consumption of foods with a high fat and sugar content.

c Explain one external benefit arising from the consumption of foods with a high fat and sugar content.

8.04 The creation of property rights

Ronald Coase argued in 1960 that if property rights can be clearly defined there is more likely to be an efficient allocation of resources. If a government can create property rights over, for instance, common land or a river, externalities can be turned into private costs and benefits. If people have property rights they can stop people using or damaging their property or can charge them for doing so. Those who improve the property can get paid for their service.

Creating property rights has the potential to increase efficiency but there will be transaction costs involved in negotiating property rights. It may, also, not always be clear who has the property rights and the measure may not be equitable as the rich are likely to have more ability to use the law to enforce their property rights.

8.05 Provision of information

A government may provide information to overcome information failure, to encourage people to consume merit goods and discourage them from consuming demerit goods.

8.03 Prohibitions and licences

If the government thinks that a market structure or the production and/or consumption of a product is very harmful it may impose a ban. For example, a government may prohibit mergers that would result in a monopoly. Some governments ban the sale and ownership of guns and others ban the production and consumption of alcohol. The success of bans on

Information may be provided through, for example, TV health campaigns and warnings on packets of cigarettes and published lists of firms that have created the most pollution.

The provision of information is designed to change the behaviour of economic agents. Its success will depend on the quality of the information provided and how consumers and producers respond.

8.06 Regulation

Regulation involves legally enforced requirements and standards implemented by governments and international organisations. Examples include a ban on smoking in public places, a limit on the amount a firm can pollute, a limit on the extent to which privatised firms can increase price, the requirement for car drivers and passengers to wear seat belts and the need for restaurants to work under hygienic conditions.

Regulation may be enforced by regulatory bodies. For instance, there may be bodies responsible for regulating utility firms and enforcing controls on uncompetitive practices.

There are a number of advantages to regulation. It is backed up by the force of law, is easy to understand and can influence people's behaviour.

Regulation has the benefits of being backed up by law, may have an immediate effect on the behaviour of economic agents and may be simple to understand. There is a problem of what is the right level of regulation. For instance, what level of air and noise pollution should airplanes be permitted to emit. It can also take time to introduce, may be costly to enforce, and may not be effective.

For regulation to be effective, governments need accurate information. Regulation is more likely to be successful if most people agree with it. If not, it can be expensive to enforce. It may take time to draw and pass legislation. Some forms of regulation are only effective if adopted globally or at least by a large number of countries; example, limits on air pollution emitted by firms producing steel.

Regulation does not raise revenue except through fines on those who do not obey the regulation. It may result in informal markets developing with banned products being sold illegally. It is a blunt instrument which works against the market.

Revision activity B

The Peruvian government, like a number of Latin American governments, is facing a conflict between energy security and environmental protection. It is seeking to increase the country's output of electricity to meet the country's increasing demand for fuel and to avoid disruptive blackouts. To generate more electricity, the government is considering building dams and flooding part of its south eastern jungle. Opponents of the proposed scheme claim that it would displace 10,000 people belonging to the Ashanikas, an Amazonian tribe, and destroy important wildlife habitats. They suggest that the government should instead promote biomass and wind power and encourage energy saving measures, in part by increasing the tax on electricity.

a   What is meant by 'energy security'?

b   Identify a first party who might benefit and a third party who might suffer from the government's proposed scheme.

c   Using a demand and supply diagram, explain how the imposition of an indirect tax gives rise to a deadweight loss.

TIP

In examining regulation, you can make use of behavioural theory. For instance, regulatory capture may occur. A regulatory agency may get too close to the producers it is regulating. If this occurs, it may protect the interests of the producers.

8.07 Deregulation

Deregulation involves removing or reducing rules and regulations that have restricted the entry into markets and/or imposed unnecessary cost. The intention is to promote competition and innovation and, as a result, increase efficiency.

Deregulation has occurred in a number of markets throughout the world. For example, the US and European air travel markets have seen a reduction in government controls over fares, routes and market entry. Reducing the barriers to entry has seen the rise in low cost airlines.

TERMS

Regulation: legally enforced requirements and standards.

Deregulation: removing or reducing rules and regulations restricting entry into markets or imposing costs.

8.08 Direct provision of goods and services

Most governments consider that everyone should have access to essential services. This is why some directly provide, at no charge or subsidised, education and healthcare services. Such direct provision is sometimes referred to as providing benefits in kind. If the goods and services provided are available to everyone, rather than targeted specifically at the poor, the policy is likely to be expensive. Universal provision, however, may enable greater advantage to be taken of economies of scale and should ensure that no stigma is attached to using the products.

As well as merit goods, governments often directly provide public goods. A government has to finance the production of public goods as there is no incentive for private sector firms to supply them. The government may supply them itself or may pay private sector firms to supply them. There is the problem of deciding what is the optimum quantity of a public good to provide. A government will seek to ensure that production of the quantity is where the marginal social benefit equals the

marginal social cost. A government may use a cost-benefit analysis in helping it determine the quantity. In considering the private benefit, it may also try to draw up a demand curve for a public good. Such a demand curve would be constructed in a different way to that of a demand curve for a private good. The latter is the horizontal summation of the quantities people are willing and able to buy at each and every price. In contrast the demand curve for a public good is the vertical summation of an estimate of the price people would be willing and able to pay for a given quantity.

Progress check C

How might knowledge of the composition of social benefits be used to decide how much students should pay towards their university tuition fees?

8.09 Pollution permits

Pollution permits allow firms in particular industries to pollute up to a certain level, for instance 80 units of carbon dioxide per year. The limit on the amount of pollution firms can create is usually reduced over time.

Tradable pollution permit schemes allow firms that pollute less than the limit to sell some of its permits to firms that would otherwise exceed the limit. The schemes will encourage firms to adopt newer, cleaner technologies if the cost of technology is less than the cost of the permits. The schemes should also reduce pollution by allowing cleaner firms to gain a cost advantage over those firms which have to buy extra permits.

Tradable pollution schemes have the potential to reduce pollution by making the polluters pay. To be effective the level of pollution permitted has to be set below the current pollution level and the level should be reduced over time. The schemes do not directly compensate those who suffer from the pollution and there are some cases where it is difficult to determine which firms have caused the pollution. Any scheme is likely to be more effective the more countries are covered by it.

Progress check D

What is meant by the 'polluter pays principle'?

TIP

Keep up to date with international agreements on climate change such as the 2015 Paris Agreement.

8.10 Behavioural theory

Governments can make use of behavioural insights to try to influence the actions of economic agents to reduce market failure. Two theories governments use are prospect theory and nudge theory.

Prospect theory is an early behavioural model was developed by Daniel Kahneman and Amos Tversky in 1979. This is the view that people dislike losses more than they like gains. It goes beyond the conventional economic theory that people may be risk-averse or risk-loving. It suggests that people will be willing to take risks to avoid losses but will not be willing to take risks to gain something. The theory helps to explain what is known as the endowment effect. This is the tendency for people to place a greater value on an object when they own it than before they possessed it. There are a number of implications of prospect theory for government policy. One is that if the government wants economic agents to stop doing something, for instance smoking, they should emphasis what people are likely to lose if they do not do so.

A more recent behavioural model is nudge theory developed by Richard Thaler and Cass Sunstein. This is the idea that people can be nudged in the right direction, that is helped to make better choices by the way choices are presented to them and providing them with indirect suggestions. For example, in the UK in 2011 tax payments were increased by 15% in some areas by the tax authorities writing to non-payers informing them that most people had already paid their tax and they were in a small minority. A year before, the UK government became the first government to set up a dedicated 'nudge unit' known as the Behavioural Insights Team.

TERMS

Pollution permits: permits allowing firms to pollute up to a certain level which is usually reduced over time.

Prospect theory: idea that people dislike losses more than they like gains.

Nudge theory: idea that people can be nudged in a particular direction by the way choices are presented to them and indirect suggestions.

8.11 Efficiency and equity

Market forces can also result in significant differences in incomes. Those who have accumulated wealth and those with skills in high demand can earn high incomes whilst the sick, elderly and unemployed may find it difficult to obtain any income. Most governments consider that everyone should have access to a minimum level of income and essential services. This is why government microeconomic policy seeks to increase both economic efficiency and promote equity.

Sometimes the objectives of increasing efficiency and promoting equity conflict. A government's decision to increase state benefits may be seen as promoting equity as it will give vulnerable groups more access to essential goods and services. Higher state benefits may, however, reduce the incentive to work.

Higher direct tax rates, to finance benefits, may also reduce the incentive to work. There is, however, the possibility that higher tax rates will encourage some people to work more in order to maintain their living standards.

A poll tax does not have any disincentive effects as it does not distort economic choices. It is, however, considered to be an inequitable tax as it is very regressive.

Revision activity C

Explain in each case whether government intervention is likely to be designed to:

i   increase efficiency

ii increase equity

iii increase efficiency and equity

  a the provision of unemployment benefits

  b the imposition of a tax on cigarettes

  c the privatisation of a profit making electricity industry

  d the provision of state education free to consumers

  e a cut in the top rate of tax

  f the granting of a subsidy to providers of public transport

TIP

Remember there is a difference between equality and equity. A perfectly equal distribution of income would not be equitable. This is because people have different needs. A disabled person who needs specialised equipment and medicines would need more income than a fit person.

8.12 Price stabilisation, means tested benefits and other transfer payments

Price stabilisation which prevents increases in prices may benefit the poor. Buffer stocks may help to prevent fluctuations in the price of food. The poor spend a higher proportion of their income on food so they are affected more by changes in the price of food. A government may impose rent controls to make housing more affordable for the poor and prevent fluctuations in rent. A maximum price on rented accommodation set below

the market price will benefit those who can find rented accommodation. It will, however, reduce the incentive for landlords to rent and will result in a shortage of rented accommodation. Figure 8.06 shows that the imposition of rent controls will cause demand to exceed supply. As a result, an illegal market may develop.

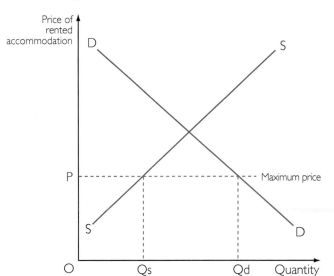

Figure 8.06

Means tested benefits are benefits that are only available to those whose incomes are below a certain level. These are targeted, unlike universal benefits, some of which go to those who do not need them. People may, however, be reluctant to apply for means tested benefits if the application is complex or if there is a social stigma attached to receiving them.

In most countries where state pensions are provided, these are universal benefits available to everyone over a certain age. The current issue with state pensions is their growing cost as most countries are experiencing an ageing population. A government could fund the increased cost by raising taxes or attracting more immigrant workers to pay tax. Alternatively, it could reduce the cost by raising the retirement age.

8.13 Progressive income taxes, inheritance tax and capital taxes

A progressive tax is one which takes a higher proportion of the income or wealth of the rich than of the poor. This is because as income or wealth rises, the marginal tax rate increases. An example in most countries of a progressive tax is income tax. Taking a higher percentage of the income of the rich results in post-tax (disposable) income being more evenly distributed than pre-tax income.

Inheritance and capital taxes can reduce the inequality of wealth. Inheritance tax is a tax on inherited assets transferred before or after death. Capital gains tax is a tax based on the increase in the value of assets between its purchase and sale. Reducing wealth inequality can also reduce income inequality as wealth generates income. Inheritance and capital taxes may reduce the incentives to work and to set up new businesses as some people are motivated by a desire to pass on wealth to their relatives. On the other hand, inheriting less may motivate some people to work harder or start up their own business.

8.14 A negative income tax and the poverty trap

A negative income tax combines the benefit system and the income tax system. It involves a government deciding on the basic amount of income people need, a benefit entitlement, and then imposing taxes from the first dollar earned. If the tax on the income earned exceeds the benefit that would be paid if income was zero, a person pays the difference to the tax authorities. If, on the other hand, the tax that would be paid is less than the benefit entitlement, the tax authorities would pay the person.

A negative income tax may be more straightforward to administer than two separate systems. It should also eliminate the poverty trap. As it involves a universal benefit system, however, it is likely to be relatively expensive to apply.

The poverty trap involves people being discouraged from working as their post-tax income is less than the income they would receive living on benefits. In this case, the marginal rates of taxation and the rate at which benefits are lost act as a disincentive to work. In some cases, high progressive tax rates can also discourage low-paid workers accepting promotion.

Progress check E

Why might an increase in unemployment benefit increase income inequality?

TERM

Poverty trap: where post tax income would be less than the income a person would receive on benefits it may discourage them from working.

8.15 The Lorenz curve and the Gini coefficient

A Lorenz curve shows the degree of income or wealth inequality. Figure 8.07 shows the line of equality, that is the line which shows that, for instance, 20% of the population receive 20% of the income and 80% receive 80% of the income. The curve shows how the actual distribution of income deviates from the 45° line of equality.

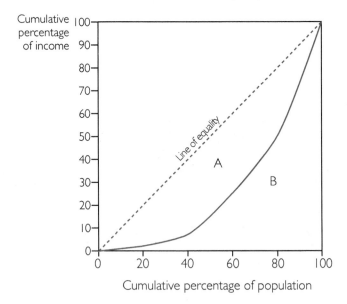

Figure 8.07

A Lorenz curve plots cumulative percentages, Table 8.01 shows how the cumulative shares of population and income are calculated.

Population groups	Cumulative percentage of population	% share of income received	Cumulative % of income received
Poorest 20%	20	2	2
Next poorest 20%	40	5	7
Middle 20%	60	18	25
Next richest 20%	80	25	50
Richest 20%	100	50	100

Table 8.01: Income distribution

The Gini coefficient is the ratio of the area between the Lorenz curve and the line of equality to the whole area below the line or equality, that is A/(A + B).

Total inequality would equal 1 whereas total equality would equal 0. The higher the figure is, the greater the degree of income inequality. So a country with a Gini coefficient of 0.48 would have a greater degree of income inequality than one with a Gini coefficient of 0.29.

The Gini coefficient is used to make international comparisons and is easy to understand. It is possible, however, that two countries could have the same Gini coefficient but a different pattern of inequality.

> **TIP**
>
> Plot a Lorenz curve for your own country and a couple of other countries.

8.16 Inter-generational equity

With ageing populations there is growing concern about a lack of inter-generational equity in some countries. Taxes on the labour force may have to be raised and government spending on, for instance, higher education may be cut to pay for increased spending on pensions and healthcare arising from greater numbers of older people. Income may be transferred from the young to the elderly at a more rapid rate due to the demographic change. The young may find themselves working longer,

paying more for their higher education and receiving less in state benefits than their grandparents.

8.17 Labour market forces and government intervention

Demand for labour

Demand for labour is the number of labour hours firms are willing and able to buy. Demand for labour is a derived demand. Labour is not wanted for its own sake but for what it can produce. If, for instance, the demand for air travel increases, demand for pilots will increase as well.

The aggregate (total) demand for labour is influenced by the level of economic activity. Demand for labour would fall during a recession. An individual firm's demand for labour is affected by a number of factors including demand for the product produced, labour productivity, the wage rate, the price and productivity of other factors of production that can be used as a substitute or a complement to labour.

Derivation of an individual firm's demand for a factor using marginal revenue product theory

The marginal revenue product (MRP) is the change in a firm's revenue which results from employing one more worker. It is found by multiplying the marginal product by marginal revenue.

Marginal revenue product theory states that demand for labour depends on its marginal revenue product. According to the theory, the quantity of labour employed is determined where MRP equals the marginal cost of labour.

Supply of labour

The supply of labour is the quantity of labour workers are willing and able to sell.

A key influence on the number of hours an individual is prepared to work is the wage rate. The backward sloping labour supply diagram suggests that as the wage rate starts to rise, a person will work longer hours. When a certain wage rate is reached, the person may choose to take more leisure. This change in how a worker responds to a rise in the wage rate is illustrated in Figure 8.08.

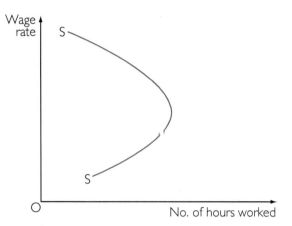

Figure 8.08

A change in the wage rate has both an income and a substitution effect. The income effect of a wage rise is to reduce the number of hours worked, as a person will buy more leisure time. The substitution effect is to increase the number of hours worked as a person substitutes the more financially rewarding work for leisure. The backward sloping supply curve suggests that at low wages, the substitution effect outweighs the income effect whereas at higher wages, the income effect outweighs the substitution effect.

Progress check F

Why does factor immobility lead to market failure?

Net advantages and the long-run supply of labour

In the long run, when people have time to change jobs, the supply of labour is influenced by the net advantages of jobs and the qualifications and skills required in doing the job. There are a number of pecuniary influences on the supply of labour. As well as the wage rate, a job may also provide overtime pay and bonuses.

Among the non-pecuniary influences are job security, promotion chances, working hours, holidays, fringe benefits (such as a company car), the training on offer, the distance required to travel to work, the convenience of the working hours and the status conferred by the job.

If the qualifications and skills required to do a job are high, there will be a limited supply of labour.

Progress check G

Identify three reasons why people may switch from a high paid occupation to a lower paid occupation.

Wage determination under free market forces

In a free market, the wage rate is determined by the demand for and supply of labour. A decrease in the demand for labour, for example, would reduce the equilibrium wage rate and result in a contraction in demand for labour as shown in Figure 8.09.

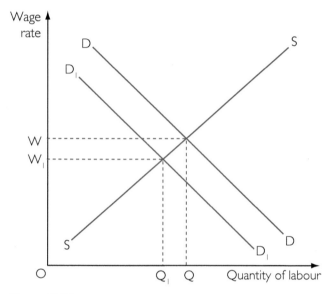

Figure 8.09

Progress check H

Explain two reasons why demand for nurses has increased in most countries in recent years.

The role of trade unions and government in wage determination

A trade union is an organisation which represents workers. It seeks to promote the interests of its members by, for example, bargaining for wage raises, improved working conditions and job security.

A trade union may raise the wage rate of its members through collective bargaining, by supporting measures to restrict the supply of labour, by taking industrial action and measures to increase the demand for labour. If a trade union pushes the wage rate above the equilibrium level, employment will fall as illustrated in Figure 8.10.

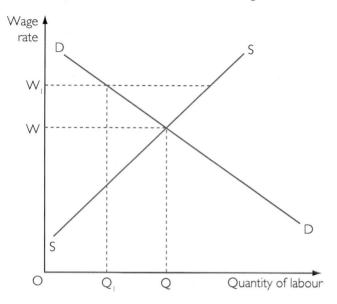

Figure 8.10

Governments influence wages in a variety of ways. They employ workers directly, they pass legislation on trade unions, some run arbitration services and some operate a national minimum wage.

A national minimum wage may increase unemployment if it results in the supply of labour being greater than the demand for labour. There is, however, the possibility that it may be accompanied by an increase in employment if the higher wage increases demand for products, if there is a monopsonist employer in the market and if the rise in pay increases workers' motivation and productivity.

Wage differentiation and economic rent

There are a number of reasons why some workers are paid more than others. One is market forces. Workers whose labour is in high demand and whose supply is limited will be paid more than those whose labour is less highly demanded and whose supply is greater. This is the main reason why skilled workers are paid more than unskilled workers. Other reasons why one

group of workers may be paid more than another group is that they have stronger trade union power, that government policy favours their group and they do not experience negative discrimination.

Economic rent arises when a factor of production is paid more than necessary to keep it in its current occupation. Transfer earnings are what the factor can earn in its next best paid occupation. So, for example, if an accountant is paid $60,000 a year and could earn $48,000 a year as a teacher, his transfer earnings would be $48,000 and his economic rent would be $12,000.

Figure 8.11 shows how wages may be divided between economic rent and transfer earnings. The more inelastic the supply of labour is, the greater the proportion of wages will be economic rent.

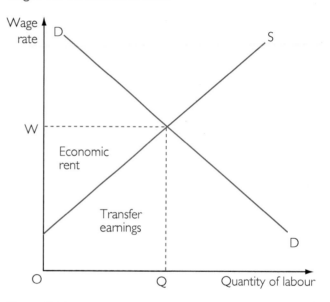

Figure 8.11

Progress check I

Why might rising educational achievements increase transfer earnings but reduce economic rent?

Monopsony in labour markets

Monopsony in labour markets arises when there is one employer, that is one buyer of labour. Being a monopsonist gives an employer market power. This means that the monopsonist may be able to pay relatively low wages.

A monopsonist is a price maker in the sense that the firm sets the wage rate. The marginal cost of labour in this case will exceed the average cost of labour. This is because to attract an extra worker, the wage rate will have to be raised. For example, if ten workers are employed the wage rate (and the average cost of labour) may be $600 a week. To attract an extra worker, the firm may have to raise the wage rate to $700. The average cost will increase to $700 and the marginal cost will be $1,700 ($700 paid to the new worker plus $100 extra paid to the original ten workers).

Figure 8.12 shows the labour market in the case of a monopsonist. The firm's level of employment is determined where the marginal cost of labour (MCL) equals the marginal revenue product (MRP). The wage rate is found from the average cost of labour (ACL) curve.

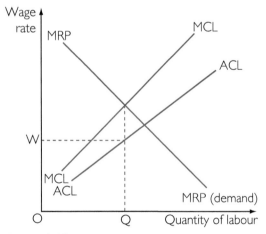

Figure 8.12

In the case of a monopsony market, the introduction of a minimum wage could raise both the wage rate and employment as shown in Figure 8.13. This is because as now all workers are paid the minimum wage, the marginal cost of labour is constant.

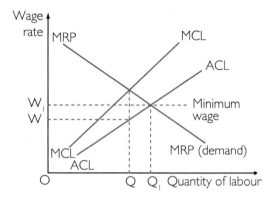

Figure 8.13

8.18 Government failure in microeconomic intervention

The use of government policies may increase efficiency by offsetting market failure. There is, however, a risk of government failure. This occurs when government intervention reduces economic efficiency.

The government may lack information about the extent of the externalities and so may set taxes or subsidies at the wrong rates and there may be time lags between deciding on the policy measure and the policy measure having an effect. Government policy measures may also have unexpected effects as households and firms may react to policy measures in ways not anticipated. In addition, government intervention may be relatively expensive and may be motivated more by a desire to be politically popular rather than to increase economic efficiency.

Progress check J

Why might the imposition of a tax on a demerit good reduce efficiency?

TERM

Monopsony: where there is only one employer buying the labour in a particular area.

Mind maps

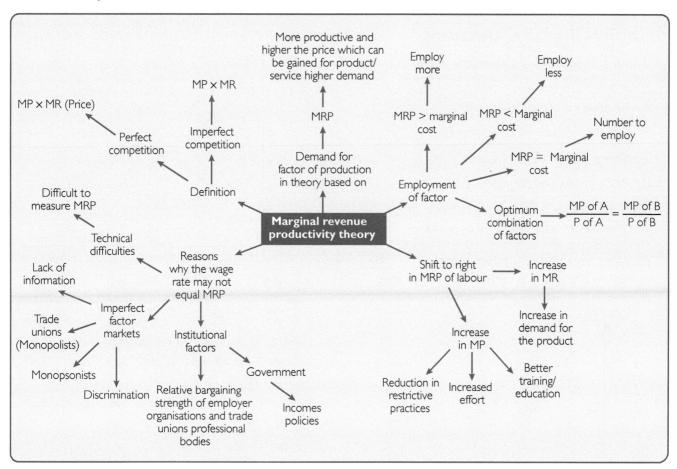

Mind map 8.01: MRP theory

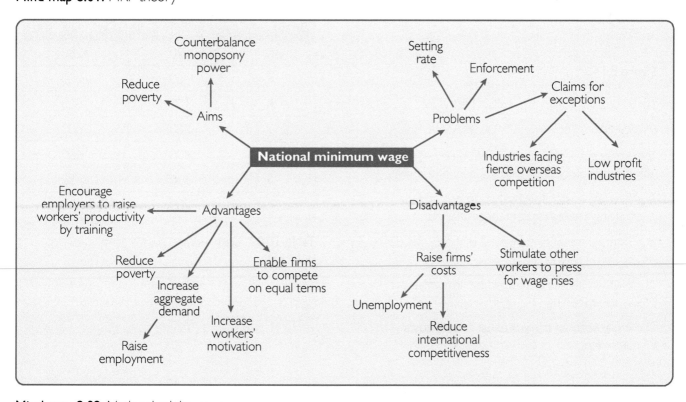

Mind map 8.02: National minimum wage

Exam-style Questions

Multiple Choice Questions

1 Which of the following is a possible source of market failure?

   A   An absence of external benefits

   B   Lack of provision of public goods

   C   Overprovision of merit goods

   D   Private costs equalling social costs

2 Figure 8.14 shows an industry producing under conditions of constant marginal cost. Under conditions of perfect competition, the industry produces an output of Y. It then becomes a monopoly producing an output of X. Which area represents the deadweight loss which occurs?

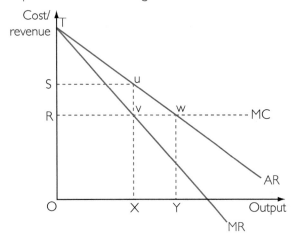

Figure 8.14

   A   STU   C   UVW

   B   RSUW   D   XVWY

3 Why may government intervention be necessary to achieve the allocatively efficient level of training?

   A   Average costs of firms that do not provide training are higher than those that do.

   B   External benefits are gained by firms that do not provide training.

   C   Private benefits are gained by firms that provide training.

   D   Social costs of training equal private costs of training.

4 Figure 8.15 shows the market for a product. What should be the subsidy per unit given by a government to achieve the socially optimum output?

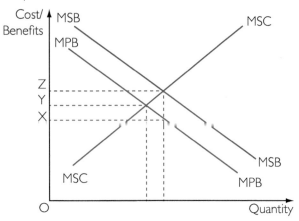

Figure 8.15

   A OX   B YZ   C XY   D XZ

5 Table 8.02 below shows the demand and supply schedules before the imposition of a tax.

If a tax of $3 is imposed on the product, what proportion of the tax will be borne by producers?

   A   The whole proportion   C   Half

                            D   One-third

   B   Two-thirds

Price ($)	Quantity demanded	Quantity supplied
10	20	1280
9	60	1000
8	150	850
7	260	600
6	400	400
5	600	150
4	900	50

Table 10.02 Demand and supply schedules before tax

6   A government decides to reduce income tax and raise indirect taxes. It raises the same amount of tax revenue. What is the likely effect on the distribution of income and work incentives?

	Distribution of income	Work incentives
A	Less equal	Decrease
B	Less equal	Increase
C	More equal	Increase
D	More equal	Decrease

7   Figure 8.16 shows the relationship between income and the amount paid in tax. Which type of tax is illustrated?

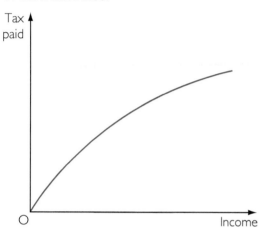

Figure 8.16

A   Flat rate   C   Proportional

B   Progressive   D   Regressive

8   What is meant by regulatory capture?

A   when a firm gains control of the market and uses its market power to push up price

B   when a regulatory agency protects the interests of producers

C   when a regulatory agency restricts the prices that producers can charge

D   when shareholders influence a firm's objectives more than managers do

9   Figure 8.17 shows the cost and revenue curves of an industry. Why would government intervention be necessary to achieve allocative efficiency?

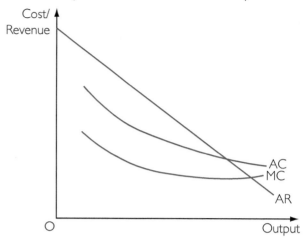

Figure 8.17

A   A profit maximising private sector firm would produce a higher output.

B   A profit maximising private sector firm would produce where average cost equals average revenue.

C   The producer would make a loss at the allocatively efficient output.

D   The producer would make supernormal profit at the allocatively efficient output.

10 Why might government intervention to correct market failure, lead to greater inefficiency?

A   The government bases its decisions on private benefits rather than social benefits.

B   The government bases its decisions on social rather than private costs.

C   There is no adverse effect on incentives as a result of redistributing income from the rich to the poor.

D   There is no time delay between recognising a problem and implementing a policy measure.

11 A firm employs two variable factors of production, Y and Z. Factor Y costs $5 per unit and factor Z $8 per unit. The marginal product of factor Y is 35 units and the marginal product of factor Z is 40 units. What should the firm do to minimise its costs of production?

A   Employ more of factor Y and less of factor Z.

B   Employ more of factor Z and less of factor Y.

C   Employ less of both factor Y and factor Z.

D   Employ more of both factor Y and factor Z.

12 Figure 8.18 shows a supply curve for labour.

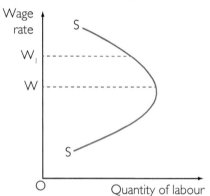

Figure 8.18

What happens when the wage rate rises from W to W₁?

A   Capital is substituted for labour.

B   Hours of leisure become more highly valued.

C   The occupational mobility of labour decreases.

D   The substitution effect becomes stronger relative to the income effect.

13 Figure 8.19 shows a firm operating in a perfectly competitive market for its product and a monopolistic labour market. What will be the wage rate paid to workers and the quantity of labour employed?

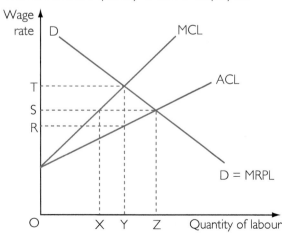

Figure 8.19

	Wage rate	Quantity of labour
A	R	Y
B	S	Z
C	T	Y
D	S	X

14 Which of the following may have monopsony power in a national labour market?

A   A national trade union

B   The army

C   The sole seller of a particular brand of orange juice

D   Workers who possess skills in high demand

15 Figure 8.20 shows the effect of an increase in demand for accountants on the market for accountants.

What is the increase in economic rent earned by accountants?

A   NPST   C   NPSVUT

B   QRST   D   TSUV

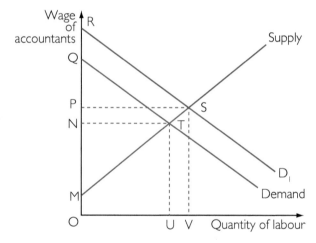

Figure 8.20

Data Response Questions

1 Intervention in the rice market

Most rice is grown and consumed in Asia. The price of rice can vary significantly in and between different Asian countries. In 2015, for instance, the price of rice in Cambodia was $0.40 a kilo and $0.70 a kilo in Indonesia. Cambodia is a net exporter of rice whereas Indonesia is a net importer. In both countries, rice accounts for a significant proportion of the diet of the poor. In 2015 15% of Indonesia's population were living on less than $2 a day.

The Indonesian government tries to help the poor by trying to keep the price of rice stable through operating a buffer stock scheme. Some economists, however, have suggested that it would be better to increase the income of the poor rather than control the prices they pay.

The Indonesian government also intervenes in the rice market to protect domestic producers to try to ensure that domestic supplies of rice are always available during times of disruption to the global supplies of rice.

Government intervention in the Indonesian rice market takes a number of forms. As well as operating a buffer stock, it restricts both the exports and imports of rice. In addition, it subsidises the fertilisers, power and water used by rice farmers and has invested directly in the industry.

a   What evidence is there in the information that the Indonesian government sees rice as a strategic industry? [2]

b   Explain two ways a government could increase the income of the poorest people in the country's population. [4]

c   Analyse how a buffer stock may help to stabilise the price of rice. [6]

d   Discuss whether providing subsidies to Indonesia's rice farmers would be likely to turn Indonesia into a net exporter of rice. [8]

2 The taxi market

In most cities in the world, there is usually a large number of taxi firms with each firm having a relatively small share of the market. The service provided by taxi firms is usually similar. There are not many barriers to entry into and exit from the market and it is possible to start a taxi firm with just one or two vehicles. Those barriers which do exist usually arise from regulation. The regulation of the taxi market can take three main forms. These are limits on the number of firms that can operate in an area, controls on the fares that can be charged and on the imposition of quality standards.

The taxi market in a number of cities and countries has been deregulated or at least partially deregulated. In April 2012 the Greek government passed legislation reducing the price of the licence needed to operate a taxi firm from €80,000 to €3,000 and increased the number of licences issued.

Deregulation may provide a number of benefits. It may make a taxi market more contestable and may increase economic efficiency. Taxi fares may fall, waiting times may be reduced and there may be innovations, for example, the introduction of taxis that cater for people in wheelchairs.

There are, however, arguments for keeping some regulation. If controls on fares are removed, passengers may find it difficult to search out the most competitive prices. Quality controls can benefit consumers. For example, a government can set standards for the road worthiness of taxis and its agencies can check that these standards are being met and that drivers possess a clean driving licence. Eliminating restrictions on the geographical coverage of taxi firms may also cause problems. There may be an over-supply of taxis and a tendency for taxi firms to concentrate their vehicles in city centres and key tourist spots. Lower profits which may be caused by greater competition may encourage taxi firms to cut out low value trips and reduce quality.

a   What is meant by deregulation? [2]

b   To what extent does the information suggest that taxi firms operate under conditions of monopolistic competition? [5]

c   Comment on whether a more contestable market will increase competition. [5]

d   Discuss whether deregulation will increase economic efficiency in the taxi market. [8]

Essay Questions

1   Discuss why wage rates are likely to differ in an economy. [25]

2   a   Explain why the price mechanism may generate negative externalities. [12]

    b   Discuss what policy measures a government could use to reduce pollution. [13]

REVISION TIP

The best place to revise is influenced by how you are revising and your level of concentration. For instance, one of your revision activities may be to write an answer to an essay question. In this case, it would be useful to write in a room where you have access to a desk. On another occasion, you may be getting a fellow student to test you with oral questions. In this case, it would be sensible to be in a room where the two of you cannot be disturbed. Besides, different people have different levels of concentration.

Chapter 9

The macro economy

Learning summary

After you have studied this chapter, you should be able to:

- distinguish between economic growth and economic development
- define sustainability
- distinguish between actual and potential growth in national output
- explain the relationship between output gaps and the business (trade) cycle
- analyse the factors contributing to economic growth
- discuss the costs and benefits of economic growth, including using and conserving resources
- analyse the use of National Income statistics as measures of economic growth and living standards
- distinguish between GDP, GNP and GNI
- describe national debt
- explain indicators of living standards and economic development
- describe the characteristics of different types of countries
- analyse the size and components of the labour force
- explain labour productivity
- define full employment and the natural rate of unemployment
- analyse the causes and types of unemployment
- discuss the consequences of unemployment
- describe the unemployment rate and the patterns and trends in (un)employment
- discuss the difficulties in measuring unemployment
- assess policies to correct unemployment
- distinguish between closed economies and open economies
- explain the circular flow of income

- analyse the multiplier, average and marginal propensities to save and consume
- explain the meaning of aggregate expenditure, the components of aggregate expenditure and their determinants
- describe income determination using aggregate expenditure and the withdrawal/injections approach
- explain inflationary gaps and deflationary gaps and their relationship between the full employment and the equilibrium level of income
- distinguish between autonomous investment and induced investment
- explain the accelerator theory
- assess the Quantity theory
- distinguish between broad money and narrow money
- explain the sources of the money supply in an open economy (commercial banks and credit creation, role of central bank, deficit financing, quantitative easing, total currency flow)
- describe the transmission mechanism of monetary policy
- distinguish between the Keynesian and Monetarist schools
- assess the liquidity preference theory
- describe types of aid and the nature of dependency
- explain the role of trade and investment, multinationals and foreign direct investment (FDI)
- examine the causes and consequences of external debt
- explain the role of the IMF and the World Bank
- describe the impact of corruption and the importance of the legal framework in an economy

9.01 Economic growth, development and sustainability

Economic growth is, in the short run, an increase in real GDP and, in the long run, an increase in productive capacity.

Economic development is an improvement in economic welfare. It is wider than economic growth and involves, for instance, a reduction in poverty, increased life expectancy and a greater range of economic and social choices.

Economic growth is often but not always associated with economic development. Higher output can lead to more employment which can move people out of absolute poverty. Increases in the quantity and quality of housing may increase life expectancy and some of the increase in tax revenue arising from economic growth can be spent on education and healthcare which can also enable people to live longer and enjoy a higher quality of life. However, a country may experience economic growth but if it is accompanied by more pollution, longer working hours and worse working conditions, it may not experience economic development. Similarly, it is possible that economic development may occur without economic growth. For instance, whilst income may not increase, a more even distribution of income may promote economic development. Greater political freedom will give people more choices. Reducing any tensions with other countries may give people a greater sense of security.

The most famous definition of sustainable development is that which was given in the Brundtland Report of 1987: 'development that meets the needs of the present without compromising the ability of future generations to meet their own needs.' For example, the living standards of a population could increase now by overfishing and by cutting down the rainforests. Such actions could, however, reduce the quality of future generations' lives.

TIP

The United Nations 'Human Development Report', which is available free online, provides useful data and analysis on changes in economic development in most countries.

Progress check A

Identify the two main reasons why a country may have a higher GNI than another country but a lower value on the HDI.

9.02 Actual versus potential growth in national output

Actual (short-run) economic growth involves an increase in real GDP. This can be illustrated by a movement of the production point from within a production possibility curve towards the curve or the rightward shift of the aggregate demand curve towards the full employment level.

Potential (long-run) economic growth involves an increase in productive capacity. This can be illustrated by a shift to the right of a production possibility curve or of a long run aggregate supply (LRAS) curve.

TERMS

Economic growth: where productive capacity and/or real GDP increases.

Economic development: an improvement in economic welfare e.g. reduction in poverty, increase in life expectancy, increase in life choices.

Sustainable development: where the aspirations of the present generation are met without compromising the fulfilment of future generations' needs.

National output: the total value of the goods and services produced by a country.

9.03 Output gaps and the business (trade) cycle

A business (trade or economic) cycle arises when economic growth fluctuates around trend (potential) economic growth (see Figure 9.01).

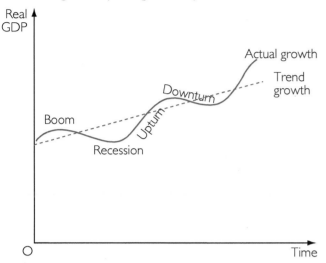

Figure 9.01

During an economic boom there is likely to be a positive output gap. This is when output is greater than the full employment level of output and actual growth is higher than trend growth. Figure 9.02 shows a positive output gap of ab. Output can be higher than the full employment level in the short run due to workers working overtime, some people being attracted into the labour force for short periods and machines may be being used flat out. This level of output will not be sustainable and is likely to be accompanied with inflation.

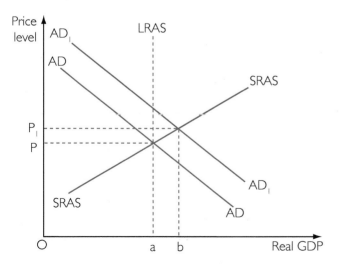

Figure 9.02

A negative output gap occurs when there is a recession. In this case, output is below the full employment level and there are unemployed resources. Figure 9.03 shows a negative output gap of yz.

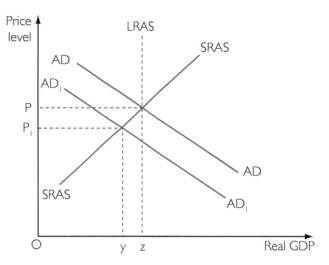

Figure 9.03

Governments aim for steady economic growth. This enables firms and households to plan ahead and avoids inflation (during a boom) and unemployment (during a recession). Governments also aim for sustainable economic growth. This is economic growth which does not endanger future generations' ability to grow by depleting resources and creating pollution.

> **TIP**
>
> Remember a fall in a positive economic growth rate from e.g. 5% to 3%, does not mean a decrease in output. It means the economy is still producing more but the rate of increase in output has declined.

9.04 Factors contributing to economic growth

If there is spare capacity in the economy, actual economic growth can be achieved by an increase in aggregate demand. A rise in consumer expenditure, investment, government spending or net exports may encourage producers to increase their output.

Potential economic growth enables real GDP to increase over time. It can be caused by an increase in the quantity and/or quality of resources. The quantity of resources may increase due to net investment, immigration of workers. The quality of resources may increase due to advances in technology, improved education and training.

9.05 Costs and benefits of growth, including using and conserving resources

Economic growth can raise living standards, reduce unemployment, make the country more powerful in global institutions and in global negotiations, increase confidence and increase tax revenue enabling governments to spend more on education, healthcare and reducing poverty.

There is a possibility that living standards may fall in the short run in order to achieve economic growth. If a country is operating at full capacity, the output of some consumer goods may have to be sacrificed in order to produce more capital goods. In the long run, of course, more capital goods will enable more consumer goods to be produced.

Economic growth may be accompanied by increased pollution, stress, longer working hours, depletion of natural resources and some structural unemployment.

Economies often face the question of whether to use or conserve non-renewable resources such as oil. Using resources now will contribute to economic growth and so generate income and raise living standards. It will also contribute to the country's export earnings and so its trade balance. Exploiting resources now may be a wise decision if it is thought that demand for the resources may fall in the future, for instance, due to the development of synthetic substitutes. Conserving resources, however, may enable future generations to enjoy income from them and may mean that the country will not become dependent on other countries for resources.

9.06 Use of national income statistics as measures of economic growth and living standards

Definitions

National income (NI) statistics cover measures of the country's output in a year.

Gross Domestic Product (GDP) is the total output produced in a country in a given time period. It can be measured in three ways. These are the output, income and expenditure methods. As these names suggest, the output method measures output directly, the income method measures all the factor payments earned in producing output and the expenditure method totals up all spending on domestically produced products.

Gross National Product (GNP) is the total output produced by the country's population, wherever they produced it. Net property income from abroad is added to GDP to calculate GNP. Net property income from abroad covers profit, interest, dividends and rent earned on the ownership of foreign assets minus payments on assets in the country owned by foreigners.

Gross National Income (GNI) is GDP plus primary incomes received from the rest of the world minus primary incomes payable to non-residents. Primary income includes compensation of employees (employment income from cross-border and seasonal workers), taxes less subsidies on production, property income and entrepreneurial income. GNI is very similar to GNP – it just makes two further adjustments in relation to GDP.

Net National Product (NNP) is GNP minus depreciation. So whilst GNP includes all investment, NNP only includes net investment that is additions to the capital stock.

Net Domestic Product (NDP) is GDP minus depreciation. It can also be calculated as NNP minus net property income from abroad.

National income figures are initially measured at market prices. This means they are measured in terms of the prices charged in shops and other outlets. The figures are then converted into factor cost, i.e., in terms of the factor incomes earned in producing the products. To convert NI figures from market prices to factor cost, indirect taxes are subtracted and subsidies are added.

National income figures are also measured at both current prices and constant prices. GDP at current prices (also referred to as money GDP) is measured in terms of the prices operating in the year in question. GDP at constant prices (also called real GDP) is GDP adjusted for inflation.

Comparisons of economic growth rates and living standards over time and between countries

Actual (short run) economic growth is measured by changes in real GDP. Living standards have traditionally been compared using real GDP per head (also referred to as real GDP per capita). More recently, GNI per head has become a popular measure.

Real GDP per head and real GNI per head are readily available indicators of living standards but they have a number of limitations. They are narrow measures as they only take into account one factor that influences living standards – income. They do not consider, for instance, pollution, the types of products produced, leisure hours and political freedom. GDP/GNI per head may also be high but if income is very unevenly distributed, only a small proportion of the population may benefit. GDP/GNI per head may also be low but living standards might be relatively high if there is a large informal economy with significant unrecorded economic activity.

Other indicators of living standards and economic development

The Human Development Index (HDI), published by the United Nations, measures more indicators of living standards than real GDP/GNI per head. It includes three major components. These are education (measured since 2010 as mean years of education received by adults aged 25 and more and expected years of schooling for children of school going age), life expectancy at birth and GNI per head.

The Index of Sustainable Economic Welfare (ISEW) is a wider composite measure. It takes into account income inequality and adds items that increase economic welfare, such as the value of unpaid housework, and deducts items which reduce economic welfare including pollution, crime and traffic accidents.

ISEW is a development of the Measure of Economic Welfare (MEW). This earlier measure started with GDP and then reduced the figure for environmental damage while adding the value of leisure time and unpaid work.

The multidimensional poverty index (MDI) classifies someone as poor if they are deprived on a third or more of ten weighted index indicators. There are two indicators of education (years of schooling and child school attendance), two indicators of health (child mortality and nutrition) and six for living standards (safe drinking water, electricity, improved sanitation, flooring, cooking fuel and assets). As with the HDI, education, health and living standards each have a weighting of one third.

The Kuznets curve is a diagram that shows how income inequality may first rise as an economy develops and then, after a certain level of income is reached, income becomes more evenly distributed. This relationship is shown in Figure 9.04.

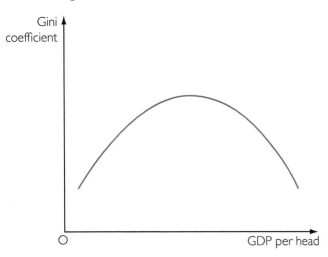

Figure 9.04

Income may initially become more unevenly distributed as the gap in earnings of agricultural sector workers and manufacturing workers widens. It is possible that when a country reaches a certain level of development it may become more evenly distributed with income being redistributed through tax and benefit systems which develop and improve education. Income distribution is, however, influenced by a number of factors and recent years have seen increasing income inequality in a number of developed countries.

TERMS

Human Development Index (HDI): measure indicators of living standards that includes GNI per head, education and life expectancy.

Index of Sustainable Economic Welfare (ISEW): a wide measure that takes into account items that increase economic welfare (e.g. unpaid housework) and deducts those that reduce it (e.g. pollution and crime).

The Multidimensional Poverty Index (MDI): takes into account 10 weighted index indicators of poverty and classes someone as poor if they are deprived on a third or more of these indicators.

9.07 National debt

National debt is the total debt of the government. It is sometimes referred to as public sector debt and is often expressed as a percentage of GDP. It changes up over time. A budget deficit adds to the national debt whereas a budget surplus can be used to reduce the national debt.

The national debt tends to rise during a recession and may be reduced during an economic boom. This is because there is likely to be a budget deficit during a recession while there may be a budget surplus during an economic boom.

A high national debt may have two major disadvantages. One is that it involves an opportunity cost. Tax revenue used to pay interest on the debt could have been used for other purposes. The other disadvantage is that it may make it difficult for the government to attract lenders.

If most of the debt is held by domestic citizens, income will be redistributed within the country whereas if most is held by foreigners, there will be an outflow of money from the country.

TIP

Remember the national debt is not the same as a budget deficit. A country may have a budget surplus but a large national debt.

Progress check B

Explain two reasons why external debt might hinder economic growth.

9.08 Characteristics of developed, developing and emerging economies

Developed economies have high income per head. They also tend to have a high proportion of their labour force employed in the secondary and, more particularly, the tertiary sector, net immigration and high rates of education, labour productivity and investment.

Developing economies may have low income per head, high population growth, high dependency ratios, uneven distribution of income, a high proportion of output and employment accounted for by the primary sector, a reliance on a narrow range of mainly primary exports, high rates of rural to urban migration, net emigration, low levels of literacy, low life expectancy and low productivity. It is important to remember that developing economies are not all the same and any one economy is unlikely to share all of the characteristics above.

Emerging economies are economies which are experiencing rapid economic growth and industrialisation. They attract flows of foreign financial investment because of their improving economic performance and status. There are a number of groups of emerging economies including the BRICS (Brazil, Russia, India, China and South Africa) and MIST (Mexico, Indonesia, South Korea and Turkey).

TERMS

Labour force: a country's working population who are employed or actively seeking employment.

Labour productivity: labour output per hour.

National debt: the total debt of government.

TIP
Developing countries tend to have high population growth rates. Be careful though, this does not mean they have large populations. For instance, in 2015 Mali had a higher population growth rate (3%) than Germany (0.2%). Its population size of 15.3 million was, however, considerably below that of Germany's 81 million.

9.09 Size and components of the labour force

A country's labour force can also be referred to as its workforce or working population. The size of a country's labour force is influenced by a range of factors including the size of its population, the age structure of the population, working age (influenced, in turn, by the school leaving age and the retirement age) and the labour force participation rate.

The labour force participation rate is the proportion of working age people who are economically active.

People are economically active, and so are in the labour force, if they are either in employment or are unemployed and actively seeking work.

The economically inactive are people of working age who are not in the labour force. This means they are neither employed nor seeking employment. The major groups who are economically inactive are people who have retired early, those in full-time education, homemakers and those too sick or disabled to work.

The labour force can be divided in a number of ways. These include those working in the primary, secondary and tertiary sectors; skilled and unskilled workers; full-time and part-time workers.

TIP
Remember the unemployed are part of the labour force. This means that a decrease in unemployment does not, in itself, increase the size of the labour force. The lower unemployment just means that more of the labour force is being utilised.

Progress check C

What could explain a country experiencing both an increase in employment and unemployment?

9.10 Labour productivity

Labour productivity is output per worker hour. It may be increased by education, training, experience and providing workers with more and better quality capital equipment.

Progress check D

Why might a country experience a decrease in production but an increase in labour productivity?

9.11 Full employment and natural rate of unemployment

Full employment is the highest possible use of a factor of production. The term is often used in relation to labour. Full employment of labour does not mean zero unemployment as there will always be some people changing jobs. Some economists suggest that full employment occurs when there is approximately 3% unemployment although the rate is likely to vary from country to country.

The natural rate of unemployment (also called the non-accelerating inflation rate of unemployment (Nairu)) is the level of unemployment which exists when the labour market is in equilibrium. In this situation, the total demand for labour equals the total supply of labour and there is no upward pressure on wages and the price level.

9.12 Causes of unemployment and types of unemployment

The three main types of unemployment are frictional, structural and cyclical unemployment.

Frictional unemployment exists even when there is full employment. It is short term unemployment which occurs when workers are in between jobs. There are many forms of frictional unemployment. These include voluntary, search, casual and seasonal unemployment. Voluntary unemployment happens when unemployed people choose not to take up the job vacancies on offer. Search unemployment occurs when workers who have lost one job do not take the first job offered to them. Instead they search around for a better job. Casual unemployment occurs when workers have periods of employment followed by periods of unemployment; for example, film actors and festival organisers. Seasonal unemployment is when people work during certain periods of the year and then are unemployed during off peak time. For instance, tour guides will find work during peak holiday times but may be out of work for the rest of the year.

Structural unemployment lasts longer than frictional unemployment and can be on a significantly larger scale. It exists due to the occupational and geographical immobility of labour. The structure of economies is always changing with some industries and occupations declining whilst other industries and occupations are developing and expanding. If workers cannot move easily from declining to growing sectors they will be unemployed.

Structural unemployment can take the forms of international, regional and technological unemployment.

International unemployment arises when workers lose their jobs because industries decline due to competition from foreign industries. Regional unemployment refers to a situation where industries and occupations decline in particular areas of the country. Technological unemployment occurs when industries and occupations disappear due to advances in technology.

Cyclical unemployment (also called demand deficit unemployment) can last for years and may be on a very large scale. It occurs due to a lack of aggregate demand and so affects most industries and occupations.

Progress check E

Why might advances in technology create rather than destroy jobs?

9.13 Consequences of unemployment

The effects of unemployment depend on the cause of unemployment, the duration of the unemployment, the scale of unemployment, the groups affected and the support given to the unemployed.

Unemployment can reduce inflationary pressure, can enable firms to expand and give the unemployed time to reflect on what they really want and to research job opportunities.

The costs of unemployment, however, are generally thought to far outweigh any benefits. The economy will lose potential output and so living standards will be lower than possible. The government will lose potential tax revenue and will have to spend more on unemployment benefits. The unemployed are likely to suffer a fall in income and may experience health problems. The longer people are unemployed, the more difficult they usually find it to obtain another job. This is because their skills may become out of date and firms tend to become more reluctant to employ them.

Progress check F

Why would unemployment cause unemployment?

9.14 Unemployment rate; patterns and trends in (un)employment

People are classified as unemployed if they are without a job and are actively seeking employment.

Two ways of measuring unemployment are the claimant count and the Labour Force Survey (LFS). The claimant count records people as unemployed if they are in receipt of unemployment benefits. The LFS measure is based on the International Labour Organisation's definition of unemployment. This records people as unemployed if they are without a job and have looked for work in the last month or have found a job which they are waiting to start in the next two weeks. This information is found from a random sample of the population.

The unemployment rate is the proportion of the labour force who are without work but who are actively seeking employment. The unemployment rate may fluctuate over time. As unemployment rises, the gap between a country's actual and potential output increases.

The young, the old and the unskilled tend to experience more unemployment than the average worker. The longer people are unemployed, the more difficulty they usually experience in finding a job. This is because they may not keep up with developments in technology and working methods, may lose the work habit and may become less attractive to employers.

As economies develop, employment tends to shift from the primary to the secondary sector and the tertiary sector. Throughout the world, more women are entering the labour force.

> **TIP**
> Keep a record of what is happening to unemployment and why in your country.

9.15 Difficulties involved in measuring unemployment

It can be difficult to ensure that any measure of unemployment does not miss out anyone who is unemployed and looking for work and does not include those who are not actively seeking employment or are working in the informal (shadow) economy but are illegally claiming benefits.

The claimant count does not include some people who are unemployed but who are not entitled to unemployment benefits. For example, workers who lose their jobs but have a partner who is employed can claim unemployment benefit for only a limited time. The claimant count also does not include those who are unemployed and actively seeking work but who are too proud to claim unemployment benefit. Some people may have savings they can draw on to support them for a period of time whilst they are seeking a new job. In contrast, the claimant count does include some people who claim the benefits illegally, either because they are not really looking for work or because they already have a job. The claimant count, however, is cheap to collect as the information is recorded every time the unemployment benefit is paid out. It also collects the information relatively quickly.

The LFS captures more of those who are unemployed and, as it is widely used throughout the world, it is good for making international comparisons. It is, however, a relatively expensive measure as it takes time to collect and it can be subject to sampling errors. As well as the risk that the sample may not be representative of the population as a whole, there may be problems in interpreting the information gathered.

Revision activity A

Selected labour market statistics 2015			
Country	Size of population	Labour force	Unemployment %
China	1.4 bn	804 m	4.2
Hong Kong	7.1 m	3.9 m	2.9
Maldives	0.4 m	0.2 m	12.0
New Zealand	4.4 m	2.5 m	5.8
Nigeria	181.0 m	57.5 m	24.0

Table 9.01

a Which country had the smallest number of people unemployed in 2015?

b Which country had the largest number of people employed in 2015?

c Which country had the highest proportion of its population in the labour force in 2015?

d Which country had the smallest proportion of its population in the labour force in 2015?

Progress check G

Identify five reasons why someone may stop being unemployed.

9.16 Policies to correct unemployment

To reduce cyclical unemployment a government will try to raise aggregate demand. It may do this by using reflationary fiscal policy and/or reflationary monetary policy. Among the measures it may employ are to increase government spending, to cut income tax and to reduce the rate of interest.

To reduce frictional and structural unemployment a government is likely to use supply side policy. For instance, it may provide more training to unemployed workers to increase their employability and may cut unemployment benefit to increase the incentive to work.

9.17 The circular flow of income between households, firms, government and international economy

The circular flow of income describes how expenditure and income moves around an economy. In a closed economy income will flow between households, firms and the government. While a closed economy is one which does not engage in international trade, an open economy does engage in trade with other countries. In the case of an open economy, income will flow between households, firms, the government and the international economy as shown in Figure 9.05.

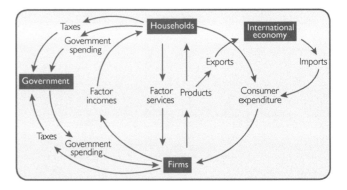

Figure 9.05

Injections are additions to the circular flow. The three injections are investment, government spending and exports. Leakages are withdrawals from the circular flow. The three leakages are saving, taxes and imports. Figure 9.06 illustrates injections and leakages.

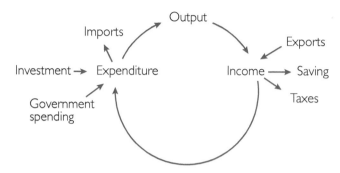

Figure 9.06

Progress check H

What are the injections and withdrawals in a closed economy with a government sector?

9.18 Aggregate expenditure

The aggregate expenditure function

Aggregate expenditure (AE) is the total planned expenditure at different levels of income. It is composed of consumer expenditure (consumption), investment, government spending and net exports.

Income determination using AE – income approach and withdrawal/injection approach

Income is determined where aggregate expenditure equals output. Figure 9.07 shows this would be at an output of Y. If aggregate expenditure rises, output will increase until the full employment level of output (Y_{Fe}) is reached.

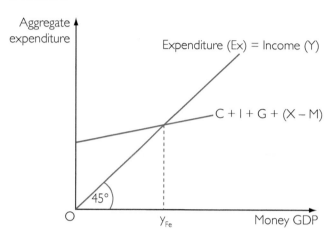

Figure 9.07

The equilibrium level of income is also where planned injections equal planned leakages (also called withdrawals), in other words, where $I + G + X = S + T + M$. An increase in injections would cause income to rise until injections again equal withdrawals as shown in Figure 9.08.

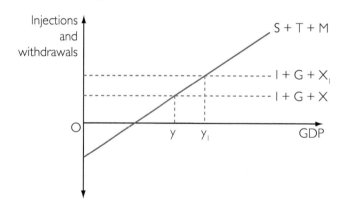

Figure 9.08

Remember an AE diagram has aggregate expenditure on the vertical axis whereas an AD/AS diagram has the price level on the vertical axis. AE rises as income rises whereas AD falls as the price level rises. Also note an AE diagram has money GDP on the horizontal axis whereas an AD/AS diagram has real GDP on the horizontal axis.

Inflationary and deflationary gaps

An inflationary gap occurs when aggregate expenditure exceeds the full employment level of income as shown in Figure 9.09. At Y_{Fe}, there is an inflationary gap of ab.

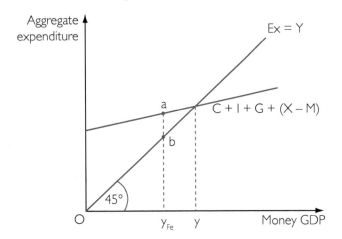

Figure 9.09

A deflationary gap is experienced when aggregate expenditure is below the full employment level of income. Figure 9.10 shows a deflationary gap of cd.

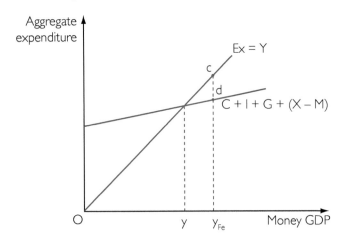

Figure 9.10

9.19 The multiplier

The multiplier is the relationship between a change in an injection and the final change in GDP. A multiplier of 3, for instance, means that an increase in investment of $10 million would result in an increase in GDP of $30 million.

The multiplier can be calculated after a rise in autonomous expenditure has worked through the economy by using the following formula.

$$k = \frac{\text{change in GDP}}{\text{change in injection}}$$

It can also be estimated before a change in autonomous spending by using the following formula.

$$k = \frac{1}{mps + mrt + mpm}$$

Here mps is the marginal propensity to save, mrt is the marginal rate of taxation and mpm is the marginal propensity to import. This is the full version of the multiplier. In a closed economy with no government sector, the multiplier is 1/mps and in a closed economy with a government sector it is 1/(mps + mrt).

Figure 9.11 shows that the multiplier is $\frac{Y_1 - Y}{r - s}$.

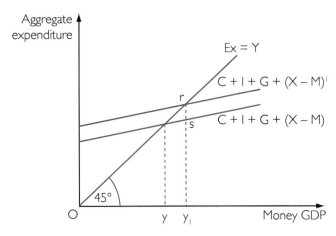

Figure 9.11

Revision activity B

a The marginal propensity to consume is 0.75 of disposable income. Initially there is no government sector and the country is a closed economy.

If investment is $50 bn, what is the value of national income?

b A government sector does develop with a marginal tax rate of 20% and government spending is $70 bn. Calculate:

  i the new multiplier figure

  ii the new level of national income

  iii the government's budget position.

c The country then engages in international trade. 1/8 or 12.5% of consumer expenditure is spent on imports and export revenue is $40 bn. Calculate:

  i the new multiplier effect

  ii the new national income

  iii the trade balance

  iv the budget position.

TERMS

Multiplier: relationship between a change in an injection into the circular flow of income and the final change in GDP.

Inflationary gap: when aggregate expenditure (AE) exceeds the full employment level of income.

Deflationary gap: when aggregate expenditure (AE) is below the full employment level of income.

TIP

It is useful to give a numerical example of the multiplier. Keep the figures simple – you are seeking to explain the concept rather than impress by, for instance, using a calculation which requires you going to six decimal places.

Progress check I

What effect would an increase in the marginal rate of taxation have on the size of the multiplier?

9.20 Investment

The difference between autonomous and induced investment

Autonomous investment is investment which occurs independently of changes in income. Advances in technology, for instance, might result in more investment at the same level of income.

Induced investment is investment undertaken because of an increase in income. With more income, firms would expect consumer expenditure to rise and so would be likely to undertake more investment.

TERMS

Autonomous investment: investment occurring independently of changes in income.

Induced investment: investment undertaken because of an increase in income.

The accelerator theory

The accelerator theory suggests that net investment depends on the rate of change in GDP and that a change in GDP will cause a greater percentage change in net investment.

The accelerator coefficient is the level of induced investment as a proportion of the increase in GDP. So an accelerator of three would mean that an increase of $3 investment would be needed to produce every $1 increase in output.

9.21 The Quantity Theory of Money

The Fisher equation of exchange is $MV = PT$ (sometimes expressed as $MV = PY$). M is the money supply, P is the general price level, V is the velocity of circulation and T or Y is the value of transactions/output.

Monetarists developed the Fisher equation into the Quantity Theory by assuming a change in the money supply will not affect V and T. With V and T constant, a change in the money supply will cause a proportional change in the price level.

Keynesians reject the Quantity Theory, arguing that V and T can be influenced by changes in the money supply and so the equation cannot be used to predict how a change in the money supply will affect the price level.

9.22 Money supply

Broad and narrow money

A country's money supply is the total amount of money in an economy. Broad money includes items which act both as a medium of exchange and store of value. Narrow money, as its name suggests, is narrower in scope and focuses on money as a medium of exchange.

The money supply may increase as a result of commercial banks lending more, the central bank engaging in expansionary open market operations and quantitative easing, a government financing a budget deficit by borrowing from the central bank and commercial banks, and more money entering than leaving the country.

TERM

Quantitative Easing (QE): a central bank creating money by buying financial assets to increase private sector spending when aggregate demand and short term interest rates are very low.

Accelerator theory: theory suggests that net investment depends on the rate of change in GDP and that a change in GDP will cause a greater percentage change in net investment.

Broad money: includes items which act both as a medium of exchange and store of value.

Narrow money: focuses on money as a medium of exchange.

Credit creation

When someone deposits money in a bank, it enables the bank to use it as the basis for loans of a greater value. Banks can lend more and so create money,

because only a small proportion of deposits are cashed. Most deposits are transferred within the banking sector. The credit multiplier shows the value of new deposits that can be created as a result of a change in a bank's liquid assets. It is calculated by the following formula.

$$\frac{100}{\text{liquidity ratio}}$$

TIP

Recent years have seen significant changes in banking, bank regulation and monetary policy. Keep up to date with developments in banking and monetary policy.

Progress check J

If there is a credit multiplier of 20, by how much can bank loans increase if there is a rise in liquid assets of $20 million?

Deficit financing

The government's budget shows the relationship between its revenue, largely tax revenue, and its expenditure. A budget surplus arises when government revenue exceeds government expenditure; a balanced budget when government revenue equals government expenditure; and a budget deficit when government expenditure exceeds government revenue.

If a government spends more than it raises in tax revenue, it can finance the deficit in four main ways. It can borrow from the central bank (sometimes referred to as resorting to the printing press), from commercial banks, from the non-bank sector and from abroad.

If a government borrows from the banking sector or abroad, it will add to the money supply. If, however, it borrows from the non-bank, domestic sector it will be making use of existing money.

Quantitative easing

Open market operations involve a central bank buying short term financial assets, most commonly treasury bills, to increase commercial banks' liquid assets, increase bank lending and lower short term interest rates.

Quantitative easing (QE) is designed to increase private sector spending when aggregate demand and short term interest rates are very low. The aim is to increase the inflation rate up to its target rate. The central bank creates money electronically to buy financial assets, such as government bonds and corporate bonds, to raise their price and so lower long term interest rates. It is hoped that the lower costs of borrowing will encourage an increase in consumer expenditure and investment.

More money entering the economy

The total currency flow is the overall balance on the current, capital and financial accounts excluding the reserves. If there is a total currency flow surplus, the money supply will increase.

The transmission mechanism of monetary policy

The transmission mechanism is the process by which a change in monetary policy works through the economy to affect the price level and real GDP. For instance, a cut in the rate of interest may increase consumer expenditure and investment. A rise in C + I will increase aggregate demand. Higher AD may increase the price level and real GDP, depending on the initial level of economic activity.

Monetarists think there is a relatively straightforward transmission mechanism between an increase in the money supply and the price level. The Keynesians think it is more complex as the influence of an increase in the money supply on the rate of interest, the effect of a lower rate of interest on C + I and the effect of higher AD on output are all uncertain.

Revision activity C

Decide whether the following statements relating to money and banking are true or false.

a Current (sight) accounts are included in both narrow and broad measures of the money supply.

b Banking is based on trust.

c In banking, there is a conflict between profitability and liquidity.

d The Fisher equation is a truism.

e A budget deficit will always increase the money supply.

f A credit crunch involves a surplus of bank loans which stimulates economic activity.

9.23 Keynesian and Monetarist schools of thought

Keynesian economists think there is a high risk of market failure and that there is no guarantee that economies will operate at full capacity. In contrast, monetarists think markets usually work efficiently and that economies will either be operating at full employment or moving towards full capacity.

Monetarists think that inflation is caused by an excessive growth of the money supply. Keynesians argue that inflation can cause an increase in the money supply, with firms and households borrowing more money to keep pace with higher costs and prices. Keynesians think inflation may be caused by cost-push or demand-pull inflation.

Monetarists think that government borrowing can result in crowding out with higher government spending leading to a reduction in private sector firms' investment. If the government borrows more, firms may find it more difficult and expensive to obtain funds. Keynesians, however, claim that government borrowing may result in crowding in, encouraging more investment. If higher government spending causes income to rise, more saving will provide the finance for investment and higher consumer expenditure will encourage more investment.

Keynesians and monetarists agree about the shape of the short-run aggregate supply curve but have a difference of opinion about the shape of the long-run aggregate supply curve. The short-run aggregate supply (SRAS) curve is drawn on the assumption that the prices of the factors of production (inputs or resources) remain unchanged. It slopes up from left to right because as output increases, average costs rise. This is because whilst the price of factors of production remains unchanged as more is produced, less efficient resources may be used and current workers may be paid overtime rates for additional output. In addition, when the price level rises, output prices usually rise relative to resource prices which increase producers' profits.

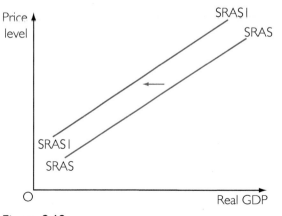

Figure 9.12

The SRAS curve may shift to the left (as shown in Figure 9.12) if there is a rise in resource prices, a decrease in labour productivity, an increase in corporate taxes and if there is a natural disaster.

The long-run aggregate supply (LRAS) curve shows the relationship between aggregate supply and the price level when there has been time for the prices of output and resources to adjust fully to changes in the economy (as shown in Figure 9.13). Monetarist economists argue that the LRAS curve is vertical. They think that, in the long run, the economy will operate at full capacity.

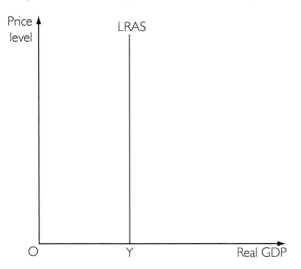

Figure 9.13

Keynesians argue that the economy can operate at any level of capacity in the long run. When there is considerable spare capacity in the economy, the LRAS curve may be perfectly elastic. This is because it will be possible for firms to employ more resources without raising average costs. As real GDP approaches the full employment level, aggregate supply becomes more inelastic. This is because firms start to experience shortages of resources which increase their price. When the economy reaches full capacity, aggregate supply becomes perfectly inelastic.

Monetarists and Keynesians agree that LRAS can increase as a result of an increase in the quantity or quality of resources. Specific reasons include immigration of workers, net investment, improved education and training, and advances in technology.

Progress check K

Why do Keynesians think that unemployment may be a more significant problem than the monetarists believe?

Revision activity D

Complete Table 9.02.

	Keynesians	Monetarists
View on market failure	Significant	
View on government failure		Significant
View on Quantity Theory		Support
Cause of inflation		Excessive growth of the money supply
Main causes of unemployment		Frictional and structural
Effects of government borrowing	Crowding in	
Shape of LRAS curve	Horizontal, then upward sloping and then vertical	
Macroeconomic policy	Favour demand management	
Government intervention		To be kept to a minimum. Main responsibilities = remove market imperfections and keep inflation low

Table 9.02

9.24 The demand for money and interest rate determination

According to the Liquidity Preference Theory, the rate of interest is determined by the demand for and supply of money. There are thought to be three main reasons why households and firms demand money (choose to hold their wealth in a money form). These are the transactions motive (money held to buy products), precautionary motive (money held in case of unexpected expenses and opportunities) and the speculative motive (money held to take advantage of changes in the price of government bonds and the rate of interest).

The Liquidity Preference Theory claims that a fall in the rate of interest can be caused by two possible changes. One is an increase in the money supply and the other is a fall in the demand for money. Figure 9.14 shows the rate of interest being reduced as a result of an increase in the money supply.

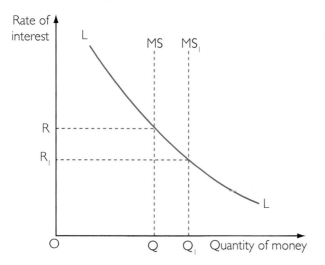

Figure 9.14

9.25 Policies of trade and aid

Trade, types of aid and the nature of dependency

International trade can bring a variety of benefits to developing countries, including opportunities to specialise and take advantage of economies of scale, increased aggregate demand, increased economic growth and increased employment.

Developing countries experience a number of disadvantages in international trade. They rely on the exports of primary products which have a lower income elasticity of demand than manufactured goods. The Prebisch-Singer hypothesis argues that the terms of trade move against developing countries resulting in them having to export more products to purchase the same quantity of imports. In addition, developed countries impose a number of trade restrictions on developing countries whilst putting pressure on the developing countries to remove trade restrictions against them.

Governments may have a number of motives for giving aid. These include altruistic, political and commercial reasons. Aid may be tied or untied, bilateral or multilateral. Untied, multilateral aid tends to be the most beneficial. Aid may compensate for a lack of saving and may provide the finance for investment in capital goods and human capital and so contribute to economic growth and development.

There is a risk that countries may become dependent on aid. Funds may flow from developing to developed countries, if the servicing of the debt arising from aid is greater than the new aid received and if the aid is used for unproductive projects.

Some developing countries may have low levels of domestic investment because of low incomes and so low savings to finance investment and a lack of financial institutions to channel any savings there are to willing investors. This is why a number of developing countries seek investment and investment funds from abroad. Some also rely quite heavily on remittances from their nationals working abroad.

TERMS

Prebisch-Singer hypothesis: argues that the terms of trade move against developing countries resulting in them having to export more products to purchase the same quantity of imports.

Liquidity preference theory: claims the rate of interest is determined by the demand for and supply of money.

Multinational companies and foreign direct investment (FDI)

Multinational companies (MNCs) are companies that produce in more than one country. An MNC setting up a branch in another country moves foreign direct investment (FDI) into that country.

In the short term, MNCs will be adding to the recipient country's balance of payments as an inflow of direct investment in the financial sector. MNCs may also bring in new technology and new management methods. They may also create employment and add to the country's real GDP and exports.

Whether the net effect of MNCs will be beneficial or not will depend on whether or not they drive domestic firms out of business, whether the wages they pay and the working conditions they provide are better than domestic employers. Their impact will also be influenced by how much of any profits they earn they return to their home country, whether they deplete non-renewable resources, whether they create pollution, how much tax they pay and how they use any influence they have on the country's government.

External debt

External debt can hinder economic development. This is because governments have to devote some of their tax revenue to servicing and repaying the debt. A high level of external debt can also make it difficult and expensive for developing countries to obtain loans for development projects.

Some governments with large external debt have defaulted on their loans rather than cutting government spending and raising taxes. Such action, however, may make it very difficult to obtain further loans.

The role of the International Monetary Fund (IMF), the World Bank and the World Trade Organisation (WTO)

The International Monetary Fund (IMF) aims to encourage the growth of world trade, promotes economic stability and helps countries with balance of payments difficulties.

The World Bank provides financial assistance for investment projects in developing countries. To obtain loans from the World Bank and the IMF, developing countries sometimes have to agree to structural adjustment programmes which require them to increase the role of market forces in their economies, to remove trade restrictions and to increase macroeconomic stability.

The World Trade Organisation seeks to promote free trade. It encourages member countries to remove trade restrictions and it presides over trade disputes between members.

International Monetary Fund (IMF): an international organisation that aims to encourage the growth of world trade, promotes economic stability and helps countries with balance of payments difficulties.

World Bank: an international organisation that provides financial assistance for investment projects in developing countries.

World Trade Organisation (WTO): an international organisation that promotes free trade by encouraging member countries to remove trade restrictions and presides over trade disputes between members.

Corruption and the importance of the legal framework in an economy

If a country does not have a developed legal framework, it can be difficult to enforce property rights and can encourage corruption.

A lack of property rights can result in a misallocation of resources and can complete non-renewable resources. Corrupt government officials can deprive development projects of some of their funds and can discourage FDI and portfolio investment.

Mind maps

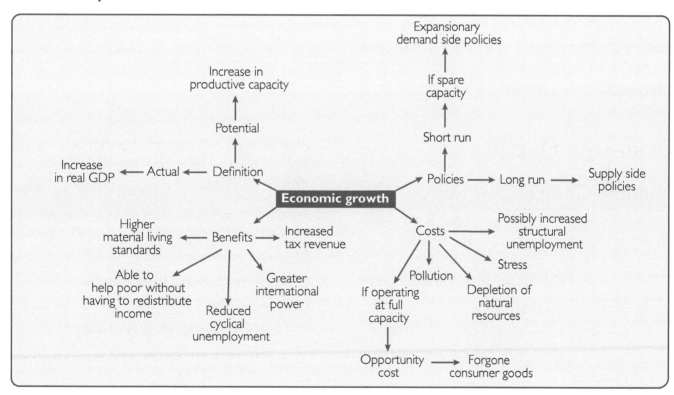

Mind map 9.01: Economic growth

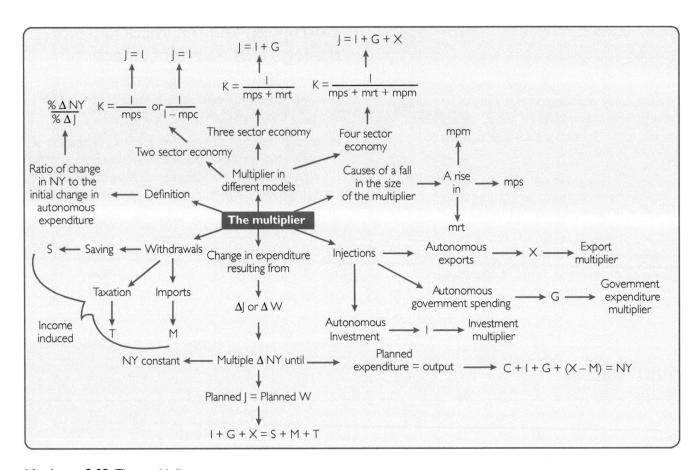

Mind map 9.02: The multiplier

Exam-style Questions

Multiple Choice Questions

1   An economy's gross domestic product is $90 billion and its net domestic product is $75 billion. What can be concluded from this information?

   A   Consumer expenditure was $15 billion.

   B   Depreciation was $15 billion.

   C   Net exports were $15 billion.

   D   Net property income from abroad was $15 billion.

2   An economy's GDP increased from $20 bn in 2002 to $30 bn in 2012. Over the same period, population increased from 20 million to 22 million and the price level increased from 100 to 125. Assuming other influences remained unchanged, what happened to living standards over this period?

   A   Decreased as real GDP fell

   B   Decreased as real GDP per head fell

   C   Increased as real GDP rose

   D   Increased as real GDP per head rose

3 Table 9.03 shows the level of consumer expenditure at different levels of disposable income.

Disposable income ($ billion)	Consumer expenditure ($ billion)
100	120
200	200
300	270
400	320
500	350

Table 9.03

What happens to the average and marginal propensities to consume as disposable income increases?

	Average propensity to consume	Marginal propensity to consume
A	Decrease	Decrease
B	Decrease	Increase
C	Increase	Increase
D	Increase	Decrease

4 What is the monetary base?

A   Notes and coins in circulation

B   Notes and coins in circulation plus the cash reserves of the banking system

C   Notes and coins in circulation, the cash reserves of the banking system and sight accounts

D   Notes and coins in circulation, the cash reserves of the banking system and sight and time deposits

5 Which way of financing a government's spending is likely to result in the greatest increase in the money supply?

A   Increasing income tax rates

B   Decreasing income tax rates

C   The sale of government bonds to the non-bank sector

D   The sale of treasury bills to the banking sector

6 Which combination of policy measures would be considered to be a Keynesian approach to reducing unemployment?

A   An increased budget deficit, increased unemployment benefits and tax cuts

B   A reduction in unemployment benefits, tax cuts and deregulation

C   A reduction in the growth of the money supply, privatisation and a rise in the exchange rate

D   An increase in information about job vacancies, a reduction in total government spending and a rise in the rate of interest

7 According to the concept of crowding out, what effect would an increase in public sector net borrowing have on the interest rate and private sector investment?

	Interest rate	Private sector investment
A	Decrease	Decrease
B	Decrease	Increase
C	Increase	Increase
D	Increase	Decrease

8 Figure 9.15 shows aggregate expenditure in an open economy. What does the distance WX represent?

A   An inflationary gap

B   Government spending

C   Savings

D   Taxes

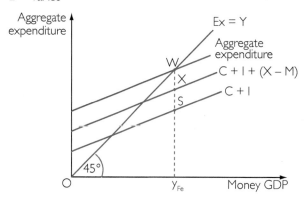

Figure 9.15

9 Government spending in an economy is initially $15 billion and national income is $90 billion. Out of every increase of $100 in national income, $10 is saved, $10 is taken in taxes and $20 is spent on imports. To raise national income to the full employment level of $140 billion, by how much will the government have to increase its spending?

A $5 billion   C $35 billion

B $20 billion   D $50 billion

10 What does the accelerator theory suggest?

A   Income is a function of the growth of investment.

B   Investment increases at a faster rate than saving.

C   Investment is a function of the growth of income.

D   Saving increases at a faster rate than investment.

11 Figure 9.16 shows the market for money is initially in equilibrium at X. Commercial banks then give more loans and the transactions demand for money increases.

What is the new equilibrium position?

A   A   B   B   C   C   D   D

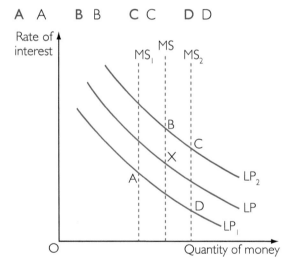

Figure 9.16

12 In a closed economy, government spending is $40 m, consumer expenditure is 0.75Y and investment is $(70 − 2r) m. The full employment level of income is $400 m. What rate of interest is required to obtain this level of income?

A   2%   B   5%   C   10%   D   15%

13 In an economy, 10% of extra income is paid in taxes, 10% is saved, 5% is spent on imports and the rest is spent on domestically produced products. If exports increase by $200 m, what is the rise in consumer expenditure?

A $150 m   C $600 m

B $160 m   D $640 m

14 Figure 9.17 shows planned investment and planned savings in an economy at different levels of income.

What is the level of actual investment at an income level of Y?

A   MN   B   NP   C   PY   D   NY

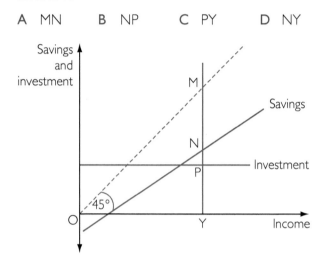

Figure 9.17

15 The growth in demand for electronic books results in a number of bookshops going out of business. How is the type of unemployment of bookshops classified?

A   Casual   C   Search

B   Cyclical   D   Structural

16 What would be most likely to reduce an economy's natural rate of unemployment?

A   An increase in the gap between paid employment and unemployment benefit

B   An increase in the gap between potential and actual output

C   An increase in net exports

D   An increase in the money supply

17 What will be the effect of a country's potential output increasing more rapidly than its actual output?

A   An increase in the inflation rate

B   An increase in the size of the output gap

C   A decrease in the unemployment rate

D   A decrease in real GDP

18 An economy is experiencing demand-pull inflation, a current account deficit, a falling exchange rate and unemployment. The government decides to increase its spending. What does this indicate is its main, short-term, macroeconomic aim?

A   To achieve price stability

B   To improve the current account position

C   To increase the value of the currency

D   To reduce unemployment

19 A country has a population of working age of 50 million. Its labour force participation rate is 55% and its unemployment rate is 8%. What are the number of people in the labour force and the number of people in employment?

	No. of people in the labour force (millions)	No. of people in employment (millions)
A	25.3	23.5
B	27.5	25.3
C	31.5	27.5
D	50.0	46.0

20 Which change would increase the size of a country's labour force?

A   A decrease in net emigration

B   A decrease in unemployment

C   An increase in the school leaving age

D   An increase in the retirement age

Data Response Questions

1 The challenges facing Brazil

At the start of 2014 Brazil experienced a recession with GDP falling over the first two quarters of the year. In response, the government increased its spending to stimulate economic activity. The rise in government spending resulted in the budget deficit doubling to 6.75% of GDP and national debt increased to 66% of GDP. The country's national debt was, in percentage terms, less than in many countries but the high rate of interest in the country meant that the cost of servicing the debt was high. Table 9.04 shows the budget position and the interest rate for a number of countries.

Country	Budget balance as % of GDP	Interest rate %
Brazil	−6.0	15.50
China	−2.7	3.04
India	−3.8	7.68
Russia	−2.8	9.45
UK	−4.4	2.09
USA	−2.6	2.33

Table 9.04: The budget position and interest rate of selected countries, 2015

In 2015 the government's fiscal stance changed. To improve its finances, it cut spending on unemployment benefit and other benefits and increased taxes, including fuel duty.

The government was also concerned about the economy's continued high inflation rate. Some economists also suggested imposing stricter rules on banks' liquidity ratios in order to reduce consumer demand but the government was concerned that such a measure might not be effective.

a   How is economic growth measured? [2]

b   Using an aggregate expenditure diagram, explain how injecting government spending into the economy might reduce a recession. [5]

c   i   Why might a large budget deficit lead to a high interest rate? [3]

    ii Explain whether the information in Table 9.04 confirms this relationship. [4]

d   Discuss whether 'stricter rules on banks' liquidity ratios' would reduce consumer demand. [6]

2 Decline in Pakistan's rate of economic growth

Pakistan's economic growth rate averaged 7.8% between 1999 and 2008. It has been lower since and has been below that of its neighbours' economic growth rates. Between 2010 and 2015, Pakistan's average growth rate was 3.8% in comparison to 6.3% for Bangladesh, 6.4% for India and 8.1% for China.

Pakistan's growth rate has been adversely affected in recent years by a series of floods. For instance, in 2016 flooding in Balochistan, Khyber Pakhtunkhwa and the Punjab destroyed housing and capital stock. Some economists attribute Pakistan's lower economic growth rate not only to the adverse effects of floods but also to the country's lack of infrastructure and underdeveloped markets. Investment in Pakistan is lower as a proportion of its GDP than in its neighbouring countries. Table 9.05 compares the components of GDP in Bangladesh, China, India and Pakistan.

Country	Consumer expenditure ($bn)	Investment ($bn)	Government ($bn)	Exports ($bn)	Imports ($bn)
Bangladesh	145	63	12	34	52
China	4324	4893	1593	2617	2084
India	1320	682	264	418	484
Pakistan	196	30	37	27	42

Table 9.05: The components of GDP in selected countries 2015

As well as the composition of the GDPs varying, the size of the four countries, and multipliers also differ.

The main industries in Pakistan are textiles and food processing. The services sector is expanding although most of it is relatively small scale and some of it operates in the informal sector.

Pakistan has a number of economic advantages. In 2015 it had a relatively small negative output gap. It has a young population with an average age of 23, compared to 25 in Bangladesh and 27 in India. It also has a range of natural resources, including copper and gas and a potential for labour productivity to increase significantly.

a   Explain the effect that a fall in capital stock will have on aggregate supply. [3]

b   i   Can it be concluded from the data in Table 9.05 that the output of Pakistan's economy was $248 bn in 2015? Explain your answer. [3]

    ii What was the level of domestic demand in India in 2015? [2]

c   Analyse why the size of the multiplier varies between countries. [4]

d   What is meant by a negative output gap? [2]

e   Discuss whether consumer expenditure is likely to increase in Pakistan. [6]

Essay Questions

1 In 2015, the GDP per head of the Netherlands was three times greater than that of Chile. Discuss whether this means that people in the Netherlands enjoyed living standards three times as great as that of people in Chile. [25]

2 a Explain the differences between economic development and economic growth. [12]

   b Discuss whether multinational companies promote economic growth in developing countries. [13]

REVISION TIP

It can be rewarding to revise with a fellow student or students. You can meet to ask each other questions on particular topics. This activity may involve you explaining points and this will really challenge your understanding.

Government macro intervention

10.01 Objectives of macroeconomic policy

Governments seek to achieve low and stable inflation, low unemployment, a balance of payments equilibrium, sustained and sustainable economic growth, avoidance of exchange rate fluctuations and economic development.

Low and stable inflation is sometimes referred to as price stability. A number of governments set an inflation target which their central banks are required to achieve.

The lowest level of unemployment possible is known as full employment. Achieving a low level of unemployment can help a government achieve the macroeconomic objective of economic growth and can help to raise living standards.

Sustained economic growth occurs when increases in aggregate demand are matched by increases in aggregate supply. Sustainable economic growth is

growth which does not damage future generations' ability to enjoy increases in output. Such growth will not conflict with promoting economic development.

The avoidance of significant fluctuations in the exchange rate promotes greater certainty which in turn stimulates investment. A large fall in the exchange rate might result in a capital outflow from the country with portfolio and direct investment being transferred to other countries. A large rise in the exchange rate, possibly caused by speculation, could reduce the country's international competitiveness. The desire to avoid sharp and sudden changes is why, on some occasions, some governments intervene in the foreign exchange market.

Governments try to promote economic development in a number of ways. As well as trying to improve people's material standards of living, they seek to increase life expectancy through encouraging healthier life styles and providing public healthcare. They also, to different degrees, provide state education and training.

Revision activity A

Complete Table 10.01 by writing low or high in each box.

Characteristic	Developed economy	Developing economy
GDP per head		
Population growth		
Proportion of population employed in agriculture		
Urbanisation		
HDI ranking		
Foreign debt as % of GDP		
Energy consumption		
Enrolment in tertiary education		
Life expectancy		
Population per doctor		
Labour productivity		
Savings ratio		

Table 10.01

Revision activity B

Classify the following into internal and external macroeconomic policy objectives.

a   Balance of payments equilibrium

b   Full employment

c   Price stability

d   Stable exchange rate

e   Steady and sustainable economic growth

TIP

Check whether the government of your country has fixed targets for economic growth, inflation, unemployment and the current account position on the balance of payments. Compare any targets you find with the targets of other economies.

Progress check A

Identify two reasons why a government may want its country's exchange rate to fall in value.

TERM

Macroeconomic policy aims: governments seek to achieve low and stable inflation, low unemployment, a balance of payments equilibrium, sustained and sustainable economic growth, avoidance of exchange rate fluctuations and economic development.

10.02 The relationship between internal and external value of money

A rise in the inflation rate will reduce the internal value of money. As a result of reducing the price competitiveness of the country's products, it is also likely to result in a fall in demand for exports and a rise in demand for imports. These changes, in turn, will reduce demand for the currency and increase its supply and so cause a fall in the exchange rate (the external value of the currency).

A rise in the external value of money will raise its internal value. An appreciation of the currency will reduce the price of imports, meaning that people will be able to buy more of them. The lower price of imported raw materials will also reduce the costs of producing some domestic products.

Progress check B

Why might the internal value of money decline but its external value rise?

10.03 Relationship between balance of payments and inflation

A current account surplus may contribute to inflationary pressure by raising aggregate demand and the money supply.

A higher inflation rate than rival countries may cause an economy to experience deterioration in its current account position. This is because its products will become less price competitive.

Progress check C

Why might globalisation put downward pressure on governments to cut their spending on education?

10.04 The trade-off between inflation and unemployment

The traditional Phillips curve suggests that it is possible for a government to reduce unemployment by increasing aggregate demand but at the expense of a higher inflation rate. Figure 10.01 shows an economy initially operating with a 9% unemployment rate and a 4% inflation rate. Expansionary fiscal or monetary policy may reduce unemployment to 3% but at the cost of an increase in the inflation rate to 11%.

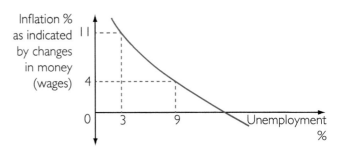

Figure 10.01

The expectations augmented Phillips curve suggests that there is no long-run trade-off between unemployment and inflation. It implies that unemployment may be reduced in the short run as a result of an increase in aggregate demand but in the long run, unemployment will return to the natural rate. Figure 10.02 shows that the natural rate of unemployment is 6%. An attempt to reduce unemployment to 4% by increasing aggregate demand may succeed in the short run at the cost of an inflation rate of 3%.

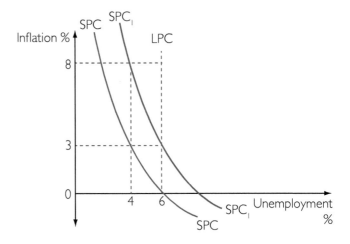

Figure 10.02

In the longer run, however, the economy will return to the natural rate of unemployment as workers and firms adjust to the new inflation rate. Some workers realising their real wages have not risen may resign. Others will press for wage rises which will raise firms' costs causing them to lower output and employment. The economy is now on a higher short-run Phillips curve with expectations of inflation built into the system. A new attempt to reduce unemployment to 4% would push up the inflation rate to 8%.

Some economists argue that with increased global competition and advances in technology it is possible to reduce unemployment close to full employment without causing inflation.

A reduction in inflation reduces unemployment as it tends to increase international competitiveness of the country's products. This may increase net exports and so raise aggregate demand and reduce cyclical unemployment.

Revision activity C

In each of the following cases, decide whether the changes would cause frictional, structural or cyclical unemployment.

a   A global recession

b   The introduction of new technology which reduces the need for labour

c   A reduction in the availability of information about job vacancies

d   A reduction in business and consumer confidence

e   A decrease in demand for fish

f   The increased popularity of biofuels over oil as a fuel

Progress check D

What could cause a conventional Phillips curve to shift to the left?

TIP

It is useful to analyse data showing the unemployment rate and the inflation rate for your country and other countries over a period of time. Remember when examining such data there may be time lags involved. There will also be the issue of causation. A reduction in the unemployment rate may be accompanied by a rise in the inflation rate – but which is causing which? In addition, both may be affected by other influences.

10.05 The problems that arise from policy conflicts

Whether the aims of government policy will conflict will be affected by the time period under consideration, the current state of the economy and the type of economic policies pursued. If there is a conflict, which aim should be given priority will again be influenced by the current state of the economy, future predictions, the costs involved and which aim the government thinks it will be most effective in achieving.

In the short run, if an economy is operating close to full employment, there may be a conflict between reducing the inflation rate or at least ensuring the inflation rate remains stable. If a government seeks to reduce unemployment by expansionary fiscal policy, the higher aggregate demand may result in inflationary pressure. In Figure 10.03 as aggregate demand (AD) increases, output moves closer to the vertical part of the aggregate supply curve (AS) and the price level rises from P to P_1.

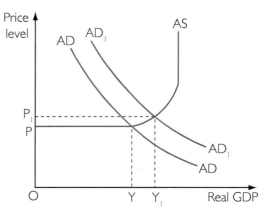

Figure 10.03

If, however, the economy has considerable spare capacity, with a noticeable output gap, it may be possible to reduce unemployment by a noticeable amount without causing inflationary pressure.

In the short run, the objectives of economic growth and a stable inflation rate may also conflict. As the previous diagram shows, higher AD causes real GDP to rise but it also pushes up the price level. As an economy's AD increases, more resources are used and they become in shorter supply and the rising competition pushes up their prices. Firms know they can charge more for their products and so they are willing to increase their prices.

Economic growth may also conflict with a balance on the current account of the balance of payments. If economic growth occurs, incomes will rise. This may result in an increase in demand for goods and services. As a result, imports of finished products and raw materials may increase. Some products originally intended for the export market may also be diverted to the home market. Of course, it is possible that economic growth may be export led and in such a circumstance may be accompanied by a declining current account deficit.

In the long run, if a government follows effective supply side policy measures it may be able to achieve most of its objectives. This is because such policies, such as improved education and training, will shift the aggregate supply (AS) curve to the right enabling AD to increase, lowering unemployment, achieving economic growth without causing inflation. Effective supply side policy measures can also improve the current account position by improving the quality and price competitiveness of domestic products. Of course, a government may also have to ensure that both AD and AS increase in line with each other. In Figure 10.04, both AD and AS rise. These shifts keep the price level at P and raises real GDP from Y to Y₁.

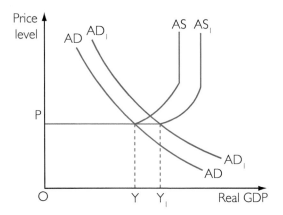

Figure 10.04

Some supply side policy measures may result in a redistribution of income from the poor to the rich, at least in the short run. For example, cuts in benefits combined with cuts in the top rates of tax, designed to increase incentives may widen the gap between the rich and the poor. Supporters of such measures, however, argue there may be a longer run trickle-down effect. The rich may start more firms and buy more products which may create employment for the poor. They also suggest that lower top rates of tax may actually increase tax revenue (see the Laffer curve below) and so provide more government funds to tackle poverty.

In practice, a government is likely to need to use a range of policy measures to achieve its objectives. In the short run, whilst unemployment and economic growth are likely to be helped by an increase in AD, a reduction in AD may be needed to reduce demand-pull inflation and a current account deficit. In the long run, however, all the objectives should benefit from an increase in AS which matches an increase in AD. This is why some economists claim that sustained economic growth should be given priority. If both aggregate demand and aggregate supply shift to the right, inflation and unemployment should be kept low and the current account close to balance. In the short run, if there is significant and rising unemployment whilst inflation is low and stable, there is still positive economic growth and the current account position is close to balance, a government is likely to prioritise reducing unemployment. If, however, unemployment is of a short-term duration and on a downturn trend whilst inflation is unanticipated and of a cost-push nature, a government may decide to concentrate on reducing inflation.

Progress check E

Distinguish between a supply constraint and a demand constraint in connection with economic growth.

TIP

Remember fiscal policy measures will be more effective, the larger the size of the multiplier.

10.06 Government failure in macroeconomic policy

Government failure in macroeconomic policy occurs when government intervention does not improve macroeconomic performance and, in some cases, makes it worse. There are a number of reasons why government failure may occur including wrong timing, a lack of or inaccurate information, economic agents not responding in the way expected, demand and supply shocks, unexpected side-effects and corruption.

Governments may use fiscal and/or monetary policy to influence aggregate demand to try to ensure that actual economic growth matches potential economic growth. This approach is known as counter-cyclical policy as it is designed to work against the business cycle and smooth out fluctuations in economic activity. When the economy is going into a downturn, a counter-cyclical policy measure would seek to increase aggregate demand. In contrast, during an upturn, a counter-cyclical policy measure may try to reduce the growth in aggregate demand. There is a risk that a government may misjudge what is happening in the economic cycle and may inject extra spending just as the economy starts an upturn. In such a case, the policy measure would be reinforcing rather than countering the cycle. This risk is reinforced by the time lag that may occur between deciding on a policy measure and that policy measure affecting the economy.

A government may think that inflation is caused by demand-pull factors and as a result may employ deflationary fiscal policy measures including higher taxes. If the inflation is actually the result of cost-push factors, the government intervention may actually cause an acceleration of the inflation rate. A government may also inject too much or too little extra spending into the economy if it has miscalculated the size of the multiplier.

If households and firms are pessimistic about future economic prospects, it may be difficult for a government to encourage higher spending through expansionary fiscal and monetary policy measures.

A government may inject sufficient extra spending into the economy to cause a significant fall in unemployment ceteris paribus. If, at the same time, however the world economy goes into a global recession aggregate demand may not increase because of a decrease in net exports. A negative supply side shock which increases costs of production might also result in cost-push inflation.

A government may raise income tax in order to reduce demand-pull inflation. This may not reduce aggregate demand and may actually cause cost-push inflation if it leads to workers pressing for and receiving wage rises. Measures to reduce income inequality may create disincentive effects. A government may impose import tariffs to protect its steel industry to maintain employment. This may have the unintentional consequence of creating unemployment in the country's car industry by pushing up the cost of domestically produced cars.

Government ministers may make policy decisions to promote their own careers rather than to improve macroeconomic performance. Some government officials may take bribes to, for example, award contracts to less efficient contractors. Regulatory capture may also occur. This where, due to the greater amount of time they spend with industry managers and the friendships they may develop, regulators favour the interests of the firms rather than consumers.

Revision activity D

A government spends $20 bn on goods and services and provides benefits which are equal to 10% of real GDP. The rate of taxation is 30%.

a At which level of real GDP would the government have a balanced budget?

b What would be the budget position if real GDP is $250 bn?

c Explain two reasons why government spending on goods and services may increase as real GDP rises.

Progress check F

Why might unemployment increase despite a rise in real GDP?

TIP

To assess how successful a government's macroeconomic policy is, examine what their objectives are and what policy constraints they have. It is also useful to compare one government's performance against that of other governments. For instance, the unemployment rate in a country may have risen but the rate in other countries may have risen by more. This may indicate that the government may have been more successful in protecting the country's employment from the adverse effects of a global recession.

10.07 Laffer curve analysis

The Laffer curve shows that tax revenue is zero when the tax rate is zero, then rises and then falls, reaching zero when the tax rate is 100 per cent. This trend is shown in Figure 10.05.

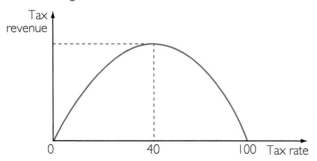

Figure 10.05

The Laffer curve suggests that a cut in a high tax rate would increase tax revenue as it would increase the incentive to work and would reduce tax evasion. It also implies that there is an optimum tax rate which will maximise tax revenue.

Economists debate how useful Laffer curve analysis is. Some dispute the shape of the curve. They claim that a curve showing the relationship between tax rates and tax revenue could be linear over part of its length and that its shape may change over time and vary between countries.

> **TIP**
>
> The Laffer curve shows the relationship between tax rates and tax revenue. Remember, however, it does not suggest that all cuts in tax rates will raise tax revenue. What it does suggest is that cuts in high tax rates will as they will change behaviour.

Mind maps

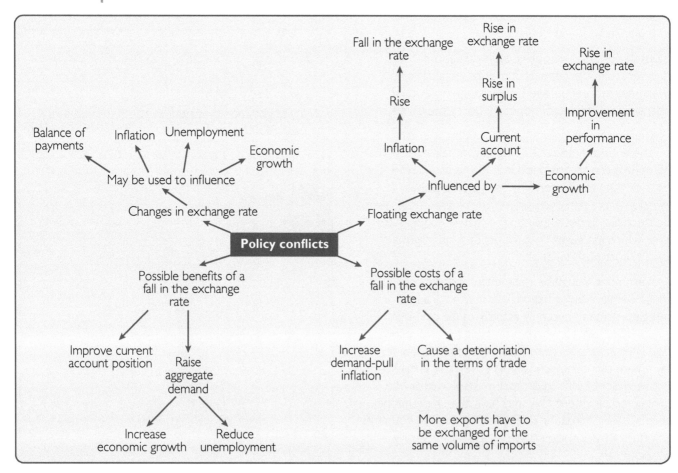

Mind map 10.01: Policy conflicts

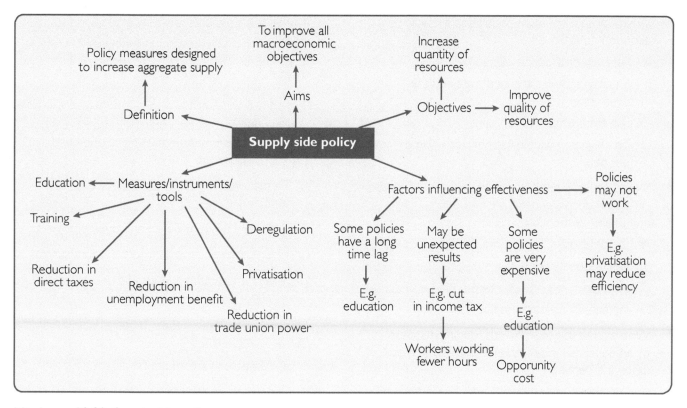

Mind map 10.02: Supply side policy

Exam-style Questions

Multiple Choice Questions

1 Which combination of economic problems would benefit from an upward revaluation of the currency?

   A   A current account deficit and inflation

   B   A current account deficit and unemployment

   C   A current account surplus and inflation

   D   A current account surplus and unemployment

2 A multinational company based in India owns a subsidiary company in Germany which in 2013 made a profit of $11 m. $6 m of that profit was sent back to the parent company in India and the remaining profit went towards the financing of a $13 m investment project in Germany. The remaining finance for the investment project was borrowed from banks, $3 m coming from German banks and the remaining money coming from India's banks. What effect would these transactions have had on India's current account, financial account and net currency flow?

	Current account	Financial account	Net currency flow
A	+ $11 m	−$13 m	+ $6 m
B	+ $5 m	−$7 m	−$2 m
C	+ $6 m	−$5 m	+ $1 m
D	+ $8 m	−$3 m	−$6 m

3 Selected data on four countries is shown in Table 10.02.

	GNI per head ($)	Life expectancy (years)	Time spent in education (years)
Country A	1,800	45	6
Country B	2,000	62	10
Country C	2,200	82	14
Country D	2,400	70	10

Table 10.02

On the information provided, which country had the highest standard of living?

A A   B B   C C   D D

4 What does an optimum population allow an economy to achieve?

   A   An even distribution of income

   B   Equality between the birth rate and the death rate

   C   Full employment of resources

   D   The highest possible level of real income per head

5 Which government policy measure would be most likely to reduce a current account deficit and unemployment?

   A   Devaluation

   B   Decrease in income tax

   C   Increase in the rate of interest

   D   Increase in corporation tax

6 Why is a rise in government spending matched by an equal rise in tax revenue likely to increase aggregate demand?

   A   A proportion of the income taken in tax would have been saved.

   B   A significant proportion of the government spending may be devoted to imports.

   C   Government spending usually accounts for a larger proportion of aggregate demand than consumer spending.

   D   Taxes are a withdrawal from the circular flow whereas government spending is an injection.

7 Figure 10.06 shows a long-run Phillips curve (LPC) and three short-run Phillips curves (SPC). The economy is initially at the natural rate of unemployment of 8% with an inflation rate of 5%.

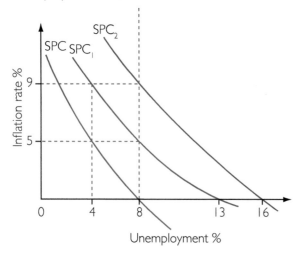

Figure 10.06

If inflationary expectations stay at 5% and the government wants to eliminate inflation, what rate of unemployment will it have to accept in the short run?

   A 4%   B 8%   C 13%   D 16%

8 Which combination of problems is most likely to result in a government increasing taxation and cutting its spending?

   A   Demand-pull inflation and a current account deficit

   B   A current account deficit and unemployment

   C   Unemployment and a current account surplus

   D   A current account surplus and demand-pull inflation

9 Which policy measure may increase the natural rate of unemployment?

   A   A decrease in income tax

   B   A decrease in the rate of interest

   C   An increase in unemployment benefit

   D   An increase in labour market flexibility

10 What would reduce the effectiveness of expansionary fiscal policy?

   A   An absence of a time lag

   B   An absence of a recession in trading partners

   C   A high marginal propensity to save

   D   A low marginal propensity to import

Data Response Questions

1 Growing inequality

The richest 1% of the global population now own as much wealth as the entire rest of the world. Seven of the world's wealthiest people live in the USA.

In 2015, the US was experiencing low but positive economic growth. Output increased most rapidly in the tertiary sector which employs 80% of the labour force. The country had a relatively low unemployment rate of 5.2% but was experiencing a relatively high poverty rate. In 2014 14.8% of the country's population were living in poverty. A family of five was considered to be living in poverty if it had an income of less than $28,960. That same year the average household income in the country was $51,939.

In a country which was ranked 8th in the Human Development Index in 2015, the number of homeless people was increasing in many cities like Detroit and Las Vegas. The number of children in these cities who qualify for free school meals increased to nearly 50%. Economists expressed concern that 21.1% of children were growing up in poverty as a significant proportion of these children are likely to be poor when they are adults.

The problem of such a high proportion of the population living in poverty was surprising in a country which is classified as a developed country. The country had an average life expectancy of 79.6 years in 2015 but the poor have a shorter life expectancy.

a   How many people were living in poverty in the USA in 2014?   [1]

b   Explain the link between unemployment and poverty.   [4]

c   What evidence is there in the extract that USA is a developed country?   [5]

d   Explain why the children of the poor tend to be poor when they are adults.   [4]

e   Discuss whether achieving the macroeconomic objectives of full employment and economic growth would reduce poverty.   [6]

2 India's strengths and weaknesses

One of the strengths of the Indian economy is its young population. The average age of the population is only 27 and 60% of the population is aged below 30. As young Indians have become richer and more educated, they are buying more items including cars, electrical goods and housing. They are also contributing to an increasing labour force.

India is, however, suffering from poor infrastructure. Its roads, railways and telephone system are of poorer quality than its economic rival, China. In an attempt to rectify this, the Indian government is increasing its spending on infrastructure.

Despite the poor infrastructure, a number of Indian industries are becoming world leaders. The country has become one of the biggest outsourcing centres in the world, with IT firms benefitting from a good supply of high skilled, relatively cheap software experts. There is a rapid growth in business processing with the number of call centres still increasing and more and more pharmaceutical research and the making of spare parts for car manufacturers being located in the country.

Table 10.03 shows the growth in labour productivity in a number of countries.

Country/area	1999–2006	2007–2012	2012	2013	2014
Bangladesh	2.2	2.6	4.3	3.5	4.5
China	9.9	9.5	7.3	7.3	7.0
India	3.2	7.4	2.7	2.8	3.8
Pakistan	1.8	0.2	1.9	4.0	2.1
UK	2.0	0.0	−0.4	0.5	0.5
USA	2.0	1.1	0.5	1.2	0.7
World	2.6	2.5	1.7	2.1	2.1

Table 10.03: The percentage growth in labour productivity in selected countries

a i Define aggregate demand. [2]

 ii Using the information provided, explain two reasons why aggregate demand has increased in India in recent years. [4]

 iii Using the information provided, explain two reasons why aggregate supply has increased in recent years. [4]

b Compare India's growth in labour productivity with that of the other countries in Table 10.03. [4]

c Discuss whether an increase in a country's labour force always benefits an economy. [6]

Essay Questions

1 a Explain how a government might seek to reduce the natural rate of unemployment. [12]

 b Discuss whether a decrease in unemployment will cause inflation. [13]

2 a Explain why an increase in taxes may cause a fall in national income. [12]

 b Discuss why the aims of government policy might conflict with each other and how a government should decide which of these aims ought to be given priority. [13]

3 a Explain how it can be decided whether an economy is a developed or a developing economy. [12]

 b Discuss whether adopting a floating exchange rate would allow a government of a developing economy to concentrate on internal policy objectives. [13]

Answers

All answers that appear in this publication have been written by the author.

Chapter 1

Answers to progress checks

A The economic problem will never be solved. This is because wants will continue to be greater than resources. Even if there are more resources, for instance, more capital goods, people would still like more goods and services. As economies grow, the goods and services considered necessary for a good standard of life increase. For example, a few years ago a family in the UK would have considered itself to be well off if it had one foreign holiday a year. Now some families have two or more foreign holidays a year and many would like to have more foreign holidays.

B Most schools engage in division of labour by employing specialist teachers e.g. economics teachers and history teachers.

C Apples do not act as money as they lack some of the key characteristics of money. They are not generally acceptable, they are not durable, they are not very portable and are not uniform.

D The cake is an economic good. It has been provided free to the customers but it is an economic good as it will have taken resources to produce it.

E Electronic road pricing is charging drivers according to where and when they drive. A person will pay more for driving into a city centre at peak times than driving on an uncongested road. Being able to charge drivers in this way indicates that those who do not pay can be excluded from consuming road space.

F A product may be treated as a demerit good in one country but not in another because governments have different views on how harmful some products are and how aware the public are of the harmful effects. For instance, Singapore bans the import and sale of chewing gum (except medicinal gum). Most other governments allow people to chew gum despite the problems caused by people disposing of chewing gum.

Answers to revision activities

A a Land: locations where films are shot.
Labour: camera operators, film directors.
Capital: cameras, editing equipment.
Enterprise: shareholders in the film company, producers.

b Capital intensive industry: the oil industry. Labour intensive industry: hotel and catering.

c A range of factors influence the supply of labour to a particular occupation including: the wage rate, bonuses, working conditions, working hours, holidays, promotion chances, job security, pensions.

d Enterprise and opportunity cost are linked as entrepreneurs will take into account the return in the next most profitable industry when considering whether to keep using their skills in a particular industry. If profit falls below the normal profit level, some entrepreneurs will switch their resources to producing other products.

e The rent of land in city centres is usually higher than that of land in rural areas as land is scarcer relative to the demand for it. In a city there are usually many competing uses for a relatively small area of land. In contrast, there is usually less competition for the use of land in rural areas.

B

A comparison of a market economy and a planned economy		
Features	**Market Economy**	**Planned Economy**
Allocative mechanism	The price mechanism	State directives
Key sector	Private	Public
Key decision makers	Consumers	The state
Other names	Free enterprise, laissez faire, private enterprise	Centrally planned, collectivist, state owned
Example	Hong Kong	North Korea
Ownership of means of production	Privately owned	State owned
Provision of public goods	No	Yes
The profit motive	Present	Not present

C **a** A constant opportunity cost – as more capital goods are produced, the same amount of consumer goods would have to be given up and as more consumer goods are made, the opportunity cost in terms of capital goods will not change.

b The movement of the PPC from AB to AC would mean that the economy's ability to produce consumer goods has increased whilst its ability to produce capital goods is unchanged.

c The PPC will have shifted either because the economy has fewer resources or lower quality resources. For instance, the decline in the quality of education may have decreased the productivity of labour and so have reduced the quantity of products that the economy can produce.

D **a** Cheques are not money. They are a means of transferring bank deposits from one person to another.

b The function of money which allows products to be bought on credit is a standard of deferred payments.

c To act as a medium of exchange money has to be divisible in order that payments of different values can be made and change can be given.

d A sight deposit (current account) is more liquid than a time deposit (deposit account).

e The general acceptability/durability and durability/general acceptability of money allows it to act as a store of value.

f Money acts as a unit of account when the value of products is compared.

Answers to multiple choice questions

1 **B** If resources that were previously unemployed are used to make agricultural goods, no manufactured goods would have to be sacrificed. In the other cases, it is possible that some manufactured goods would have to be forgone to make the agricultural goods.

2 **A** A is a matter of opinion – a value judgement. In contrast, B, C and D are all factual questions.

3 **B** Complete specialisation means devoting all resources to producing one type of product. B shows that all available resources are employed providing capital goods. A and C show a combination of consumer and capital goods being produced – with A indicating some resources are unemployed. D is an unattainable position.

4 **C** A mixed economy has both a private sector and a public sector. The private sector covers firms that are owned by individuals. In this sector, decisions on the allocation of resources are based on the market forces of demand and supply. The public sector covers state run organisations in which the allocation of resources is determined by state planning. A and B are likely to apply to market, mixed and planned economies whereas it is unlikely that D would be found in any type of economic system.

5 **D** In a planned economy, it is the government/state that determines what products are produced, how they are produced and for whom.

6 **C** As not all wants can be met, choices have to made.

7 **A** If an item is not generally acceptable as money, people will not be prepared to exchange products for it. Some early forms of money, e.g. gold and silver did have intrinsic value, but most forms of money today such as banknotes do not. Other characteristics of money include divisibility rather than indivisibility. Divisibility enables payments of different values to be made and change to be given. Limited supply, rather than unlimited supply. Is an important characteristic linked to acceptability. If an item is in unlimited supply, it will not be generally acceptable.

8 **B** Land covers natural resources. A beach is an example of a natural resource. In contrast, A, C and D are human made goods used in the production of the holiday and so are capital goods.

9 **B** To raise the production of capital goods from 20m to 50m, resources have to be switched away from producing capital goods. The output of consumer goods has to fall from 100m to 60m and so 40m consumer goods have to be forgone in order to make 30m more capital goods.

10 **C** As it is not possible to charge directly for a public good, there is a risk that some people will consume the product without paying for it.

Answer to data response question

1 a Removal of price controls, removal of subsidies and privatisation (sale of state owned enterprises).

b Primary

c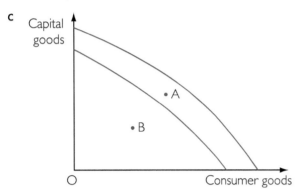

The ability of the Russian economy to produce products is likely to have decreased, shifting the PPC to the left. This is because life expectancy fell which probably reduced the size of the labour force. The rise in unemployment would have moved the production point further inside the curve, as shown by the movement from point A to point B.

d The inhabitants of Poland enjoyed a higher life expectancy in 2014 than those in Russia. The economic growth rate was also higher in Poland than in Russia. Russia had the lowest growth rate out of the four countries shown while Poland's was the second highest. The unemployment rate was higher in Poland than in Russia.

It would have been useful to have additional data including the countries' current account position and inflation rate, to make a fuller comparison of the two countries' economic performance.

e Reasons why the sale may benefit the economy:

- There may be competitive pressure on firms in the private sector to be allocatively, productively and dynamically efficient
- Private sector companies may provide more choice, higher quality and lower prices for consumers.
- There will be saving of government revenue if the firms had been loss making.

Reasons why the sale may not benefit the economy:

- There may be a reduction in social provision for workers if an adequate state welfare system is not developed.

- Private sector firms may not take externalities into account.
- Private sector monopolies may develop which charge high prices and produce low quality products and do not provide choice.
- There will be a loss of government revenue in the long run if the state owned enterprises had been profitable.

Answers to essay questions

1 a A production possibility curve (PPC) shows the amount of two types of products that can be produced with existing resources and technology. In practice, most PPC are bowed outwards. This is because the opportunity cost of producing one type of product increases the more of it that is produced. The best resources are employed first, so as more is made, the more resources that have to be used and so the more of the other product that has to be given up.

The figure below shows the PPC of an economy that can produce capital and consumer goods.

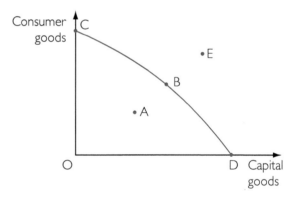

Production point A shows unemployed resources. Points B, C and D are all productively efficient points and point E is unattainable.

A PPC will shift to the right if the quantity or quality of resources used in producing both types of products increases. If the ability to produce only one type of product increases, the shape of the PPC will change. If there is an advance in technology affecting capital goods, the amount of capital goods that can be produced will increase. The figure below shows that the rise in the productive capacity of producing capital goods will pivot out the PPC on the horizontal axis.

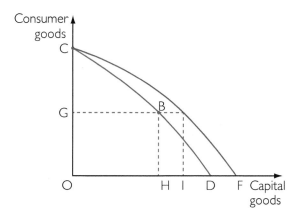

The maximum amount of consumer goods that can be produced remains at C whilst the maximum amount of capital goods that can be produced increases from D to F. If originally, the economy had selected to produce at point B, it would have made G quantity of consumer goods and H quantity of capital goods. After the advance in technology, G quantity of consumer goods could now be combined with a higher quantity of capital goods – I amount.

b The economic problem is that wants are infinite whilst resources are finite. It is very unlikely that the problem of scarcity will ever be solved as whilst the quantity and quality of resources tend to increase over time, so do wants. Different economic systems seek to manage the problem of wants exceeding resources in different ways.

In a market economy the market forces of demand and supply determine how resources are allocated. These forces work through the price mechanism. Those whose services are most in demand will earn the highest wages and will have high purchasing power. If demand for a product decreases, its price will fall which will result in a contraction in supply. As a result, scarce resources will not be wasted producing products that consumers are not willing and able to buy. In contrast, if demand for a product increases, the resulting rise in price and profitability will encourage producers to make more of the product.

In coping with the economic problem, the price mechanism has a number of advantages. It rations out goods and services. Those who can afford the products can buy them. It provides an incentive for firms and workers to be efficient. The more productive workers are, the more they will earn and the more responsive firms

are to changes in consumer demand, the higher the profits they will earn. The price mechanism also works automatically and quickly, moving resources away from products declining in popularity towards those increasing in popularity.

In practice, though, there may be market failure with the price mechanism not resulting in productive, allocative and dynamic efficiency. Monopoly power may develop which can distort the allocation of resources. A monopoly firm may create an artificial shortage in order to drive up prices. A pure market system would fail to produce public goods, and would under-produce merit goods as they would be under-consumed and would over-produce demerit goods as they would be over-consumed. Linked to merit goods and demerit goods, consumers and producers in a pure market system would also not take into account positive and negative externalities. The greater the extent of market failure, the less efficiently resources will be used and the greater will be the problem of scarcity.

In addition, in a pure market economy, different groups will be affected by the problem of scarcity to different degrees. Whilst the rich may be able to satisfy most of their wants, the poor may not be able to meet even their basic needs. The price mechanism reflects effective demand, that is not only the willingness to buy products but also the ability to buy them. It may be claimed that there is consumer sovereignty but consumers do not have equal purchasing power. It is the poor which experience scarcity to the greatest extent.

An advantage claimed for a planned economy is a relatively even distribution of income. State planning may also mean that externalities are taken into account, wasteful duplication may be avoided, there may be full employment of resources, public goods will be produced and the consumption of merit goods will be encouraged whilst the consumption of demerit goods will be discouraged.

Relying on state planning and directives to allocate resources, however, is not guaranteed to be more efficient in tackling the problem of scarcity than a market economy. Whilst all resources may be employed, they may be underemployed or not employed in the most productive uses. There may be an overconcentration on capital goods. State planning can be slow and may not accurately assess consumers' wants. The lack of incentives for workers and SOEs may also mean that output is lower than possible and so scarcity is more of a problem than necessary.

Which type of economic system is more effective in dealing with the economic problem depends on the degree of market failure and government failure. As there are advantages and disadvantages of market and planned economies, most countries operate mixed economies. Such an approach may result in greater equity and a more beneficial provision of products than in a market economy and may provide more incentives and less bureaucracy than in a planned economy. No type of economic system, however, can eliminate the problem of scarcity.

2 a The basic economic problem is scarcity. Wants exceed resources meaning there are not enough resources to produce everything that people want. As a result of the problem, all economies have to make choices. The three fundamental questions they all have to answer are what to produce, how to produce and for whom to produce.

If there was enough land, labour, capital and enterprise to make all the products people desire to have, economies would not have to answer the question of what to produce. In practice, economies have to decide what they are going to use their resources to make. If, for instance, an economy decides to make more capital goods, the opportunity cost would be consumer goods. The following figure shows that making full use of its resources, an economy is producing 30m capital goods and 40m consumer goods. To produce additional 10m capital goods, 12m consumer goods have to be forgone.

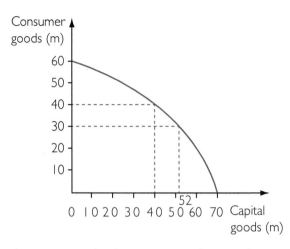

An economy also has to answer the question of how to produce. It has to decide which resources to use and in what combinations. Its decision will be influenced by what resources are available to it. For instance, an economy which has a plentiful supply of labour and a shortage of capital is more likely to make use of labour intensive methods of production rather than capital intensive methods. It is important to use the most efficient methods so that the gap between what is produced and what people want is minimised.

Economies have to answer the question of who should receive the output produced as consumers will be competing for a limited number of goods and services.

Different economic systems answer the three fundamental economic questions in different ways but the existence of the economic problem means that no type of economic system can avoid finding answers to these questions.

b The price mechanism is used to answer the three fundamental questions which arise because of the economic problem of scarcity in a market economy and in the private sector of a mixed economy. The market forces of demand and supply, operating through the price mechanism, determine the allocation of resources, the methods of production and the distribution of income.

Consumers indicate their choices by the prices they pay, and the possibility of earning profit provides the incentive for firms to respond to their choices. The price of resources and their productivity influence the methods of production and goods and services are distributed on the basis of who can pay for them.

The price mechanism is not the only way to tackle the basic economic problem. State planning is used in a planned economy and a combination of state planning and the price mechanism is used in a mixed economy. No mechanism can solve the basic economic problem as wants will always exceed resources.

The price mechanism does have a number of advantages. It is an automatic method of allocating resources and one which enables consumers to decide what is produced. If a product becomes more popular, consumers will compete for it, bidding up its price. A higher price will encourage firms to produce more of it.

The price mechanism also promotes efficiency, innovation, enterprise and hard work. If firms produce what consumers are willing and able to buy at the lowest possible prices, they can earn high profits. If, however, they produce unpopular products or fail to keep their costs down, they may be driven out of business. Entrepreneurs that develop new products and new methods of production and workers who are very skilful and diligent can be well rewarded.

The price mechanism does also, however, have disadvantages. The price mechanism does not take into account externalities. In cases where there are negative externalities such as pollution, there will be overconsumption and overproduction with too many resources being devoted to such products. Merit goods will be under-consumed and demerit goods will be over-consumed. There will be no financial incentive for private sector firms to produce public goods. There may be abuse of market power, with monopolies restricting output and driving up prices. People who have the highest incomes are able to buy the most products and the poor may not be able to purchase many products.

The price mechanism has the potential to tackle the basic economic problem in an efficient manner but it cannot solve it and there is no guarantee that relying on market forces will result in the best outcome. The extent to which the price mechanism is effective depends on the degree of market failure which occurs.

Chapter 2

Answers to progress checks

A Three factors that influence demand for air travel are the price of air travel, the price of foreign holidays and income. A rise in the price of air travel would be expected to cause a contraction in demand for air travel. Foreign holidays are a complement to air travel. If foreign holidays rise in price it is likely that demand for foreign holidays will contract and so demand for air travel will decrease. Air travel has positive income elasticity of demand and so a rise in income would usually result in an increase in demand for air travel.

B A contraction in demand for ice cream is caused by an increase in the price of ice cream. Less ice cream is demanded because it is more expensive. In contrast, a decrease in demand for ice cream is caused by a change in any influence on demand for ice cream other than a change in its price. For instance, a decrease in demand for ice cream may be caused by a spell of cold weather.

C Two factors that could make demand more price inelastic is a reduction in the degree to which other products are substitutes and an increase in the extent to which the product is seen to be a necessity. If, for instance, the number of hotels falls from six to one, demand for room bookings in the remaining hotel will become more price inelastic. As visitors will not be able to stay elsewhere, the remaining hotel would be able to raise its price without losing many bookings.

Over time changes in, for instance social attitudes, income and lifestyles, can turn products that were regarded as luxuries into necessities. For instance, in a number of developed countries, dishwashers are now regarded as a necessity by many households. A rise in the price of dishwashers in these countries will cause a smaller percentage fall in demand.

D An income elasticity of demand which is both positive and greater than one means that as income rises, demand increases by a greater percentage. Demand for a number of services is both positive and elastic, making them superior products.

E The cross elasticity of demand between one model of car and petrol would be negative as they are complements. In contrast, the cross elasticity of demand between the model and other models of cars is positive. This is because they are substitutes.

F Three factors that could cause an increase in the supply of rice are the granting of a government subsidy, a fall in the costs of production and a period of suitable weather. The granting of government subsidy would provide an incentive for farmers to grow more rice. Lower costs of production would make farmers more willing and able to grow rice. In addition, good climatic conditions would be likely to increase the amount of rice grown successfully.

G A fall in the price of blankets would lead to a contraction in the supply of blankets. Some resources used to produce blankets are likely to be shifted to producing duvets. This would increase the supply of duvets.

H The price mechanism rations products by limiting their consumption to those who can afford to pay the prices. If demand for a product increases, initially demand will exceed supply. Price will rise until demand equals supply again.

I The amount of consumer surplus received from the purchase of a product differs between consumers because people have different purchasing power and value the product differently.

Answers to revision activities

A a It would be expected that luxury wrapping paper would be more elastic than standard wrapping paper. The information does, however, suggest that the standard wrapping paper has a closer substitute as it has a higher positive XED figure.

   b To raise revenue the firm should raise the price of the luxury wrapping paper as demand will fall by a smaller percentage than the rise in price. In contrast, it should lower the price of standard wrapping paper, as demand is elastic.

   c The firm should lower the price of the firm's standard gift tags as this would significantly raise sales of its standard wrapping paper. It should leave the price of the luxury gift tags unchanged.

   d In the long run, the firm should concentrate on the luxury wrapping paper. This is because the product is more income elastic and would, therefore, benefit to a greater extent from rises in income over time. It also faces less competition in producing this type of wrapping paper.

B a PES + 20%/25% = 0.8.

   b Supply is inelastic.

c The car firm would want to make its PES more elastic. It would want to be able to take full advantage of a rise in price and to minimise the risk of making a loss if price falls.

d The firm could seek to make its supply more elastic by cutting its production time. This might be achieved by introducing more advanced equipment and training workers.

C a An increase in the cost of paper will raise the cost of producing newspapers. This will lead to a decrease in supply, which in turn will raise price and cause demand to contract as shown in the figure below.

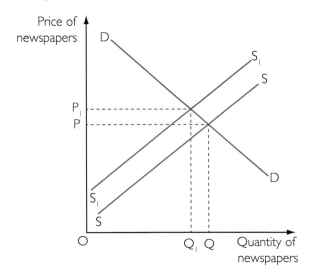

b Newspapers and internet websites are substitutes, a reduction in the quality of internet websites may encourage people to switch to newspapers. This would increase demand for newspapers, raise their price and cause supply to extend.

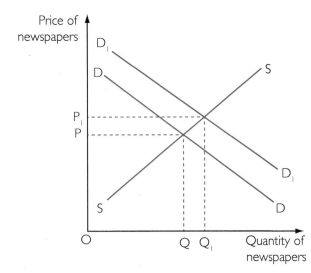

c Free gifts provided by newspapers are designed to increase demand. Higher demand will push up price and cause a rise in quantity supplied.

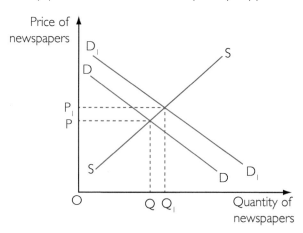

d The introduction of more efficient printing presses will reduce costs of production. Lower production costs will increase supply which will lower price and cause demand to extend.

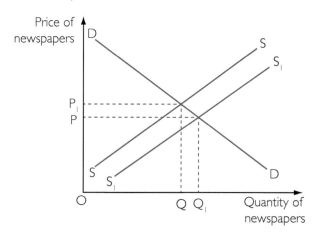

Answers to multiple choice questions

1 **D** A shift to the right of the demand curve shows an increase in demand. Popular films will encourage people to buy more cinema tickets. A and C would cause a movement along the demand curve and B a shift to the left of the demand curve.

2 **D** If total expenditure remains unchanged when price falls by 8%, it must mean that the quantity demanded has risen by 8%. An equal percentage change in price and quantity demanded means that PED is unitary.

3 **C** 80 units is 40% of 200. To raise sales by 40%, price would have to fall by −0.8 = 40%/? = −50%. So price would have to fall by 50% i.e. by $5.

4 **A** If demand is inelastic, a rise in price will cause a smaller percentage rise in demand and so total revenue will rise. Demand is not perfectly inelastic and so a rise in price will cause demand to contract.

5 **D** The existence of close substitutes would mean that a rise in price would cause a greater percentage fall in demand and a fall in price would cause a greater percentage rise in demand. A, B and C would be likely to cause a low PED.

6 **B** The price of Product X rises by 50%. Demand for Product Y increases by 20%. So XED = 20%/50% = 0.4.

7 **B** A negative figure shows two products are complements. −0.2 is low and so this suggests the two products are distant complements.

8 **C** Price rises by 50%. With PES being 0.8, supply would increase by 40%. This means supply rises to 2,800. The firm's revenue is $30 × 2,800 = $84,000.

9 **B** A rise in incomes would increase demand for laptops, shifting the demand curve to the right. A reduction in the cost of producing laptops would increase supply, shifting the supply curve to the right. The new curves intersect at K.

10 **C** The consumer surplus is initially PWZ. After the rise in price, the consumer surplus falls to P1WX. This is a decrease of PP1XZ.

Answers to data response questions

1 a Pakistan's share of the global cotton market was 11m/120m = 9.2%.

b A fall in the price of cotton may be caused by a rise in the supply of cotton and/or a decrease in demand for cotton. In 2015 the supply of cotton increased due to a bumper harvest in India and due to China selling some of its stockpile of cotton.

c Spices are an ingredient in national colouring. A rise in their price would increase the cost of producing natural clothing and so increase its price.

d The information suggests that the supply of spices is inelastic. It mentions that it 'takes some time to increase the quantity supplied'. Indeed, it states that it takes five years to grow nutmeg. With such a long growing period, it is difficult to adjust supply to changes in demand.

e   The price of spices rose in 2015 because of an increase in demand. The figure below shows the demand curve shifting to the right which would have caused the price to rise and supply to extend.

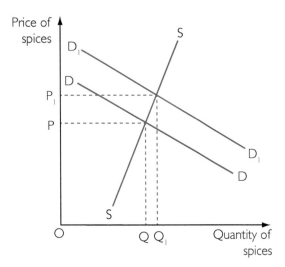

f   Whether farmers will benefit from a rise in the price of their products will depend on the cause of the rise and the duration of the higher prices. A rise in price which results from an increase in demand is likely to be more beneficial than one which has been caused by a decrease in supply. Higher demand will raise revenue and may reduce cost per unit. A decrease in supply which results from bad weather and flooding would raise the price and possibly revenue of those farmers who are not so badly affected. It may, however, destroy most or not all of the crops of other farmers.

If farmers decide to restrict supply in order to raise price, their total revenue will increase if demand is price inelastic. As they are likely to be producing less, their total costs would be expected to fall (although average cost may rise). With higher total revenue and lower total cost, their total profit would increase.

A rise in price may encourage farmers to plant more crops. If price remains high, they may be able to increase their revenue. If, however, price falls in the future they may receive less revenue than they expected and may make a loss.

Answers to essay questions

1   a   Cross elasticity of demand (XED) is a measure of the responsiveness of demand for one product to a change in the price of another product. It is measured by the formula:

$$XED = \frac{\% \text{ change in quantity demanded of product A}}{\% \text{ change in the price of product B}}$$

Cross elasticity of demand indicates not only whether products are substitutes, complements or independent goods but also the extent of any relationship. The sign shows the relationship and the figure the extent of the relationship.

Substitutes have positive XED. For instance, a 10% rise in the price of holidays in Thailand may cause a 2% demand for holidays in Sri Lanka. This would give a positive XED of 0.2. Some people who might have visited Thailand may now switch to Sri Lanka. The following figure shows this positive relationship.

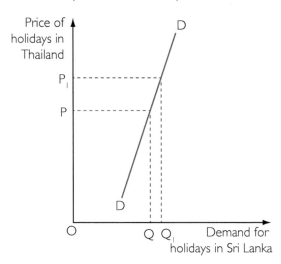

The figure indicates that the two holiday destinations are not very close substitutes. The more similar consumers view products to be, the higher the degree of positive XED they are likely to have.

Complements, in contrast, have negative cross elasticity of demand. This means that a change in the price of one product will cause demand for the related product to change in the opposite direction. For instance, the 10% rise in the price of holidays in Thailand may result in a 20% decrease in demand for flights to and from Thailand. This would give an XED figure of − 2.0. This would suggest that the two products are close substitutes. The following figure shows this inverse relationship between the changes in the price of holidays in Thailand and flights to and from Thailand.

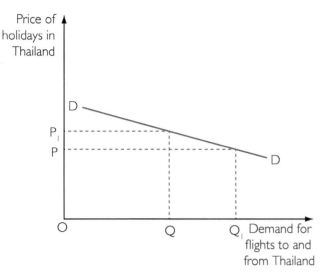

If products are unrelated, there will be a XED of 0. The following figure shows that the rise in the price of holidays in Thailand leaves demand for pineapple juice unchanged.

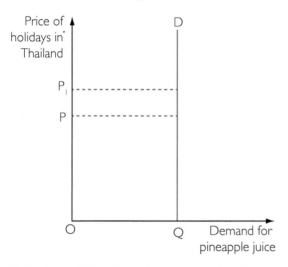

b Whether a fall in the price of a product is accompanied by a reduction in the quantity traded will depend on the cause of the fall. A fall in price caused by a decrease in demand will result in a contraction in supply. The following figure shows that the decline in demand results in a reduction in the quantity traded of 50,000 units.

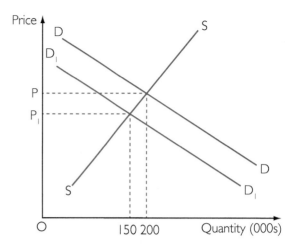

A fall in price caused by an increase in supply would, however, lead to a rise in the quantity traded. The figure below illustrates how a shift to the right of the supply curve causes price to fall to P_1. And the quantity traded to increase by 80,000 units.

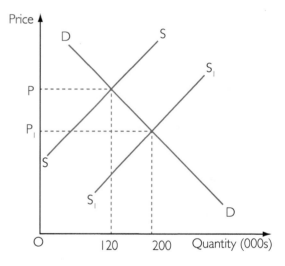

It is also possible that a fall in price and an increase in the quantity traded may be caused by a combination of an increase in supply and an increase in demand. For this to occur, supply would have to increase by more than demand.

The removal of a minimum price set above the equilibrium price would increase the quantity traded. The figure below shows that price is initially set at PX. At this price, there is a surplus of 10,000 units. 25,000 units are supplied but only 15,000 units are purchased. Removing the minimum price would permit the price to fall to the equilibrium price of P. The quantity traded now rises by 6,000 units to 21,000 units.

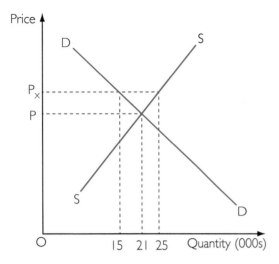

The relationship between a fall in price and the quantity traded will depend on the cause of the fall.

2 **a** Equilibrium price occurs where demand and supply are equal. If the price is above or below the equilibrium, market forces will move it to the equilibrium level. The figure shows a market initially in disequilibrium with supply exceeding demand at a price of P.

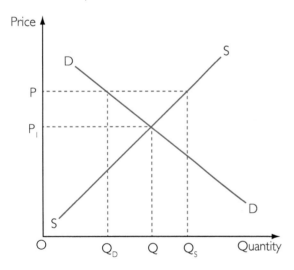

The unsold surplus will drive down price to P_1. At this price, there will be no tendency for price to change. At P_1 firms will be able to sell all that they are prepared to supply and consumers will be able to buy all that they are willing and able to purchase.

If price is below the equilibrium level, there will be excess demand. The figure shows demand being greater than supply at a price of P. The shortage created will lead some unsatisfied consumers offer to pay higher prices and so the

price will be driven up. This will cause demand to contract and supply to extend until demand and supply are again equal. In this case, this is at a price of P1.

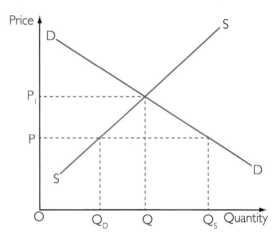

Over time price moves from one equilibrium to another equilibrium level and so on. What causes the equilibrium price to alter are changes in market conditions. If, for instance, demand increases, there will initially be a shortage. The following figure shows that at what was the equilibrium price of P, demand (Qa) will now exceed the quantity supplied (Q_1). As indicated above, this situation will drive up the price to a new equilibrium of P_1.

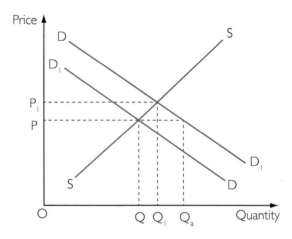

A decrease in supply will also cause the market to move to a new, higher equilibrium price. A lower equilibrium price will occur if either supply increases and/or demand decreases.

b A change in income can have a major influence on demand for a firm's products. Some firms produce products which have income elastic demand. This means that a change in income causes a greater percentage change in demand.

To decide how firms will be affected by a change in people's income, it is necessary to examine not only the degree of income elasticity of demand their products have but also the type of income elasticity of demand they possess and whether the country is experiencing economic growth or a recession.

Inferior goods have negative income elasticity of demand. This means that demand falls as income rises. In contrast, normal goods have positive income elasticity of demand, with demand and income moving in the same direction. Normal goods which have an income elasticity of demand of more than one are referred to as superior goods or luxury goods.

During a recession, a firm's revenue would increase if its product is an inferior one. Demand will increase as income falls and this increases the firm's revenue. Most years, however, income rises and during times of economic growth, a firm's revenue earned from the sale of a normal good will increase and may increase significantly if the product is a superior good. For instance, if income elasticity of demand is 3, a 10% rise in income will lead to a 30% increase in demand which will have a noticeable impact on total revenue. As income usually rises, a firm is likely to want to concentrate on products with positive income elasticity of demand.

Over a given income range, some products may have zero income elasticity of demand. This means that as income rises, demand does not change. For instance, a rise in income may have no effect on demand for soap in a developed country.

As income changes over time, what are perceived to be superior, normal and inferior goods may change. For example, as income continues to rise in China, bicycles are beginning to be seen as inferior goods, as more people start to buy cars. Technological advances can also affect how products are perceived and so their income elasticity of demand. In a number of countries, digital radios have positive income elasticity of demand whilst analogue radios now have negative income elasticity of demand.

Chapter 3

Answers to progress checks

A Operators of a buffer stock more often buy the commodity than sell it because the limits are usually set too high, relative to the long-run equilibrium level. This means that they have to intervene to buy the commodity to stop its price falling.

B In the case of the imposition of both a specific tax and ad valorem tax, the supply curve will shift to the left. The shift, however, will be a parallel one in the case of a specific tax but a non-parallel one in the case of an ad valorem tax.

C The tax base is the coverage of tax i.e. what is taxed. For example, if the purchase of books was not initially taxed and the government decides to tax the purchase, the government will be widening the tax base. The tax burden is the amount of tax paid as a proportion of GDP. It is how much tax is paid. (Tax incidence is who pays the tax.)

D A government may provide free primary school education because parents may undervalue the private benefits their children will receive. Another reason is that parents will not take into account the external benefits of education when they make decisions about whether to send their children to school. In addition, a government may want to provide free education on the grounds of equity. Education is such an important product, that a government may consider that every child should have access to it, whether their parents could afford to buy it or not.

E Privatisation increases the role of the private sector in an economy. A programme of privatisation will increase the size of the private sector in a mixed economy and will move it closer to a market economy.

Answers to revision activities

A a The woman has $42,400 of taxable income.

   b The woman pays $13,000 tax in total.

   c The average tax rate is $13,000/$50,400 = 25.8% or 0.258.

   d The woman's marginal tax rate is 50% or 0.5.

   e The tax system is progressive as the proportion of tax paid rises with income. The marginal tax rate exceeds the average tax rate.

B 1, 4, 5 and 6 are transfer payments. They involve payments given to people not in return for a good or service.

2, 3, 7 and 8 are all non-transfer payments. In each case, the people are receiving a payment in return for providing a service.

C a A buffer stock.

b A smoking ban.

c Higher state pension.

d Government provision.

e Government subsidy to dentists.

Answers to multiple choice questions

1 A The equilibrium price is $3. Setting a maximum price above the price will have no effect on the market. The market will clear at the equilibrium price and there will be no shortage or surplus.

2 A A government is likely to tax a demerit good in order to discourage its consumption. A public good will not be provided by the market and so a government is likely to either provide it directly or pay a private sector firm to provide.

3 B At a price of P_F, supply will exceed demand. Consumers will purchase YZ amount in order to maintain the price of P_F.

4 C The tax per unit is $5 and so the tax revenue is $5 × 100.

5 A A subsidy granted to the consumers of the product would increase demand and so shift the demand curve to the right. B would shift the supply curve to the right, C the demand curve to the left and D the supply curve to the left.

6 D The original four canons of taxation are certainty, convenience, economy and equity. General acceptability is the key characteristic an item needs to possess to act as money.

7 A The granting of a subsidy would increase supply, lower price and result in a rise in the quantity traded. B would raise price and reduce the quantity traded. C would lower price but also reduce the quantity traded. D would increase price and the quantity bought in the market would fall, with the government or a buffer stock purchasing any unsold stock.

8 C Progressive taxes make income more evenly distributed while regressive taxes make income less evenly distributed. The marginal rate of taxation is likely to fall as, in the case of a progressive tax, the marginal tax rate is below the average tax rate whereas, in the case of a regressive tax, the marginal tax is lower than the average tax rate.

9 D The removal of a price floor, minimum price, would cause the price to fall to the equilibrium level. Demand would extend but supply would contract. A lower quantity would be sold.

10 C A subsidy causes an increase in supply which is shown by a shift of the supply curve to the right. An ad valorem subsidy causes a non-parallel shift to the right. This is because a given percentage accounts for a greater value, the higher the price. A shows the effect of the imposition of a specific tax, B the effect of the imposition of an ad valorem tax and D the granting of a specific subsidy.

Answers to data response questions

1 a Removing a subsidy will lead to a decrease in supply. The reduction in supply will raise price and cause demand to contract as shown in below.

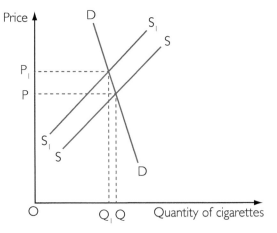

How much price rises and demand contracts will be influenced by how large the subsidy was and the price elasticity of demand. As demand for cigarettes is price inelastic, the main impact is likely to be on price rather than quantity.

b The price of soap rose less in actual amount than the price of toothpaste but by a greater amount in percentage terms – 600% as opposed to 300%.

c The information does not suggest that subsidy given to soap and toothpaste was sufficient to achieve the price the government wanted. Although the government had subsidised the products and imposed maximum prices, the products were sold illegally on shadow markets.

d It is probably more justifiable to subsidise soap than potatoes. Soap is a necessity. It may also be considered to be a merit good. Some people may not fully appreciate the need to wash on a regular basis. Keeping clean can cut down on the transmission of diseases and reduce health costs. Some people may also not be able to afford soap.

Potatoes are eaten in greater quantities by the poor than the rich. So there may be a case for subsidising them on the grounds of equity. There are, however, substitutes for potatoes which provide greater health benefits.

2 a A goods and services tax is an indirect tax. This is because it is a tax on expenditure and because the burden, or at least some of the burden, can be passed on to consumers. The nature of the tax means that some people pay it not directly to the government but indirectly through the sellers of the product.

b Incorporating the education cess into the services tax is likely to have increased the tax burden on the poor. This is because the services tax is a regressive tax. Before the incorporation, the education cess was added to income tax, which is a progressive tax.

c India's wealth tax would not have been classified as a good tax. It lacked two of the qualities of a good tax. It was not very economical as it had a high cost of collection. It was also not convenient for taxpayers as the forms that people had to fill out were too complex.

d India's tax revenue rose over the period. It increased in every year, except 2011 when it was the same as the previous year. The rise in tax revenue was particularly noticeable between 2011 and 2012. It cannot be concluded, however, from the information that tax rates increased over the period. This is because tax revenue may have increased because the government has increased the tax base, tax evasion has fallen or incomes have increased. A government can gain more tax revenue by taxing a greater range of products or lower the tax threshold at which people and firms pay tax. Greater penalties for, or more success at detecting, tax evasion may reduce the problem. A rise in GDP per head will increase tax revenue, sales tax revenue and probably corporation tax revenue since as well as incomes rising, expenditure and profits may increase.

e Subsidies on basic foods have the potential to increase the availability of the foods and to lower their price. The poor spend a high proportion of their income on food. Lower prices may enable those who did not have access to sufficient food to now eat a sufficiently nutritious diet. Some of the poor, now possibly able to spend less on food, may have sufficient money to buy other basic necessities. Subsidies given to farmers may also raise the incomes of farmers and farm workers who may initially have had low incomes. A higher output of basic foodstuffs may also increase employment.

The amount of subsidies passed on to consumers will be influenced by price elasticity of demand. Demand for food is price inelastic which suggests most will be passed on to consumers. There is a risk, however, that subsidies may reduce the incentive for farmers to be efficient and there is the risk that farmers will produce food of a lower quality. Food prices may still be too high for the poor to afford.

Cash payments provide the poor with greater freedom as to what they buy. They may, for instance, spend some of their money on educating their children which would increase their chances of getting out of poverty. If they spend it on better housing, better food or healthcare, it could increase their earning capacity. There is a risk, however, that some of the poor may spend it in ways that do not reduce their poverty. They may, for instance, spend more money on demerit goods or non-nutritious food. There is also the risk that cash benefits may reduce the incentive for those who are unemployed to search for work.

If people do not have sufficient income to buy sufficient food, there is an argument for subsidising food. For those retired from the labour force or too sick to work, cash benefits may help them without having a disincentive effect. To reduce poverty in the long run, government spending on education might be more effective than either of the two measures.

Answers to essay questions

1 a A maximum price is a price limit or ceiling. Sellers are not allowed to charge more than this price. In contrast, a minimum price is a price floor. Sellers are not permitted to charge less than this.

To have any effect on a market a maximum price has to be set below the equilibrium price whereas a minimum price is set above the equilibrium price.

Setting a maximum price below the market equilibrium price will cause demand to extend and supply to contract.

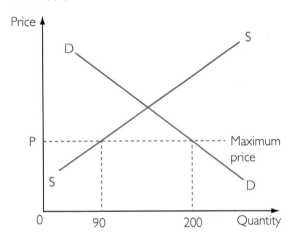

Demand will exceed supply and there will be a shortage. The diagram shows there is unsatisfied demand of 110. This gap between demand and supply would tend to push up price. To prevent this happening, a government would have to pass legislation so that it can penalise any seller who charges more. It may also introduce a rationing system to determine who will receive the product at the lower price. The excess demand may result in a shadow market developing with some sellers selling the product above the legally enforced maximum price.

Setting a minimum price above the market equilibrium price will result in supply extending and demand contracting. The diagram shows how this results in a surplus of 70 units.

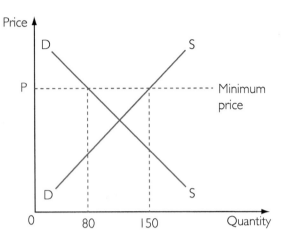

This time market forces will put downward pressure on the price. To stop this happening, the government would have to buy up the surplus. Costs may also be incurred storing the product. Again a shadow market may develop, but this time with sellers selling at below the legally enforced price.

b The introduction of a minimum price is likely to benefit the producers of the product. They will receive a higher price and so enjoy higher producer surplus if the rise in the quantity supplied is purchased.

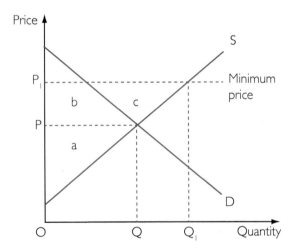

The diagram shows that the price received by producers rises from P to P1 and the quantity they sell rises from Q to Q1. It also shows that producer surplus increases from a to a, b and c. Producer surplus will provide a greater return to producers and would provide them with a greater ability to reinvest.

A minimum price may be in the form of a minimum wage. The introduction of a minimum wage may initially increase the cost of producers if they had been paying less than the minimum wage. If, however, higher paid workers increase their productivity, unit wage costs may be unchanged or may even fall. Some producers may also benefit from the higher demand which is likely to follow an increase in the minimum wage.

If a minimum price is put on a raw material, producers of finished products that use the raw material will be disadvantaged. They will experience a rise in their costs of production. To maintain the minimum price, the government may impose a tariff on imports of the raw material. The higher price of the raw material could reduce the international price competitiveness of the finished products.

A minimum price may result in a large stockpile. This is particularly likely to occur if supply is price elastic. In such a case, the gap between the quantity supplied and the quantity demanded may be large. If the surplus is sold on the world market at a lower price, foreign producers may experience a fall in demand. Alternatively, the stockpile may be stored which will involve an additional cost or may be thrown away which is clearly a waste. The government may not be able to afford to continue to buy up the surplus. If the government decides to stop buying up the surplus, the price might fall significantly.

A minimum price may reduce the pressure on the producers to be efficient. The higher price may result in the producers not keeping their costs low and not innovating. The lack of productive and dynamic efficiency would be a disadvantage for producers should the minimum price be removed in the future.

A minimum price is likely to benefit the producers of the product in the short run but may disadvantage them in the long run and will harm firms that purchase the product as a raw material.

2 a Adam Smith identified four characteristics of a good tax and economists have since added other characteristics. The four described by Adam Smith are certainty, convenience, economy and equity.

A tax is certain if tax payers understand how much they have to pay and when they have to pay it. The rate of indirect taxes that people have to pay is usually relatively well understood but in many countries, there is confusion about the amount of income tax that people have to pay. In the case of a progressive income tax, people often think they are paying a higher proportion of their income in tax than they actually are. For example, someone having a taxable income of $50,000 in a country with income tax rates of 10% on the first $10,000 of taxable income, 25% on the next $20,000 and 40% on higher income may think s/he is paying 40% of their income in tax. In fact, s/he is paying $14,000 in tax and her/his average tax rate is 28%. The person is confusing the average tax rate with the marginal tax rate. A proportional tax is likely to lead to less confusion. In most tax systems, people are usually aware of when they have to submit their tax returns.

Most countries now allow people to submit their tax returns online. This makes the process more convenient than having to file paper forms. Paying taxes through employers and indirect taxes through sellers is convenient for workers and consumers and cuts the government's administration costs. It does, of course, impose an administrative cost on employers and sellers.

A good tax is one which is economical in the sense that the revenue collected is greater than the cost of collecting it. Indirect taxes are usually cheaper to collect than direct taxes as sellers do most of the work.

While indirect taxes tend to be economical they are not considered to be equitable. The quality of equity mentioned by Adam Smith refers to a tax being based on the ability to pay. Economists now distinguish between vertical equity and horizontal equity. Vertical equity is based on the idea that the rich should pay more than the poor. In contrast, horizontal equity is based on the idea that people in the same circumstances should pay the same amount of tax.

Since Adam Smith's time, economists have suggested that a good tax should be flexible. A flexible tax is one which adjusts to changing economic circumstances. Revenue from income tax, for instance, rises automatically during an economic boom at a time when the government would want to reduce the amount people are spending.

Some economists also suggest that a tax should be neutral in that it should not alter what jobs people do, how long they work, where they live and what they buy. While it is generally accepted that it would be best if taxes could avoid disincentive effects, many economists think that there are circumstances when taxes should affect people's behaviour. For example, taxes may be imposed to discourage the consumption of demerit goods.

b To correct market failure in the case of merit and demerit goods a government may provide information, grant a subsidy or impose an indirect taxation or use regulation.

In the case of a merit good, a government may provide information, subsidise its production or consumption or make its consumption compulsory. Providing information about the beneficial effects of a merit good is designed to increase demand. The following figure shows the demand curve shifting to the right, moving the market closer to the allocatively efficient level of Q_X.

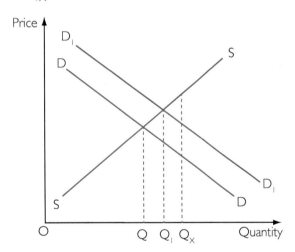

The provision of information works with the market and can help to reduce information failure. To be effective, however, the government must itself have accurate information. It can be debated who is a better able to judge how beneficial a product is – consumers themselves or the government? There is also no guarantee that consumers will be persuaded by the information.

A subsidy given to consumers is also designed to increase demand. Higher demand will again move the market closer to the allocatively

efficient level. It may, however, be difficult for a government to calculate the amount of the subsidy. If it is too high, the product may end up being over-consumed.

A subsidy given to producers would be designed to encourage higher consumption by reducing its price. The following figure shows a subsidy would shift the supply curve to the right, lower price and cause demand to extend.

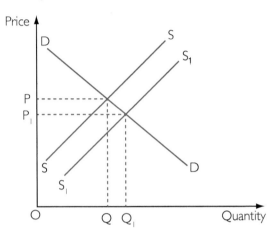

A subsidy to a producer is a market based solution and the resulting lower price can particularly benefit the poor. The more elastic demand is, the larger the impact on the quantity bought and sold is likely to be. A subsidy has to be set at the right level and may involve a relatively high cost. It may also take time to introduce and will be less effective if demand is inelastic.

If it is thought that the product is very important for people to consume, a government may make it compulsory for people to consume it. For example, a government may require people to send their children to school, wear seat belts in cars and install smoke alarms in their homes. Using regulation has the benefits of being backed by law and simple to understand. It does, however, require monitoring and if a significant proportion of the population are not in favour of the law, may require a high cost of enforcement.

To discourage consumption of a demerit good, a government may provide information about the harmful effects of consuming the product. This may discourage demand and move the market to the allocatively efficient level. As with providing information about a merit good, however, the government must have accurate information and consumers may not respond in the way expected.

A government may also use regulation by banning the consumption of the product or not permitting children to consume the product. Sometimes a ban can have a significant impact on people's behaviour. For instance, the smoking ban in public places in Ireland has reduced smoking. There is a risk, however, that a ban may give rise to a shadow market. For example, the ban on the sale of ivory has resulted in an illegal trade in ivory.

In addition to providing information and using regulation, a government may impose a tax on a demerit good. The imposition of an indirect tax will cause the supply curve to shift to the left, price to rise and demand to contract as shown in the figure.

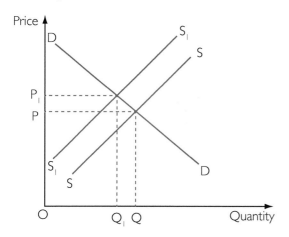

This measure works with the market and raises revenue for the government. It may not, however, be very effective if demand is inelastic, will fall more heavily on the poor and may contribute to inflation.

All policy measures have some advantages and some disadvantages, and governments often use a combination of measures. For example, governments run anti-smoking campaigns using TV advertisements, tax cigarettes and some require cigarette producers to put health warnings on their packets, ban children from smoking and ban smoking in public places.

Chapter 4

Answers to progress checks

A A fall in profit levels will reduce the willingness and ability of firms to invest. Firms will have less incentive to invest and will have lower amounts to spend on investment.

B A widespread flood would cause a decrease in aggregate supply as it would damage and destroy some of the country's resources. The top soil would be removed from farmland, factories and other capital goods would be damaged and some workers may lose their lives.

C In most countries, the weight attached to food declines over time. This is because as people get richer, they may spend more in total on food but a smaller proportion as they are likely to spend even more on other items.

D A fall in the real price of laptops would mean that laptops have risen in price less than the inflation rate.

E A consumer boom may cause demand-pull inflation if the higher aggregate demand is not met by an equal increase in aggregate supply.

F A rise in wages may not result in cost-push inflation if the rise is matched by an increase in labour productivity. In this case, wage costs per unit will not rise. It is also possible that other costs may have fallen.

G A balance of trade deficit means that the value of imported goods is greater than the value of exported goods. If a country has a balance of trade deficit and a current account surplus, it must have a greater overall combined surplus on the three other parts of the current account balance. The three other parts are trade in services, primary income and secondary income.

H Two reasons why someone may sell US dollars to the UAE's dirham is because she or he may want to go on holiday to the UAE or because she or he may want to buy property in the UAE.

I Factor endowments influence what a country is good at producing. For instance, if a country has good quality, fertile land with a good climate, it may have a comparative advantage in producing agricultural products.

J A supermarket may buy food from abroad because it may be cheaper, may be of a better quality and may not be available in the domestic market.

K Trading blocs consist of countries which are geographically close to each other.

L A recession in one country would reduce spending in that country including spending on imports. A main trading partner may experience a decline in its net exports and so in its aggregate demand.

M A tariff is a tax on imports whereas a quota is a limit on imports.

N Imposing trade restrictions on a country that employs child and slave labour may make the offending country poorer and worsen its people's living conditions. It is, however, generally thought that it is legitimate to impose trade restrictions on countries which engage in illegal labour market conditions.

Answers to revision activities

A
a An increase in AD and later an increase in AS.

b An increase in AD.

c An increase in AD.

d An increase in AD and an increase in AS.

e A decrease in AD.

B
a Trade in goods, credit item.

b Trade in goods, debit item.

c Trade in services, debit item.

d Trade in services, debit item.

e Financial account, credit item.

f Primary income, debit item.

g Secondary income, debit item.

C
a False. The overall balance of payments always balances but the current account is more commonly in deficit or surplus.

b False. Transactions in assets involve money leaving the country and as such they appear as a debit item in the balance of payments.

c True. The total value of debit items equals the total value of credit items.

d False. A government may not be too concerned about a short-run, relatively low current account deficit or surplus. It may want to give priority to another objective. For instance, it may want to focus on reducing inflation and a current account surplus may be the result of this and a current account deficit may result from a government concentrating on reducing unemployment.

e False. The merchandise balance is the difference between the value of exports of goods and the value of imports of goods.

f True. Devaluation may not reduce a trade deficit. If PED for exports and imports is less than one, devaluation will increase a trade deficit.

D
a The trade balance is initially 400 m pesos − 500 m pesos = a trade deficit of 100 m pesos.

b The trade balance changes to 600 m pesos − 450 m pesos = a trade surplus of 150 m pesos.

c The change in the trade balance indicates that the combined price elasticities of demand for exports and imports is greater than one. This is because the fall in the price of the currency has moved the current account position from a deficit to a surplus.

E
a Country X has the absolute advantage in producing both products as it can make more of both.

b In Country X the opportunity cost of product A is 2B whereas in Country Y it is 6B. In Country X an increase in 16 units of A involves sacrificing 32 units of B, a ratio of 1:2. In Country Y, to produce 2 more units of A involves giving up 12 units of B, a ratio of 1:6.

c Country Y has the comparative advantage in producing product B as it can produce it for a lower opportunity cost – one sixth as opposed to a half.

d An exchange rate of 7 units of product B for 1 unit of product A would not benefit both countries as it lies outside the countries' opportunity cost ratios. The exchange rate has to be more than 2 units of product B and less than 6 units of product B to benefit both countries.

F Figure 4.12 shows that the country produces copper more cheaply than the world price.

a   Domestic consumers would be faced with a higher price and lower quantity.

b   Domestic producers would benefit from selling a higher quantity at a higher price.

c   Foreign producers would face more competition and their share of the market would be reduced.

Answers to multiple choice questions

1   **A**   A decrease in income tax would raise disposable income which would be likely to increase consumer expenditure. B, C and D would all be likely to reduce aggregate demand.

2   **B**   The weights in a consumer price index reflect spending patterns. These spending patterns change over time and so the weights have to be changed.

3   **C**

Product	Weight		Price change (%)	Weighted price change (%)
Food	2/5	×	15%	6
Electricity	1/10	×	10%	1
Transport	1/5	×	20%	4
Entertainment	1/10	×	−10%	−1
Clothing	1/5	×	30%	6
				16

The overall rise in the cost of living (the inflation rate) was 16%.

4   **C**   A fall in the price of the currency will increase import prices including the prices of imported raw materials. More expensive raw materials will push up costs of production. A, B and D may cause demand-pull inflation.

5   **B**   Between January 2009 and January 2010, Pakistan experienced a lower rate of inflation. This meant that the price level was still increasing albeit at a slower rate. Higher prices will increase the cost of living. The internal purchasing power of the Pakistani rupee will have fallen, the Pakistani consumer price index will have increased. Costs of production are likely to have risen with inflation.

6   **C**   Insurance is included in the trade in services (invisible) section of the current account of the balance of payments, A the primary income of the current account, B the trade in goods balance of the current account and D the financial account.

7   **D**   The current account has a surplus of $30 bn (trade balance = $20 bn + net income −$20 bn + current transfers $30 bn). The financial account balance has a deficit of −$10 + −$20 bn + −$10 bn + $20 bn = $20 bn.

8   **C**   A trade weighted exchange rate is the price of a currency, in terms of a basket of currencies of the main countries, the country trades with.

9   **A**   If the value of Argentine imports increases, more Argentine pesos will have to be sold to buy the foreign currency needed to produce the imports. B would increase demand for the Argentinian pesos. C and D would decrease the demand for the Argentine pesos.

10   **A**   A decrease in foreign direct investment in Bangladesh would reduce demand for takas and so may result in a fall in the price of the taka. B, C and D could also lead to an increase in demand for the taka and so a rise in the value of the taka.

11   **D**   A fall in the price of a country's currency would lower export prices. To take advantage of the likely rise in the demand for exports, it is important that the supply of exports is elastic. A and B would result in a deterioration in the trade balance and are not directly linked to a fall in the price of the currency. C would mean that the value of net exports would fall and so the trade balance would deteriorate.

12   **B**   Egyptians taking more holidays abroad would increase the supply of the Egyptian pound as Egyptians sell the currency to purchase the currencies of the destinations they are going to. Egyptian firms selling fewer products will result in a fall in demand for the Egyptian pound. An increase in supply of and a decrease in demand for the currency would push down its price.

13   **C**   Country Y has an absolute advantage in both products as it can make more of both products. It has a comparative advantage in producing chairs as it can make these at a lower opportunity cost – 1 chair equals a quarter of a TV as opposed to 1 chair equals half a TV.

Country X has the comparative advantage in producing TVs – 2 chairs as opposed to 4 chairs.

14 B If there is perfect mobility of factors of production between the countries, the resources may move rather than the products. A and D would make trade more likely. In the case of C, trade is based more on comparative rather than absolute advantage.

15 B Country Y has the absolute advantage in producing both products. Initially, its comparative advantage is in producing manufactured goods and X's comparative advantage in producing agricultural goods. In Country Y, the opportunity cost of producing 1 manufactured good is $\frac{3}{5}$ of an agricultural good whereas it is 2 agricultural goods in Country X. The opportunity cost of producing agricultural goods is lower in Country X – $\frac{1}{2}$ manufactured goods as opposed to $1\frac{1}{4}$ in Country Y. After the change in technology, the opportunity cost ratios change for Y but X continues to have the lower opportunity cost in producing agricultural products ($\frac{1}{2}$ manufactured good as opposed to now $1\frac{1}{2}$ in Country Y). Country Y also continues to have the comparative advantage in producing manufactured goods (now $\frac{2}{3}$ as opposed to 2 agricultural goods).

16 C The tariff per unit is UX and XY quantity of goods are imported so tax revenue is UVXY.

17 B The main difference between a customs union and a free trade area is that a customs union requires member countries to impose the same tariff on non-members whereas a free trade area does not. A, C and D are possible features of an economic union.

18 B The terms of trade is a measure concerned with export and import prices. A favourable movement occurs when the number gets larger. If initially the index of average export prices is 100 and the index of average import prices is 100, the terms of trade would be 100. Then if export prices fall to 90 and import prices fall to 60, the terms of trade would increase to 150.

19 C In year 1, the terms of trade was 400/500 × 100 = 80 and in year 2 the terms of trade changed to 560/600 × 100 = 93. The balance of trade changed from a deficit of $3m ($4m − $7m) to a deficit of $2.8m ($5.6m − $8.4m).

20 A A credit item involves money coming into the country. Money spent in Pakistan by Egyptian tourists brings money into Pakistan and would appear in the trade in services balance of the current account. B and C would appear in the current account (trade in services and trade in goods) but as credit items. D is a credit item but one which would appear in the financial account.

Answers to data response questions

1 a A base year is a year used at the start of an index series of economic data. It is given value of 100 and then other years are compared to it.

b It can be concluded that the people of Pakistan spent a higher proportion of their income on food than people in India. It cannot, however, be concluded that people in Pakistan spent more on food than people in India. To determine how much was actually spent in the two countries, it would be necessary to know the income levels in the two countries.

c The weighting given to recreation and culture in India would be expected to increase over time. This is because incomes per head would be expected to rise. As people get richer they tend to spend a higher proportion of their income on leisure activities.

d A 10% rise in the price of health in 2015 would have affected people in India more than people in Pakistan. This is because people in India spend a higher proportion of their income on food.

e i A change in relative prices means that the price of some products has altered at a different rate to others. A relative fall in the price of car travel, for instance, may not necessarily mean that car travel is actually falling in price, but is rising more slowly than bus and train travel.

ii A 10% rise in the price of housing and household utilities would have more of an effect on Pakistan's inflation rate than on India's inflation rate. This is because spending on housing and household utilities accounts for 29.41 of total spending in Pakistan but only 16.91% in India. With a weighting of 29.41/100, a 10% rise in the price of housing and household utilities would contribute 29.41/100 × 10% = 2.941% points to the inflation rate of Pakistan. With a weighting of 16.91/100, it would only contribute 16.91/100 × 10% = 1.691% points contribution to the UK's inflation rate.

f   No consumer prices index provides a totally accurate measure of inflation. There may be sampling errors and whilst weights are reviewed on a regular basis, there is nevertheless a time lag. This can give rise to what is called a substitution bias. A CPI has a fixed basket of goods and services for at least one year. This means that it cannot reflect within that time period the likelihood that consumers will switch away from buying products which are becoming relatively more expensive to those which are becoming relatively cheaper. Prices are selected from a range of retail outlets but again these may not fully reflect short-term changes in where consumers buy their products from, including from cheaper outlets.

There is also the problem that the quality of products changes over time. For instance, a television set produced now may be more expensive than one produced a year before but it may have more advanced features, so like is not really being compared with like.

The CPI is based on a basket of goods and services purchased by a 'typical' household. Different types of households and households in different regions are, however, likely to experience differences in the changes to their cost of living. Pensioners, for example, will suffer a higher rise in their cost of living than the inflation rate indicates if they spend more than the average on food and the price of food rises significantly.

In addition, there are variations in how different countries measure their consumer price indices with some differences in components. This can make international comparisons difficult.

2 a i   Two ways the Chinese government could intervene in the foreign exchange market to prevent the yuan rising in value against the US dollar are to sell yuan and lower the rate of interest.

   ii   A currency is described as undervalued if the exchange rate does not reflect its purchasing power parity and if it gives rise to a current account surplus over time. For instance, if a basket of goods and services

is priced at $100 in one country and 1,000 rupee in another country, the exchange rate would be expected to be $1 = 10 rupee. If the exchange rate was $1 = 15 rupee, the rupee would be regarded as undervalued. A country which continues to experience a current account surplus, such as China in recent years, may be claimed to be operating an undervalued exchange rate.

b i   The table does support the statement. The value of the pound only varied by $0.04 over the period.

   ii   Over the whole period the value of the pound fell very slightly with one dollar being able to purchase a greater proportion of a pound. The size of the current account deficit increased by a significant amount of the period both in terms of an actual amount and in terms of a percentage of GDP. The slight yearly variations in the value of the pound did not seem to make any difference to the continuing growth of the deficit. This lack of a relationship suggests that there were other causes of the increasing deficit including possibly an appreciation of the pound against other currencies and a fall in income of some of the country's trading partners.

c   A depreciation in the exchange rate is likely to increase the rate of inflation for two main reasons. One is the higher price of imports. More expensive imports that the country's consumers buy will directly push up the country's consumer price index. A rise in the price of imported raw materials will push up costs of production and can result in cost-push inflation. Domestic firms may also be tempted to raise their prices now they are competing with more expensive imports.

The other reason why a depreciation may increase the rate of inflation is because it may result in a rise in net exports which will increase aggregate demand. If the economy was initially operating close to full capacity, it will be difficult to match the higher aggregate demand with higher aggregate supply and demand-pull inflation may occur.

There is a chance, however, that a depreciation in the exchange rate will not result in a rise in the inflation rate. If the country is an important market for the products of other countries, their firms may cut their prices in terms of their own currency, so that they remain at the same price when sold in the country. Even if the price of imported raw materials rises, it may not have much effect on the country's inflation rate if firms can switch to domestic producers. Higher aggregate demand may also not have much impact on the price level if there is considerable spare capacity in the economy.

Answers to essay questions

1 a Absolute advantage occurs when a country can produce more of a product per resource unit. In the example below, Country A has the absolute advantage in producing cars whilst Country B has the absolute advantage in growing wheat.

Output per resource unit		
	Cars	Wheat
Country A	50	100
Country B	20	400

It is thought, however, that comparative advantage explains a greater proportion of international trade. A country is said to have a comparative advantage in a product when it can produce it at a lower opportunity cost and is even better at producing the product or not so bad at producing it. In the example below, Country X has the absolute advantage in producing both TVs and rice.

Output per resource unit		
	TVs	Rice
Country X	20	500
Country Y	5	250

Country X has the comparative advantage in producing TVs. It can make four times as many TVs than Country Y whereas it can only make twice as much rice. It has a lower opportunity cost in producing TVs – 25 rice as opposed to 50 rice in the case of Country Y.

Country Y has the comparative advantage in producing rice. It can make only a quarter as many TVs but half as much rice. It has a lower opportunity cost – 1/50 of a TV as opposed to 1/25 of a TV in the case of Country X.

Comparative advantage theory suggests that international trade is beneficial for two countries even if one of them has the absolute advantage in both products produced as long as two conditions are met. These are that there should be a difference in the relative efficiencies and that the exchange rate should lie between the two countries' opportunity cost ratios. In the example above, the exchange rate would have to be 1 TV exchanges for more than 25 rice and less than 50 rice.

b The main reason why a government may wish to pursue a policy of free trade is that unrestricted international trade has the potential to increase the living standards of its citizens.

Free trade can allow a country to exploit fully its comparative advantage. It can concentrate on producing what it is best at producing and import products at a lower opportunity cost. If other countries follow a policy of free trade, there can be an efficient global allocation of resources. Global output can rise and people can consume more products.

Higher level of competition which results from free international trade can drive down prices, raising consumer surplus. It can also raise the quality of what is produced.

There are, however, a number of reasons why it may not always be to a country's advantage to engage in free trade. If other countries are imposing trade restrictions, the country may need to protect its industries. If other countries are subsidising their firms or dumping products in the country, its firms may not be able to compete even if they have a comparative advantage.

It may also be thought that some of the country's firms may be able to grow and develop a comparative advantage. An infant (sunrise) industry may experience a fall in average cost when it expands as it would be able to exploit economies of scale to a greater extent. If it is not protected at the start, it may be competed out of the market. It may, however, be difficult to spot which new industries have the potential to develop a comparative advantage. There is also a risk that even if the industries with potential are selected, the protection may make them become complacent and so they may not go on to lower their average costs significantly.

A government may also want to protect a declining (sunset) industry to prevent a sudden and large increase in unemployment. By allowing an industry to decline gradually, the number of workers can be allowed to fall through what is called natural wastage. Over time workers who leave through retirement and moving to other jobs may not be replaced. There is a risk, however, that those involved with the industry will fight to keep the industry going. It may also be argued that it would be better to keep unemployment down by giving support to infant rather than declining industries.

In addition, a government may want to protect its strategic industries, including agriculture, to ensure their survival. A government may not want to become reliant on imports for essential products in case, for whatever reason, the supplies are cut off.

In theory, free trade has the potential to create significant benefits but in practice there are reasons why a government may not always pursue a policy of free trade. Indeed, no government in the world pursues a policy of completely free trade.

2 a The terms of trade is the ratio of average export prices relative to average import prices. A deterioration in the terms of trade means that the number gets smaller and results from export prices falling relative to import prices.

There are a number of possible causes of deterioration. One is devaluation. A government may decide to lower the value of its currency from one fixed rate to a lower one in order to reduce a current account deficit.

Export prices may also fall relative to import prices as a result of rising labour productivity in the country or higher inflation in other countries from which the imports are purchased. As with devaluation, these causes are likely to increase the volume of exports sold and reduce the volume of imports purchased. Whether export revenue rises and import expenditure falls will depend on the price elasticity of demand for exports and imports.

A less beneficial cause of deterioration is a fall in the relative price of exports resulting from a decrease in demand. In this case, fewer exports will be sold at a lower price, causing export revenue to decline. A deterioration caused by higher demand for exports may also have a harmful effect on the current account of the balance of payments, although the effect is more uncertain. This is because some of the imports may be capital goods or raw materials which may later contribute to the country's exports.

b The effect that the formation of regional trading blocs will have on competition will depend on the nature of the trading blocs and may differ between those countries inside the blocs and those outside.

A free trade area seeks to achieve free trade between member countries. All the member countries agree to remove trade restrictions on the free movement of products between each other. This should promote competition within the free trade area as now competition will not be distorted by protectionist measures. If the firms in one member country produce a product at a higher cost, the country's government cannot discourage its citizens from purchasing imports by, for instance, imposing tariffs. The member countries are, however, free to set whatever restrictions they want on non-members. This means that the formation of a free trade area may have a neutral effect in terms of competition with non-members.

A customs union involves not only removing trade restrictions on fellow members but also agreeing on imposing the same tariff on the products of non-member countries. Again this trading bloc should increase competition between the members.

An economic union takes integration even further than a customs union. As well as removing trade restrictions on other member countries and imposing a common external tariff, it involves the countries moving towards operating as one economy. It has not only free movement of products but also the free movement of labour and capital. People can work in other member countries, with their qualifications recognised, and firms can set up branches in other member countries.

An economic union involves the use of a common currency. This means that a member country cannot gain a competitive advantage over its fellow member countries by devaluing its currency. A common currency contributes to a level playing field of competition and reduces transaction costs and promotes price transparency. The harmonisation of economic policies, such as minimum wage rates and similar tax rates, also make it difficult for one government to protect its industries from competition from other member countries.

The effect that the formation of regional trading blocs will have on non-members will depend on whether any external tariff is higher or lower than the average tariff member countries were charging before their formation.

It will also be influenced by whether the increased internal competitive pressures raise the efficiency of member countries' firms. If they do, firms in one trading bloc may be able to compete more effectively with firms from other trading blocs. Those countries outside of major trading blocs may, however, have greater difficulty competing.

Chapter 5

Answers to progress checks

A Devaluation would lower the external value of the currency. So by avoiding devaluation, the government is seeking to maintain the external value of the currency. Adopting deflationary fiscal policy would imply that the government is trying to prevent the internal value of the currency falling.

B A central bank may seek to reduce a current account deficit by attempting to reduce the exchange rate. It may try to do this by selling the currency and/or lowering the rate of interest. Selling the currency may increase the domestic money supply if some of the extra money comes back into the country. A rise in the money supply can cause an increase in aggregate demand. A cut in the rate of interest can also raise aggregate demand by encouraging an increase in consumer expenditure and investment. Higher aggregate demand can result in demand-pull inflation if there is a lack of spare capacity in the economy.

C A rise in the rate of interest may reduce spending on imports. It will discourage borrowing and encourage saving and so may reduce spending on both imports and domestically produced products. There is a possibility, however, that it may increase expenditure on imports. This is because a higher rate of interest may attract hot money flows from abroad and drive up the exchange rate. A higher exchange rate will lower import prices and so may encourage people to switch from buying domestically produced products to buying imports.

D Moving from a current account deficit to a current account surplus could create inflationary pressure as it would increase aggregate demand and bring more money into the economy.

E Exchange controls are an expenditure switching policy measure. They are designed to encourage people to switch from imports to domestic products by restricting how much of the domestic currency can be changed into foreign currency to spend on imports and investment abroad.

F The imposition of import restrictions may increase the inflation rate by raising both the price of imported products and the price of domestically produced products. A tariff is a tax on imports, and at least some of this tax may be passed on to the consumer in the form of a higher price. Observing that the price of imports has increased may encourage some domestic firms to increase their prices.

G The expenditure dampening measure is to change the rate of interest and the expenditure switching measure is devaluation.

Answers to revision activities

A
  a A depreciation. A rise in the US rate of interest may encourage some Australians to place money in US financial institutions. In this case, they will sell Australian dollars to buy US dollars. The rise in the supply of Australian dollars is likely to reduce its price.

  b An appreciation. If incomes rise in the European Union, demand for Australian exports is likely to rise. This will increase demand for the Australian dollar.

c A depreciation. Demand for Australian exports will fall, resulting in a fall in demand for the Australian dollar. Australian demand for imports will increase, causing an increase in the supply of Australian dollars.

d A depreciation. Successful expenditure policies would result in lower spending by Americans, including lower spending on imports. Demand for Australian products would fall, causing a fall in demand for Australian dollars.

e An appreciation. A large number of tourists would come to Australia to witness events at the global sporting event. This will increase demand for Australian dollars.

f An appreciation. Multinational companies will demand Australian dollars to spend on setting up their overseas branches.

B Sale of the currency by the central bank

↓

Increase in the supply of the currency

↓

Depreciation of the currency

↓

Fall in export prices and rise in import prices

↓

Rise in net exports

↙ ↓

Reduction in current account deficit

Rise in aggregate demand

↙ ↘

Increase in demand-pull inflation   Fall in unemployment

C Decrease: **b**, **c** and **d**

Increase: **a** and **e**

D

Policy measure	Pairs of government macoeconomic policy objectives
A cut in the rate of interest	Reduce cost-push inflation Reduce unemployment
An increase in government spending on education	Increase economic growth Increase net exports
A rise in income tax	Reduce demand-pull inflation Reduce income inequality
The removal of tariffs	Reduce a current account surplus Reduce cost-push inflation

Answers to multiple choice questions

1 A A devaluation of the currency would reduce export prices and raise import prices. If demand for exports and imports is elastic, this will result in an improvement in the balance of trade position. B, C and D would all increase spending on imports and might divert products from the export market to the domestic market and so would tend to increase a balance of trade deficit.

2 A Moving to a deficit would result in money leaving the country. A trade deficit would tend to increase unemployment, reduce the exchange rate and reduce real GDP.

3 B A government subsidy to domestic producers would reduce the price of their products and so may encourage both domestic consumers and foreigners to buy more domestically produced products and fewer foreign produced products.

4 D By lowering export prices and raising import prices, devaluation will lower the terms of trade. Devaluation may raise employment. It may be caused by a fall in the rate of interest but is unlikely to cause it. If devaluation stimulates economic activity, it may increase a budget surplus.

5 B An expenditure dampening policy would reduce consumer expenditure. With consumers spending less, imports are likely to fall and domestic firms may put more effort into selling products to other countries.

6 **C** An upward revaluation of the currency would raise export prices and lower import prices. This will reduce a current account surplus if demand for exports and imports are elastic. Lower import prices will reduce the prices of some finished products produced, and may lower the prices of some domestically produced products if they use imported raw materials. Higher export prices do not affect the country's inflation rate as the country's population does not buy exports.

7 **A** Devaluation would reduce the price of exports and increase the price of imports. These price changes could result in an increase in net exports. Such a change would improve the current account position and the resulting higher aggregate demand would reduce cyclical unemployment.

8 **C** An automatic stabiliser is a form of government spending or tax revenue which changes, without an alteration of government policy, to dampen down economic fluctuations. Income tax and sales tax revenue will automatically rise whilst unemployment benefit will automatically fall during an economic boom. Higher tax revenue and lower government spending will reduce the growth of aggregate demand. In contrast, the amount paid out in a state retirement pension is influenced by the age of the population rather than economic activity.

9 **C** A deflationary monetary policy measure is a measure designed to reduce aggregate demand by reducing the money supply/growth of the money supply and/or raising the rate of interest. A sale of government securities by the central bank would take money out of circulation and, by lowering the price of government securities, raise the rate of interest. A is an expansionary monetary policy measure, B is a deflationary fiscal policy measure and D is a supply side policy measure.

10 **A** A rise in the rate of interest may reduce consumer expenditure and investment and so reduce demand-pull inflation. It will, however, push up the costs of production of firms which have borrowed in the past and so may raise cost-push inflation. B may increase demand-pull

inflation in the short run but reduce cost-push inflation in the long run. C and D may reduce cost-push inflation.

Answers to data response questions

1 **a** A cyclical budget deficit is an excess of government spending over tax revenue resulting from an economic downturn or recession. A fall in economic activity will result in a decline in direct taxes and indirect tax revenue and a rise in government spending on unemployment benefit. A cyclical deficit will disappear as economic activity picks up.

b Economic growth is likely to increase the value of a country's imports. Higher incomes are likely to result in a rise in spending on both domestic and imported goods and services. Firms will increase their output, purchasing more raw materials and more capital goods. Some of these may be imported. Economic growth may be export-led. In this case, the growth of exports may outstrip the growth of imports.

c The extract suggests that the BRICS as a group are relatively open economies in the sense that international trade accounts for quite a significant proportion of their economic activity. The degree of openness varies with Russia and South Africa being the most open and Brazil the least open. The extract does also mention that all the economies impose trade restrictions. This indicates that they are not completely open in the sense of engaging in free trade. More information would be needed on the trade restrictions to determine the extent to which they reduce their openness.

d The extract mentions a number of similarities. All the BRICS had experienced a cyclical budget deficit and initially all had high rates of economic growth. The extract does, however, mention that their macroeconomic performance has varied. Brazil, India and South Africa have had a deficit on the current account of the balance of payments while China and Russia have had surpluses. The table gives a snapshot of the countries' macroeconomic performance in 2015. Brazil and Russia experienced negative economic growth (and probably a recession). South Africa experienced a moderate rate of economic growth while China and India had relatively high rates of economic growth. China had a low rate of inflation. India's and South Africa's inflation rates were a little high and of a similar rate. In contrast, Brazil and particularly Russia had worryingly high inflation rates. The unemployment rates were relatively similar between four of the countries but South Africa had a very high rate with a quarter of its labour force not being utilised. There were some notable variations in income per head with Russia having an income per head nearly four times as high as India's. To make a fuller comparison of the countries' macroeconomic performance, more information particularly on trends in economic growth, inflation and unemployment rates would have been useful.

2 a A budget deficit arises when government expenditure exceeds government revenue. The main source of government revenue is tax receipts. This is why a budget deficit is often described as a government spending exceeding tax revenue.

b The type of inflation caused by an increase in the money supply is demand-pull inflation. More money circulating in the economy would be likely to mean that banks will have more money to lend and so the rate of interest is likely to fall. A lower interest rate may encourage higher consumer expenditure and investment. The higher aggregate demand may push up the price level if aggregate supply does not respond in line with aggregate demand.

c A rise in the rate of interest would be expected to reduce the inflation rate. Indeed, this is why central banks often increase the rate of interest to reduce inflationary pressure. A higher interest rate is likely to lower consumer expenditure and investment as the reward for saving will rise and the cost of borrowing will increase. There is some evidence in Figure 5.02 to support the expected inverse relationship. The evidence occurs at the start and at the end of the period shown. Between 2011 and 2012 the rate of interest rose while the inflation rate fell and between 2014 and 2015 the interest rate fell and the inflation rate rose. Between 2012 and 2014, however, both the interest rate and the inflation rate rose. Over the whole period the interest rate rose by 57% while the inflation rate rose by 2014%. This indicates that the rise

in the interest rate from 7% to 11% either did not have the expected effect or that there was time lag involved.

d Venezuela's exports are dominated by oil. Demand for oil tends to be price inelastic. As a result demand is likely to fall by a greater percentage than the fall in price and so export revenue is likely to decrease. Lower export revenue will reduce demand for the currency, the bolivar. Lower demand for the bolivar will result in a depreciation in the currency.

e Subsidies given to farmers have the potential to reduce inflation. A subsidy will, in effect, reduce the cost of producing food. This may cause supply to increase and price to fall as shown in the diagram below.

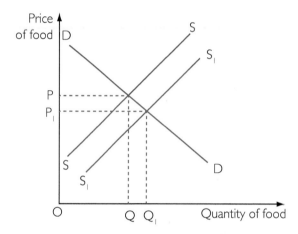

Food appears as a category in the consumer price index of countries and so a lower price of food would put downward pressure on the inflation rate. A lower price of food may also reduce claims for wage rises which could prevent cost-push inflation occurring.

There is the possibility, however, that subsidies given to farmers may not reduce inflation especially over time. The subsidies may encourage farmers to become more inefficient and possibly expand into areas where they do not have a comparative advantage. This may mean that the cost of food would increase, despite the subsidy, in the long run. A lower price of food might also encourage consumers to spend more on other items so that the overall pressure on prices remains unchanged.

Answers to essay questions

1 a The exchange rate is the price of one currency in terms of another currency or currencies. If the currency is a freely floating one, its value is determined solely by the market forces of demand and supply. If it is a fixed exchange rate, the price is set by the government, or central bank acting on behalf of a government, or group of governments. The price of a managed exchange rate will be influenced by the government or central bank.

A floating exchange rate will fall if demand for it decreases and/or supply of it increases. There are a number of reasons why these changes may occur. If the prices of the country's products are rising and demand for its exports is elastic, foreigners will spend less on the country's exports and so will buy less of the currency. Inflation can also result in an increase in the supply of the currency if it leads to a rise in import expenditure. This is because more of the currency will have to be sold to purchase foreign currency in order to try to buy imports. The effect of a loss in price competitiveness on the price of a currency is illustrated in this figure.

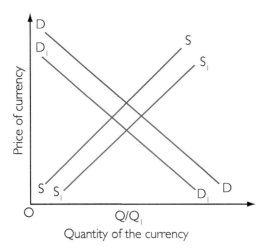

A relative fall in the quality or marketing of the country's products would have a similar effect.

The demand for and supply of currency is not only influenced by changes in demand for the country's products and foreign products but also by direct, portfolio and other investment flows and by speculation. If the country's interest rate falls, 'hot money' is likely to flow out of the country. Financial investors will sell the currency to buy the currencies of those countries which offer a higher rate of interest. If the economic performance of the country declines, some firms may be encouraged to move abroad. This would again result in an

increase in the supply of the currency and a fall in its value.

A large part of the activity in the foreign exchange market is accounted for by speculation. If people believe that the value of a currency will fall in the near future, they will sell it now to prevent encountering a loss. Of course, their action can contribute to the very outcome they are expecting.

In the case of a fixed exchange rate or managed exchange rate, a government or central bank may lower the price either because the price cannot be sustained or because it is thought that a lower value will help improve the country's macroeconomic performance. If there is widespread selling of the currency because it is thought to be overvalued, there may not be sufficient reserves of foreign currency to maintain the exchange rate and raising the rate of interest may also prove ineffective. A government may also encourage a central bank to move its exchange rate to a lower price to improve its current account position or stimulate economic growth and employment.

b   Whether a fall in its exchange rate will reduce a deficit on the current account of the balance of payments will depend on the price elasticities of demand for exports and imports, how domestic firms respond, what is happening to incomes in other countries, any changes in trade restrictions and the level of spare capacity in the economy.

A fall in the exchange rate will reduce the price of the country's exports, in terms of foreign currency, and will raise the price of imports, in terms of the domestic currency. A fall in the price of exports should make them more price competitive and lead to higher demand. Whether revenue will rise or not depends on whether demand is elastic or inelastic. If demand is elastic, a fall in price will cause a greater percentage rise in demand and so result in an increase in revenue. A rise in import prices should lead to a fall in demand for imports. The effect on expenditure of imports will again depend on price elasticity of demand. If demand is elastic, import expenditure will fall.

The importance of elastic demand is emphasised in the Marshall-Lerner condition. This states that a fall in the value of a currency will lead to an improvement in the trade balance only if the sum of the price elasticities of demand for exports and imports is greater than one.

The J-curve effect suggests that a fall in the exchange rate may initially worsen the trade position before it improves it. This is shown in the following figure.

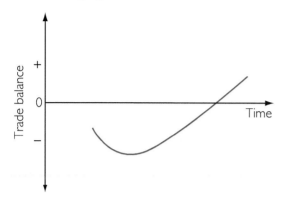

When the exchange rate first falls, there is not sufficient time for consumers to make much of an adjustment to the change in prices. It can take a while for households and firms to notice price changes, to change contracts and to find new suppliers. With inelastic demand, export revenue will fall and import expenditure will rise. Then as time progresses and buyers find alternative sources, demand is likely to become more elastic. This may cause export revenue to rise, import expenditure to fall and so the trade balance to improve.

If demand for a country's exports are price inelastic in the long run, export revenue could rise if firms keep the price of their exports unchanged in terms of foreign currencies. For example, initially £1 might exchange for $2. The UK could have sold three million products to the US at an average price of £15 ($30). The UK would have earned £45 million ($90 million). If the pound depreciated to £1 = $1.5 and UK firms keep the price unchanged at $30 in the US, firms would still earn $45 million but this would now be converted to £60 million.

A lower exchange rate may be ineffective in reducing a current account deficit if incomes in other countries are falling. In such a circumstance, export revenue may fall by more than import expenditure.

Reducing the exchange rate, in the hope of increasing sales of exports may also not work if foreign governments increase trade restrictions imposed on the country's products or if the economy is working at full capacity. Foreign governments may try to discourage imports by, for instance, increasing tariffs on the country's exports. Such a measure could offset the increased price competitiveness gained by the fall in the exchange rate.

In addition, if resources are fully employed, firms may experience a rise in demand for their products in other countries but may not be able to produce more to meet the extra demand.

A lower exchange rate has the potential to reduce a current account deficit given the right conditions. It will provide firms with the opportunity to raise export revenue if they respond in the appropriate way given the price elasticity of demand for their products, if incomes abroad do not fall, additional trade restrictions are not imposed and there is the capacity to increase output. Import expenditure will fall if demand for imports is price elastic and foreign firms adjust their prices in the country in line with the fall in the exchange rate.

In the long run, however, if a current account deficit has arisen because the country's products lack price and/or quality competitiveness, the deficit is likely to reappear.

2 a An appreciation of a currency means that its exchange rate rises with each unit of the currency purchasing more of another currency or currencies. It will result in a rise in export prices in terms of foreign currencies and a fall in import prices in terms of the domestic currency.

Domestic citizens do not buy their country's exports and exports are not included in the consumer price index, an important measure of inflation. The citizens do buy imports and lower import prices are likely to reduce inflationary pressure in the country. This is for three main reasons. One is that some of the products consumers buy will fall in price. The more imports they do buy, the larger this impact will be.

The price of imported raw materials will also fall. This will reduce domestic firms' costs of production. This may enable them to reduce their prices and possibly increase their profit levels.

In addition, lower import prices will put pressure on domestic firms that produce substitute products to avoid price rises. So both directly and indirectly an appreciation can lower a country's inflation rate. The extent of its influence will depend on the size of the appreciation and what proportion of raw materials and products purchased by consumers are imported.

b A rise in an economy's inflation rate may result in a depreciation of the floating exchange rate. If the economy's price level is rising more rapidly, this may make its products less internationally competitive. This may result in a fall in demand for its exports and a rise in demand for imports. Demand for the currency will fall whilst the supply of the currency will rise. As shown here, these changes will cause the value of the currency to fall.

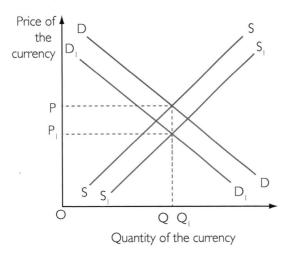

A rise in an economy's inflation rate may put downward pressure on a fixed exchange rate but may not cause the exchange rate to change. This is because a central bank may buy up the currency or raise the rate of interest to offset the downward pressure.

Even in the case of a floating exchange rate, a rise in an economy's inflation rate will not necessarily cause a depreciation in the exchange rate. Other countries may be experiencing even higher rates. It is also possible that despite a high inflation rate, other countries will still want to purchase the country's exports. This may be because incomes abroad are increasing or the quality of the country's products is improving.

As well as trade flows, there are other influences on the exchange rate. An economy may currently be experiencing a rise in its inflation rate, but if its economic performance is forecast to improve, speculators may increase demand for the currency. In addition, foreign multinational companies may be encouraged to set up in the country if consumer expenditure is rising. This would again increase demand for the currency.

For an economy operating a floating exchange rate, a rise in an economy's inflation rate might be expected to cause depreciation in the external value of the currency. There are a number of reasons, however, why this might not be the case.

Answer to Activity 5.01

	Demand-pull inflation	Cost-push inflation
Definition	An excess of aggregate demand	A rise in the costs of production
Illustrated by	A shift to the right of the AD curve	A shift to the left of the AS curve
Examples of causes	A consumer boom	Rise in wages
	Increase in net exports	Rise in price of imported raw materials
	Rise in government spending	Rise in indirect taxes
Impact on real GDP	Increase up to the FE level	May reduce
Policy to reduce	Deflationary fiscal policy	Supply side policy
	Deflationary monetary policy	

Chapter 6

Answers to progress checks

A The existence of unemployed resources means that national output is lower than possible. The country will be producing below its productive potential and will be productively inefficient.

B A reallocation of resources would increase economic efficiency if allocative efficiency is not being achieved. If, for instance, the MSC exceeds MSB in the case of Good X while the MSB exceeds the MSC in the case of Good Y, some resources should be transferred from producing Good X to producing Good Y.

C An increase in government spending on education may increase dynamic efficiency by making workers and entrepreneurs more inventive.

D It is difficult to achieve allocative efficiency in the case of public goods as it is difficult to assess how much consumers value the products. This is because they do not have to reveal their preferences.

E If social costs are equal to private costs, it means there are no external costs.

F A first and second party involved in the production and consumption of air travel are the airline and a passenger. A third party is someone living near the airport who experiences air, noise and visual pollution.

G A CBA takes into account social costs and social benefits while a private sector investment project only takes into account private costs and benefits.

Answers to revision activities

A **a** A reduction in unemployment would increase productive efficiency. More use would be made of factors of production and output would increase.

b Reallocating resources from producing demerit goods to producing merit goods would increase allocative efficiency. This is because resources would be moved from producing products that are over-produced to those that are under-produced.

c A reduction in surpluses would increase allocative efficiency. Resources would not be wasted.

d A reduction in labour productivity would reduce productive efficiency. Costs per unit would be driven up above the minimum level.

e A switch from producing less popular to more popular products will increase allocative efficiency. Producers will be responding more effectively to consumer demand.

f Organisational slack can also be referred to as X inefficiency. It arises when firms do not minimise average costs due to a lack of competitive pressure. It may involve managers permitting some spare capacity to exist. If too much organisational slack exists, a reduction may increase both productive and allocative efficiency. If, however, all organisational slack is eliminated, it may become difficult for firms to adapt to market conditions and so both allocative and productive efficiency may be reduced.

B **a** False. A shift to the right in the production possibility curve shows that the economy is capable of producing more. It does not in itself, however, indicate an increase in productive efficiency. To assess whether productive efficiency is being achieved or not, it would be necessary to assess where the production point is relative to the production possibility curve.

b True. If average revenue is above marginal cost, not enough resources are being allocated to producing the product. Consumers are valuing the product more than it is costing to produce it – there is a welfare loss.

c True. When allocative efficiency is achieved, consumers are paying an amount for the last unit consumed which matches society's valuation of the resources used to make that unit.

d False. To achieve economic efficiency, marginal social cost should equal marginal social benefit.

e True. Information failure can result in people under-consuming merit goods and over-consuming demerit goods. This causes too few resources being devoted to consumer goods and too many resources being devoted to demerit goods.

C **a** Private benefits: 2, 7.
Private costs: 6, 9.

External benefits: 5.
External costs: 1, 3, 4, 8.

b

Output	Social benefit	Marginal social benefit	Social cost	Marginal social cost
20	100		90	
21	120	20	100	10
22	150	30	120	20
23	200	50	150	30
24	240	40	190	40
25	260	20	220	30

The allocatively output is 24 units since this is where MSB = MSC.

Answers to multiple choice questions

1 **C** If more people travel by train, others will benefit from their action. These include road users. A is a private cost and B and D are private benefits.

2 **D** If there is a net social benefit, it means that social benefits exceed social costs. Social benefits are private benefits plus external benefits. In this case, social benefits are $600 m + $700 m = $1,300 m. As private costs are $500 m, it means that external costs must be less than $800 m.

3 **B** A more efficient allocation of resources will enable an economy to produce more goods and services with existing resources.

4 **C** Points X and Y are both productively efficient as they both occur on the production possibility curve. To know what effect the movement along the production possibility curve has on allocative efficiency, it would be necessary to have information on consumers' preferences.

5 **B** A Pareto improvement occurs when a change in the use of resources causes at least one person to be better off without causing anyone else to be worse off. A movement from X to B increases person R's utility, whilst leaving person T's utility unchanged. A movement from X to A reduces both people's utility. A movement from X to C increases person R's utility but reduces person T's utility. Finally, a movement from X to D leaves person R's utility unchanged but reduces person T's utility.

6 **D** The tax on the substitute good might initially have meant that its price exceeded its marginal cost and that it was under-consumed. The introduction of a tax on a rival product may increase the demand for the substitute moving consumption closer to the efficient level. A tax on a complementary good may also mean that this product was initially under-consumed. This time, however, the introduction of a tax on a product which is in joint demand will reduce demand for the complementary good. A and D would also increase inefficiency as they would move price away from marginal cost.

7 **D** Producer surplus rises by PPxUV whilst consumer surplus falls by PPxTV, giving a net benefit of TVU. The cost to the government is Px multiplied by quantity purchased which is YZ – giving a total cost of YTUZ. So the net loss to society is YTUZ – TVU which is equal to YTVUZ.

8 **C** Moving from production point X to production point Y would result in a rise in the output of vegetables. As most of the population are vegetarians such a change in the allocation of resources is likely to increase their economic welfare. At point Y, however, there are unemployed resources whereas at point X there is full employment of resources.

9 **A** If the benefit of consuming the last unit equals the cost of producing the last unit, it will not be possible to increase welfare either by reducing or increasing output. A reduction in output would mean that production would be at a point where the benefit would exceed the cost and so insufficient resources would be being devoted to the product. Producing where the cost of the last unit exceeds the benefit gained would mean too many resources are being devoted to producing the product. The cost of producing an extra unit may be zero but if the benefit is greater, more should be produced until the two are equal. The gap between social benefit and social cost could be a positive or a negative gap and the key determining factor in deciding the output which maximises economic welfare is the equality between marginal social cost and marginal social benefit.

10 **D** A relatively straightforward question. Social cost is private cost ($90,000) plus external cost ($60,000 + $85,000) = $235,000.

Answers to data response questions

1 a In the short run, firms are regarded as being productively efficient when they produce any given output at minimum cost. In the long run, productive efficiency is achieved by producing at the lowest point on the lowest average costs curve. To be allocatively efficient, firms have to produce where price equals marginal cost.

b The information mentions that a lack of competition reduces the pressure on firms to keep their costs low. This indicates that at least some Latin American firms might not have been productively efficient. It also mentions that the lack of competition reduces pressure on firms to 'respond quickly and fully to changes in consumer demand'. This implies that firms may be allocatively inefficient – not producing the right products in the right quantities.

c Latin American governments could increase spending on education and training and could provide investment subsidies to increase efficiency. A more educated and better trained labour force should have higher productivity. This should reduce firms' costs of production. A more educated and better trained labour force should also be more geographically and occupationally mobile, should adapt more quickly and fully to changes in consumer demand and so increase efficiency.

Investment subsidies should encourage firms to undertake more investment. New investment also often embodies advanced technology. Having more and better quality capital equipment should cut costs of production and may increase flexibility of production. If this is the case, again productive efficiency and allocative efficiency should increase.

d i The information in the table is inconclusive. Venezuela has by far the highest inflation rate but only the third highest unemployment rate. Colombia has the second lowest inflation rate but the highest unemployment rate. Chile does, however, have the lowest inflation rate and the lowest unemployment rate but only by a small margin.

ii A high unemployment rate is an indication of productive inefficiency. When an economy has a high unemployment rate, it will be producing inside its production possibility curve. With unemployed resources, actual output is below potential output.

A high inflation rate may indicate inefficiency but this is not necessarily the case. Producers becoming more productively inefficient can contribute to cost-push inflation. This type of inflation, however, may also be caused by external shocks. Domestic producers may be relatively efficient but a rise in the price of imported fuel may drive up costs. In addition, inflation may be of a demand-pull nature. Producers may be producing the right products in the right quantities and at the lowest possible cost. If, however, aggregate demand exceeds the maximum output the country can produce, inflation will occur.

2 a High income elasticity of demand occurs when a change in income results in a greater percentage increase in demand. In other words, demand is income elastic and the YED figure is high.

b Half of the highest paid sports leagues in 2014–2015 were football leagues. Three different sports were in the top three highest paid. The figures show only the average player salary and some individual footballers may be paid more than some individual basketball and cricket players but more information would be needed to determine this. The table also shows that, on average, footballers in the UK's Premier League are paid more than footballers in the CSL in China. This picture could change in the next few years as more money is being put into the Chinese league.

c Firms in the US cricket market are seeking to be more innovative. The Times of India Group has put on high profile cricket matches with world stars in an effort to attract more spectators. They are also considering building specialised stadiums to cater for the needs of cricket fans.

d One private benefit of playing sport is the enjoyment the people may gain. Other potential private benefits are the health benefits and the social contacts the people may gain. The external benefits that may arise from people playing sport are reduced healthcare costs and increased output arising from healthier and more productive workers.

e A cost-benefit analysis (CBA) would be useful in helping to decide whether to build a cricket stadium. Seeking to identify and compare the social costs and social benefits that are likely to arise from the building and operating the stadium would enable the decision to be based on more than just the private costs and benefits. As a result, a decision is more likely to be made where economic welfare will be maximised.

It is, however, difficult to identify and to attach a monetary value to some external costs and some external benefits. It is also difficult to decide on how to value benefits and costs that will occur in the future.

A CBA is not a perfect tool but it can help in determining whether an investment decision will improve the economic welfare of a community.

Answers to essay questions

I Market forces may result in an efficient allocation of resources. A rise in demand will cause price to rise. The higher price will signal to producers that consumers are willing and able to buy more of the product. The higher profit that may be earned from producing the product will provide an incentive for firms to produce more of the product. More resources will be devoted to the product's production.

If a product becomes less popular, market forces should mean that its price will fall. Firms may experience losses making it which will encourage them to use their resources to make other products.

Market forces should promote consumer sovereignty, enabling consumers to decide how resources are allocated and producers to respond to their changes in demand.

There are, however, a number of reasons why the market forces might fail to achieve an efficient allocation of resources. One is that there may be information failure about the benefits and costs of consuming a product. In the case of merit goods, too few resources are devoted to the production of the product. This is because consumers do not fully appreciate the benefits they gain from consuming the product. As a result, the products are under-consumed and so under-produced. Demerit goods, in contrast, will have too many resources allocated to them. Consumers do not

recognise the full costs of consuming the product and so their demand is above the allocatively efficient level.

Market forces reflect consumer demand and producer supply. When making their decisions on what to buy and what to produce, consumers and producers usually only take into account private costs and benefits. This means that the existence of positive and negative externalities can result in inefficiency. The following diagram shows that the presence of positive externalities will result in too few resources being devoted to the output of the product.

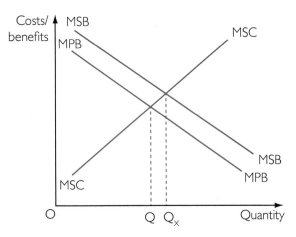

The allocatively efficient output is Q_X since this is where marginal social benefit equals marginal social cost. Consumers, ignoring the external benefits arising from consuming the product, however, will only demand Q amount and this is the quantity producers will provide.

The following diagram shows a firm seeking to maximise profits where marginal private cost equals marginal private benefit.

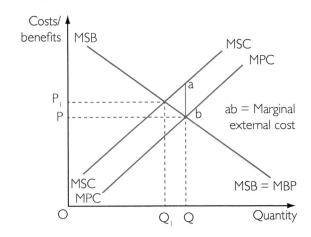

The output of Q is above the allocatively optimum level of QX. The price of P also fails to reflect the social cost and is below the allocatively efficient price of PX.

There is likely to be an even more significant failure in the case of public goods, i.e., goods which are both non-rival and non-excludable. As people can act as free riders, it is very difficult to make consumption dependent on payment. This problem may discourage private sector firms from providing public goods.

Private sector firms may also use any market power they possess to restrict output below the allocatively efficient level. They may do this in order to drive up price and increase their profits. A lack of competitive pressure may also mean that firms do not strive to keep their costs low.

Firms may want to respond to consumer demand in an efficient manner, but a lack of factor mobility may prevent them doing so. Workers, for instance, may lack the skills necessary to move from declining to expanding industries.

To work efficiently, market forces need perfect information, the absence of externalities and possibly perfect product and factor markets.

2 a   Efficiency in the use of resources covers both allocative efficiency and productive efficiency. The following diagram shows the allocatively efficient output is X At this level of output the value people place on the last product consumed is equal to the cost of that last unit. The right quantity of output is produced.

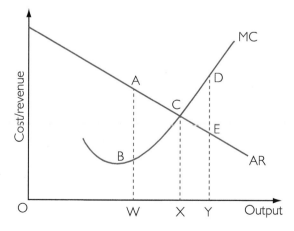

An output of W would be allocatively inefficient. This is because consumers value

the product more than it is costing to make it. There is an insufficient quantity of resources devoted to making the product and there is a welfare loss represented by the area ABC. Mutually beneficial transactions are being forgone. An output of Y would also be allocatively inefficient. In this case, the cost of producing the product exceeds the utility consumers gained. There is overproduction and a welfare loss of CDE is created.

Productive efficiency occurs when firms are producing the maximum output for a given quantity of resources and producing that output at the lowest possible cost. This can also be viewed as producing a given level of output with the minimum quantity of resources.

Productive efficiency in an economy takes place when production occurs on the production possibility curve as illustrated by point Z in the following diagram.

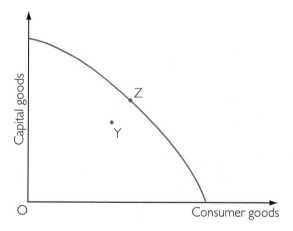

If the economy is producing at point Y, there are unemployed resources and some industries may be losing more resources than necessary for the output they are making. By employing all resources and by ensuring all industries are productively efficient, the economy's output can rise to Z. At production point Z, it will not be possible to make more capital goods without making fewer consumer goods and vice versa.

For an individual firm, productive efficiency occurs when it produces any given output at the lowest possible average cost. Productive efficiency is sometimes defined as producing at the lowest point on the lowest average cost curve. This is shown as point X in the following diagram.

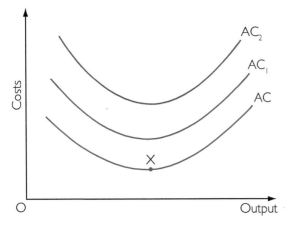

Information failure can result in market output being above or below the allocatively efficient level. Information failure often occurs when there are negative and positive externalities. A lack of awareness of effects on third parties can result in an inefficient use of resources. If not all costs are taken into account, output will be too high. In contrast, if not all benefits are considered, output will be too low.

b Information failure may result in market failure in the case of merit goods. These products generate externalities but are also more beneficial or harmful to consumers than they themselves realise. Consumers lack information or have inaccurate information about merit goods and so they under-consume them. The diagram below shows that actual demand is DD whereas demand based on full and accurate information about the merit good is D_XD_X.

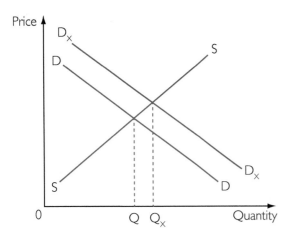

The allocatively efficient output is Q_X but the market output is below this at Q. The product is under-consumed and so under-produced.

The existence of positive externalities in the case of merit goods such as healthcare and education increases the extent of market failure. In the absence of government intervention, the failure to take into account the benefits to others means that the quantity traded will be even further below the optimum level.

It is, of course, difficult to measure positive externalities and so to assess the extent of market failure. There is also some debate as to whether people should be allowed freedom to act in their own best interests or whether the government should, in some cases, make decisions on their behalf. This choice is influenced by the degree of information failure and the view on who is best informed – consumers or the government. Different governments and societies have different views on what are merit goods and the extent to which they are under-consumed. For example, entry to most museums in the UK is free whereas most museums in France charge entry fees. This suggests that visiting a museum is regarded as more of a merit good in the UK than in France.

The extent to which market failure exists will be influenced by how well-educated the population is. The more educated people are, the less information failure there should be.

Merit goods do provide evidence of market failure but there is some debate as to the extent to which merit goods exist.

Answer to Activity 6.01

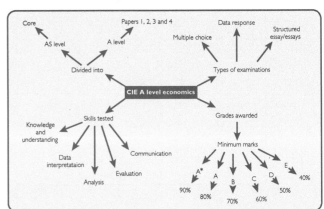

Chapter 7

Answers to progress checks

A A person would be unlikely to consume a quantity of a product where total utility is falling as this would mean that marginal utility is negative. Consuming the last unit would have reduced total satisfaction which would be irrational.

B If a consumer is getting more satisfaction per dollar spent on apples than on oranges, she should buy more apples and fewer oranges. As she switches her purchase, the marginal utility per dollar spent will fall as apples and rise on oranges until they are again both equal.

C If the price of one of the two products falls, the budget line will rotate outwards. This shows that a larger amount of the product can be purchased with a given level of income.

D A straight, downward sloping indifference curve would indicate the two products are perfect substitutes for each other.

E More capital-intensive methods of production and improvements in the capital equipment used have raised agricultural output.

F Diminishing returns give rise to increasing costs of production. If adding more of a variable factor gives rise to a smaller increase in output, the cost per unit produced will increase.

G Financial economies of scale, managerial economies of scale, staff facilities economies of scale and, of course, risk bearing economies of scale.

H Two possible barriers to exit from an industry are long-term contracts and sunk costs. A long-term contract will mean that a firm may have to continue to provide a good or service for at least a year, for example. Sunk costs are costs which are not recoverable should the firm leave the industry. Spending on market research and the cost of firm specific equipment are examples of sunk costs.

I The theory of contestable markets suggests that privatisation may make a market efficient even if the state owned enterprise is sold off to one firm provided there is free entry into and exit from the market. In such a situation, potential competition may be sufficient to keep the market allocatively and productively efficient.

J Among the factors that may prevent a firm from expanding are demand for a product not increasing, a lack of finance and difficulty in attracting factors of production.

K A perfectly competitive firm's marginal revenue and average revenue are equal and both will remain constant if the firm increases its output. In contrast, in a firm operating under conditions of monopolistic competition, its average revenue will exceed its marginal revenue. Average revenue and marginal revenue will also fall with output.

L A firm might stay in an industry, despite making a loss, as long as it can cover its variable costs and believes that in the longer term it will return to profitability.

M The prisoners' dilemma can be applied to emphasise the interdependence of oligopolists. It suggests that firms consider how their rivals will respond to their actions.

N Perfect competition is the highest level of competition possible but it is not perfect. Whilst it offers consumers a choice of producers, it does not provide a choice of differentiated products. In addition, although firms will be allocatively efficient in the sense of producing where price equals marginal cost, they will not necessarily produce where marginal social benefit equals marginal social cost.

Answers to revision activities

A

Output	Total cost	Fixed cost	Variable cost	Average cost	Average variable cost	Average fixed cost	Marginal cost	Marginal variable cost
0	100	100	–	–	–	–	–	–
1	150	100	50	150	50	100	50	50
2	180	100	80	90	40	50	30	30
3	201	100	101	67	33.67	33.33	21	21
4	220	100	120	55	30	25	19	19
5	280	100	180	56	36	20	60	60
6	360	100	260	60	43.33	16.67	80	80

B

a True. A fall in the price of a product, for instance, will increase people's purchasing power (income effect) and will encourage them to switch from substitutes to this product (substitution effect).

b False. Average fixed costs always fall with output. Average variable costs, however, tend to fall at first and then rise.

c True. Demand for skilled labour is usually more inelastic than demand for unskilled labour. This is because it is more difficult to replace skilled labour with machinery and with new workers.

d False. If the supply of labour is perfectly elastic, all of the workers' earnings will be transfer earnings.

e False. Although seeking to raise wage rates is a major function of trade unions, it will not pursue this aim at all times. During a recession, trade unions are more likely to pursue job security for their members.

f True. One reason why small firms survive is that they cater for a market which has a relatively small demand. Larger firms may not find it profitable to make products for such a market.

g True. If marginal revenue is zero and PED is unitary, selling one more unit will not add to total revenue. Total revenue will be at its highest level.

h True. A perfectly competitive firm is a price taker. A change in the quantity it sells would be too insignificant to influence price. What determines the amount it sells at the market price is the relationship between that price and its marginal cost (MR = MC). In contrast, a monopolist is a price maker. To encourage people to buy more of the product, it would have to lower price.

i False. It is true that a perfectly competitive market is a contestable market as both lack barriers to entry and exit. It does not, however, follow that a contestable market is a perfectly competitive market. It is possible for other market structures to be contestable markets. What is significant in the case of contestable markets is not the actual competition in the market but the potential competition.

C

Comparison of market structures				
Feature	Perfect competition	Monopolistic competition	Oligopoly	Pure Monopoly
No. of firms in the market	Very many	Many	Dominated by a few large firms	One
Market concentration ratio	Very low	Low	High	100%
Barriers to entry and exit	None	None or low	High	Very high
Type of product produced	Homogeneous	Differentiated	Differentiated and homogeneous	Unique
Influence on price	Price taker	Price maker	Price maker	Price maker
Ability to earn supernormal profit in the long run	No	No	Yes	Yes

Answers to multiple choice questions

1 **D** The person is receiving a higher utility per $ spent on product Y than on products X and Z. The marginal utility per $ spent on product Y is 8 whereas it is 5 on each of the other two products.

2 **D** This is the paradox of value. Whilst food has a high total but low marginal utility, the reverse is true for diamonds.

3 **B** The total cost when output is zero is 20. The total cost and average cost of the different units is shown below.

Units of X	Total cost	Average cost
1	60	60
2	90	45
3	120	40
4	180	45
5	260	52

4 **C** The firm's average fixed cost (AFC) is $2 ($10 − $8). AFC is total fixed cost/output. In this case, $2 = $8,000/output. So output is 4,000 units.

5 **A** A definition question. B is decreasing returns to scale. There are no specific terms for C and D.

6 **D** People prefer points further away from the origin. Combination W is further from the origin than Y. Whether the individual could afford it or not would be shown by combining the budget line with the indifference curves that apply. To determine whether Product S is more expensive than Product T, it would be necessary to see the budget line. An indifference curve diagram does not provide any information on costs of production.

7 **B** The diagram shows that after the changes, the same amount of ice cream is purchased whilst more fruit is purchased. If income is increased and the price of fruit remains constant, it will be possible to buy more fruit. If the price of ice cream increases, however, it may be the case that only the same quantity of ice cream can be purchased.

8 **B** Increasing returns to scale occur when output increases by a greater percentage than inputs. The table below shows this occurs when output rises from 400 to 600.

Output	% increase in output	Inputs	% increase in inputs	Returns to scale
200		60		
	100		100	constant
400		120		
	50		25	increasing
600		150		
	33.3		40	decreasing
800		210		
	25		50	decreasing
1,000		315		

9 **A** As AR > MR, the firm is a price maker. A monopoly can be a price maker but a firm operating under conditions of perfect competition is a price taker. As AR = AC, the monopoly is making normal profit.

10 **C** A kinked demand curve shows that if an oligopolist raised its price, competitors would not do the same and so demand is likely to fall by a large percentage. In contrast, if the oligopolist lowered its price, demand would be more inelastic as competitors would also be likely to lower their prices and so the fall in its price would cause a smaller percentage rise in demand. Consumers are more sensitive to price changes in the long run when they have more time to find substitutes. In imperfect competition AR falls as more units are sold.

11 **D** Marginal cost is zero. This means that profit will be maximised where marginal revenue is zero and this occurs where total revenue is at a maximum.

12 **A** The supply curve shows the different quantities which will be supplied at different prices. A profit maximising firm will produce where marginal cost equals marginal revenue. Under conditions of perfect competition, average revenue equals marginal revenue. So the supply curve can be plotted from where the average revenue and marginal revenue line cuts the marginal cost curve. In the short run, a firm will continue in production if it can cover its variable costs and therefore, its supply curve is based on its marginal cost curve above the average variable cost curve.

13 **A** The firm will produce where MC = MR. This is where output is M. Average cost is F and total cost is OFKM.

14 **B** At Q supernormal profit is GPJN. When the firm cheats, it will produce where MC = MR and earn supernormal profit of PKLH. So there is extra supernormal profit of JKLM minus the loss of HMNG supernormal profit.

15 **B** The profit maximising output is where MC = MR, which is the case at V. The allocatively efficient output is where MC = P (AR) – which, in this case, is at Y.

Answers to data response questions

1 **a** Aviation fuel is a variable cost for an airline. The more flights the airline operates the more aviation fuel it will use. As a result, the cost of the aviation fuel it uses varies with output.

b The four firm market concentration ratio was 68% (22% + 18% + 17% + 11%). This means that the largest four airlines carried just over two-thirds of passengers at US airports.

c Collusion is more likely to occur if there are only a few firms, or only a few dominant firms in the market. This is because it will make it easier for the firms to communicate and because the firms may know more about each other's costs and strategies. Similar costs and strategies would make it easier to agree on, for instance, pricing strategy. Additional factors that would encourage collusion are that most of the firms in the market are involved in the collusion, it is possible to stop new entrants from coming into the market and that collusion is either not illegal or difficult to detect.

d High barriers to entry into a market can increase the opportunity of firms to earn supernormal profit and protecting the supernormal profit. They do not, however, guarantee that supernormal profit will be earned.

High barriers to entry may enable the firms to collude and push up prices and earn supernormal profit. If new firms cannot come into the market, they cannot compete away any supernormal profit the firms are earning.

If the firms are in oligopoly market, however, a firm may lose consumers if a rival cuts its price and the firm does not do the same. A loss in demand may also result from a change in taste away from the product. Increases in the cost of production may also eliminate any supernormal profit earned.

A state-owned monopoly will also have a legal barrier to entry but may not aim to earn supernormal profit as its main aim may be to promote economic welfare.

Firms operating under conditions of monopoly and oligopoly can protect any supernormal profit being earned in the long run because of barriers to entry. The existence of barriers to entry, however, do not ensure that supernormal profit will be earned in either the short run or the long run. A fall in demand or a rise in costs of production could result in the firms earning only normal profit or even making a loss.

2 a The information indicates that Coca-Cola is not a pure monopoly. It does, however, indicate that it had a dominant monopoly position in 2015 as it had a market share of 48%.

b A price war may be risky as it can result in all the firms that engage in it losing out. There are circumstances, however, when a firm may benefit from engaging in a price war. If a firm has lower costs, more retained profits than its rivals or can cross subsidise its products, it may be able to drive its rivals out of business by reducing its price. If it does succeed in forcing its rivals out of the market, it could then increase its price.

c There is some evidence in the information that Pepsi-Cola is becoming more allocatively efficient. Allocative efficiency occurs when resources are allocated in a way that maximises consumer satisfaction. Resources are devoted, in the right quantities, to producing what consumers are willing and able to buy. The information mentions that consumer demand is switching away from making fizzy drinks to making healthier drinks. Pepsi-Cola is seeking to produce a higher proportion of healthier drinks in order to respond to a change in demand.

d It is uncertain whether increasing spending on advertising will increase a firm's profits. It will do so if it increases revenue by more than costs. There is a chance, however, that it may not result in a significant rise in demand if the advertising campaign is not popular. There is also the possibility that one firm's increase in expenditure on advertising may be less than the rise in a rival's advertising expenditure.

e Pepsi-Cola's approach to diversification is to diversify not only into other soft drinks but also into food. Pepsi-Cola has a wider product range than Coca-Cola. This has some advantages. It means that its risks are spread. If, for instance, demand for fruit drinks declines, the impact on the company's profit may not be very significant and resources could be shifted from fruit juices to, for example, breakfast cereals. Wide diversification may also enable workers to develop a range of skills, will permit cross fertilisation of ideas and may provide savings in advertising costs since advertising one product may promote the whole company.

On the other hand, adopting Coca-Cola's approach to specialising in soft drinks, has a number of potential advantages. It may be easier to manage and co-ordinate a more focused range of products. The firm may also be able to build up expertise and may gain a good reputation in producing soft drinks.

Answers to essay questions

1 a According to utility theory, consumers would change their spending patterns if the satisfaction they gain from the products or the prices of products alter. For instance, initially a consumer may be allocating her spending between three products, X, Y and Z such that:

$$\frac{\text{Marginal utility of X}}{\text{Price of X}} = \frac{\text{MU of Y}}{\text{P of Y}} = \frac{\text{MU of Z}}{\text{P of Z}}$$

$$\frac{20}{4} = \frac{35}{7} = \frac{15}{3}$$

She is maximising her total utility, as changing her purchases cannot increase her satisfaction. She is gaining the same marginal utility per dollar spent i.e. 5 units. If, however, the price of product X fell to $2, she would not be maximising her utility if she did not alter her purchases.

$$\frac{20}{2} > \frac{35}{7} = \frac{15}{3}$$

She is gaining more satisfaction per dollar spent from X. She will reallocate some of her spending from Y to Z and Z to X. As she consumes more of X the marginal utility she gains from it will fall. As she consumes less of Y and Z, the marginal utility she gains from them will rise until she is again in equilibrium with her purchases.

$$\frac{12}{2} = \frac{42}{7} = \frac{18}{3}$$

A change in the satisfaction she gains from one or more of the products she buys would also cause her to alter her spending pattern. If, from the above position, she gained more satisfaction from product Y than before, perhaps because of a rise in its quality, she would again be encouraged to alter her spending pattern. For instance, if the marginal utility of Y rose to 56 she would gain 8 units of marginal utility per $ spent but only 6 from X and Z. This would encourage her to buy more of Y and less of X and Z.

b Reducing the scale of production will reduce total costs of production. With less being produced, less resources will be employed and so total costs will be lower. What is more uncertain is what will happen to average costs of production. If economies of scale are being experienced, a fall in output will raise average costs of production. For instance, less discount might be given on the purchase of raw materials if less are purchased. Few specialist workers may be employed, banks may charge higher interest rates and may be more reluctant to lend to smaller firms and capital equipment might be used less efficiently.

A smaller industry may also mean that less advantage can be taken of external economies of scale. With fewer potential students, colleges might decide to stop running courses. Specialist services provided by financial institutions may be withdrawn and specialist markets may be closed.

It is, however, possible that a fall in the scale of production may lower average costs if the firms and/or the industry was initially too large. Smaller firms may have less managerial problems. With fewer managers, decisions might be made more quickly. With fewer workers and closer contact between workers and managers, industrial relations might be better.

With a smaller industry, external diseconomies of scale may be reduced. Firms may find that they have to pay less for factors of production and may have reduced transport costs due to less congested roads and less demand for rail services.

2 a Monopoly and monopolistic competition are two types of market structure. In both cases, each firm in the market is a price maker. A rise in its output will lower price. As a result, its average revenue will exceed its marginal revenue and both will decline with output.

A monopoly and a monopolistically competitive firm will be likely to produce where neither allocative nor productive efficiency is achieved. In the private sector, a monopoly and a monopolistically competitive firm are likely to be profit maximisers and will produce where

marginal cost equals marginal revenue, but also where price exceeds marginal cost and where average cost is greater than marginal cost.

In a pure monopoly, however, there is only one firm in the industry whereas in monopolistic competition there is a relatively high number of firms. This means that in a monopoly there is a high degree of market concentration. Indeed, in the case of a pure monopoly there will be a one firm market concentration ratio of 100%. Even if a monopoly is defined in terms of a firm with a share of 25% or more of the market or a 40% plus share, one or two firms are likely to account for a large share of the market. On the other hand, in monopolistic competition the firms are small relative to the size of the industry. As a result the market concentration ratio is low.

In a pure monopoly, there is a unique product with only one firm producing the product. In monopolistic competition, consumers can enjoy variations in the product. This is because the firms produce slightly differentiated products.

A major difference between the two types of market structure is that whilst there are high barriers to entry and exit in the case of monopoly, there are no or low barriers to entry and exit in the case of monopolistic competition. This difference explains why a monopoly can protect any supernormal profit in the long run but a monopolistically competitive firm cannot. If a monopolistically competitive firm does earn supernormal profit in the short run, new firms will enter the market and compete it away. The diagram here shows how the long run equilibrium output of a monopolistically competitive firm which is producing where MC = MR and where it is earning only normal profit.

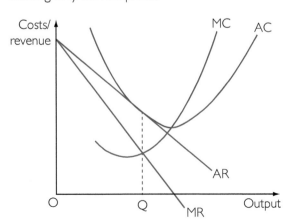

b A monopoly may disadvantage consumers in a number of ways. It may mean that consumers have a limited choice of products. They may also have to pay a high price. This is because a monopoly may restrict output below the efficient level in order to drive up price.

There is another reason why price may be higher under conditions of monopoly than under a more competitive market structure. This is because average costs of production may be higher under monopoly. Higher costs may result from x-inefficiency or diseconomies of scale. X-inefficiency refers to a lack of drive to keep costs low. Without the threat of competition, a monopoly may not spend time and effort searching for the cheapest raw materials, its managers may take long breaks and it may employ out of date equipment and too many workers. A monopoly may also experience diseconomies of scale if it grows too large. The firm may become difficult to manage and there may be more industrial disputes.

Not all monopolies, however, are large and those that are may experience economies of scale. A monopoly may earn supernormal profit but if its average cost is significantly lower than would be the case under more competitive conditions, price might also be lower. The existence of supernormal profit may also allow a monopoly to spend more on research and development and innovation. This means that it is possible that quality may be higher under conditions of monopoly. A monopoly may also seek to improve the quality of its existing products and develop new products in order to strengthen barriers to entry. In addition, a monopoly may choose to produce a range of products so that whilst consumers may not have a choice of producers, they may have a choice of products.

In the case of a natural monopoly, long-run average costs will be lower if one firm controls the market than if a number of firms supply the market. One firm operating in a natural monopoly market allows economies of scale to be exploited fully and for wasteful duplication to be avoided. A state run monopoly may also benefit consumers if it bases its production and pricing decisions on social costs and social benefits.

There is the possibility that a monopoly may disadvantage consumers by limiting choice, reducing quality, restricting output and charging a high price and so reducing consumer surplus. The outcome, however, is uncertain as it is possible that a monopoly may result in lower average costs, lower prices and better quality.

Chapter 8

Answers to progress checks

A A government's ability to raise the rate of corporation tax may be restricted by other countries' corporation tax rates. A government may be worried that if it raises its corporation tax rate above other countries' tax rates, firms may move abroad.

B The sale of cigarettes to children is banned by many governments whilst adults are allowed to buy cigarettes because it is thought that information failure is more significant in the case of children.

C If private benefits form a high proportion of social benefits, students might be expected to pay a high proportion of tuition fees.

D 'The polluter pays principle' is the idea that those who create an external cost should pay for it. In other words, an external cost should be converted into private cost.

E An increase in unemployment benefit may increase income inequality if it encourages some people to become voluntarily unemployed.

F Factor immobility leads to market failure because it stops markets making full adjustment to changes in demand. If there is difficulty moving resources from making less popular products to more popular products, there will be surpluses and shortages.

G Three reasons why people may switch from a higher paid to a lower paid occupation are that they may believe they will gain more job satisfaction from it, it may provide more job security and it may provide a better pension.

H One reason why demand for nurses has increased in most countries in recent years is due to increase in life expectancy. With people living longer, demand for healthcare has increased. Another reason why demand for healthcare has increased and so demand for nurses has also increased is a rise in income. As people get richer they demand more and better healthcare.

I Raising educational standards should increase workers' skills and mobility. This is likely to mean that there will be a range of well-paid jobs they can do. The gap between what they are earning now and what they could earn in their next best paid job should narrow.

J The imposition of a tax on a demerit good may reduce efficiency if it causes the quantity traded to fall by too much. The problem may change from over-consumption of the product to under-consumption with the marginal social benefit from consuming the product exceeding the marginal social cost of producing the product.

Answers to revision activities

A a The information indicates that ice cream in China has positive income elasticity of demand and is a normal good. As income increased in the past, demand for ice cream increased.

b One external cost arising from the consumption of high fat and high sugar foods is the increased burden placed on health services. Those who do not consume the foods may have to pay higher taxes or higher prices because of the increased burden and may also experience delays in medical treatment.

c Firms selling dental products and diabetes testing devices will benefit from increased sales. This rise in their sales is a spillover effect resulting from the increased consumption of the high fat and high sugar products.

B a Energy security means that a country has sufficient supplies of its own. It is not dependent on other countries for its energy supplies.

b A first party is either an energy firm or a consumer of energy. A third party who might suffer from the government's proposed scheme is a member of the Ashanikas tribe.

c The imposition of an indirect tax of $P_Y P_1$ per unit will cause the supply curve to shift to the left as shown in the figure below. This will raise price from P to P_1 and cause demand to contract from Q to Q_1. The price the producer receives falls to P_Y.

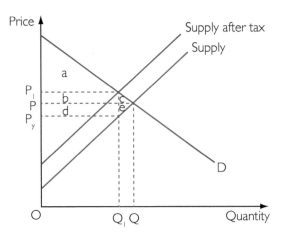

Consumer surplus falls by b + c amount and producer surplus by d + e amount. The government receives tax revenue of b + d amount and so there is a deadweight loss of c + e.

C a ii Unemployment benefits are designed to provide the unemployed with a basic income.

b i A tax on cigarettes is designed to discourage the consumption of a demerit good and move the market towards the allocatively efficient output.

c i One of the motives behind privatisation is to put market pressure on firms to respond to consumer demand and to keep costs down.

d iii Providing state education free helps the poor and helps increase labour productivity.

e i A cut in the top rate of tax would benefit the well paid and would be designed to increase incentives.

f iii A subsidy to providers of public transport will help the poor and will increase the output of a product which was previously under-consumed.

Answers to multiple choice questions

1 B Market forces will not provide public goods as it would not be possible to charge directly for them. A and D would enable markets to work more efficiently and merit goods are under – provided rather than over-provided.

2 C The monopolisation of the industry causes consumer surplus to fall by RSUW. Of this, RSUV is converted into producer surplus and UVW is lost.

3 B Firms may be reluctant to train their workers for fear that once trained, they will move to another firm and that firm will reap the benefits of the training. A, C and D would encourage firms to provide training and would not necessitate government intervention.

4 D The socially optimum output is achieved where marginal social cost equals marginal social benefit. To encourage people to buy this quantity, the price would have to fall to X and this would require a subsidy of XZ per unit.

5 D

Price ($)	Original quantity demanded	Quantity supplied	Quantity supplied after tax
10	20	1280	600
9	60	1000	400
8	150	850	150
7	260	600	50
6	400	400	
5	600	150	
4	900	50	

After tax, if a firm sells a product for $10, it will only receive $7 as the $3 will have to be passed to the government. So the firm would now supply at $10 what before it had supplied at $7 and so on. The price rises by $2, so consumers are bearing two thirds of the tax and producers are bearing the remaining third.

6 B Moving towards greater reliance on indirect taxes is a regressive move as indirect taxes tend to take a higher proportion of the income of the poor. Lowering income tax may encourage people to work longer hours and accept promotion.

7 D As income rises the tax payment is rising but at a decreasing rate. This means that the rich will be paying proportionately less and the poor proportionately more.

If progressive taxes act as a disincentive to work and effort, a redistribution of income to the poor would reduce real GDP.

8 B There is a risk that a regulatory agency may get too close to the producers it is regulating. If this occurs, it may protect the interests of the producers.

9 C The allocatively efficient output is achieved where marginal cost equals price (average revenue). In the case of a natural monopoly, such as illustrated in Figure 14.07, this may be where average cost is still falling and a loss would be made as average cost is greater than average revenue.

10 A Failure to take into account social benefits may result in allocative inefficiency. B, C and D would all increase the chances of government intervention increasing efficiency.

11 A The marginal product received per dollar spent on factor Y is 7 whereas it is 5 for factor Z. The higher return from factor Y suggests more of it should be employed and less of factor Z.

12 B A backward sloping supply curve shows that at first a rise in wages will encourage workers to work longer hours. At this stage the substitution effect is dominant. Between W and W_1 the income effect becomes dominant and workers, in effect, buy more leisure time.

13 A The number of workers employed is determined where the marginal cost of labour (MCL) equals the demand for labour (marginal revenue product of labour MRPL). The wage rate is then found from the average cost of labour curve below where MCL crosses the MRPL curve.

14 B The army is likely to be the only buyer of the labour of soldiers. A national trade union may have monopoly power in the sale of labour. The extent to which workers who possess skills in high demand may have some degree of monopoly power will depend on whether they negotiate collectively. The sole seller of a particular brand of orange juice is likely to be competing to buy the services of workers with other firms producing orange juice.

15 A The initial economic rent earned is MNT. It then rises to MPS – an increase of NPST.

Answer to data response question

1 a The information suggests that the Indonesian government sees rice as a strategic industry as it mentions that the government wants domestic supply of rice to be available at all times, even when it is difficult to get imports.

b The government could increase the income of the poorest people in the short run by providing them with state benefits. The government could also provide training for the poor which could increase their skills and so increase their earning potential.

c A buffer stock may seek to stabilise the price of rice by setting an upper and a lower price limit. If there is a risk that the price will fall below the lower price limit, the buffer stock operators would buy some of the product to stop its price falling. In contrast, if the price is in danger of rising above the upper limit, the buffer stock operator would sell some of the product.

d Subsidies might turn Indonesia into a net exporter of rice if the subsidies are large enough to lower its price below those of rival producers. Domestic firms would also need to possess the capacity to increase supply to meet both domestic and foreign demand.

If incomes rise in Indonesia, domestic demand may account for most of the rice produced in the country. Indonesia may also not be able to become a net exporter if the rice crop is hit by bad weather or a disease. A fall in incomes abroad would reduce the amount Indonesia could export. Tastes could change with foreign demand for rice decreasing. In addition, a rise in Indonesia's exchange rate could offset the cost advantage provided by the subsidies. Foreign governments may respond to the Indonesian government providing subsidies by imposing trade restrictions on Indonesian rice. A tariff may keep Indonesian rice uncompetitive in price terms and a quota will restrict the quantity of rice purchased.

2 a Deregulation involves the removal of legal restrictions on firms usually with the intention of increasing competition in markets.

b The information largely suggests that taxi firms operate under conditions of monopolistic competition. It indicates that there is a low market concentration ratio as the industry has a large number of small firms, which is a key feature of monopolistic competition. It also mentions that the firms produce a slightly differentiated product and that it is possible to enter the market with one or two vehicles.

The information does, however, mention that regulation can create a barrier to entry. It would be expected that monopolistic competition would either have no barriers to entry and exit or only low barriers. In order to judge whether any remaining regulation in this case is consistent with monopolistic competition, it would be necessary to assess how strong a barrier it creates.

c A more contestable market means that it is easier to enter and exit a market and that firms that come into the market will not be at a disadvantage compared to incumbent firms. A more contestable market will increase potential but not necessarily actual competition. If supernormal profits are being made new firms will come into the market. Indeed, there may be hit and run competition. Firms may enter and then leave when the circumstances that gave rise to the supernormal profits disappear.

At any one time, however, a more contestable market does not necessarily mean that there will be more firms in the market. Indeed, a contestable market may consist of only one firm. What will provide the competitive pressure will be the threat from outside the market.

d Economic efficiency is achieved when both productive efficiency and allocative efficiency are achieved. Deregulation may increase economic efficiency in the taxi market. Removing restrictions on the number of firms that can operate in the market will be likely to increase competition. Greater competitive pressure can make firms more sensitive to changes in consumer demand and more determined to keep costs low. It can also push down fares and may encourage firms to innovate to increase the quality competitiveness. In addition, more firms in the market can reduce waiting time for passengers.

There is, however, no guarantee that deregulation will increase economic efficiency. Any increase in the number of firms in the market may cause congestion in city centres and tourist spots. Removing controls on the geographical coverage of taxi firms may result in more remote areas not being covered. Allowing taxi firms to charge whatever fares they want may also cause problems. Fares to destinations without a return fare may rise significantly. Consumers may not have the time or confidence to find the lowest fare, especially if they have to hail down taxis in the street.

Answers to essay questions

I   Inequalities in wage rates in an economy occur for a number of reasons. Market forces explain why some workers are paid more than other workers. Workers whose skills are in high demand and in short supply are likely to be paid more than those whose skills are demanded less and which are in greater supply. Marginal revenue productivity theory suggests that demand for labour will be high if labour productivity is high and/or the product provided is in high demand. For example, top lawyers are highly skilled and their services are in high demand. The supply of top lawyers is also limited, with not many people possessing the necessary skills, qualifications and experience. In contrast, the supply of cleaners in many countries is high relative to demand for their services. The following figures show that the wage rate of top lawyers is significantly higher than that of cleaners.

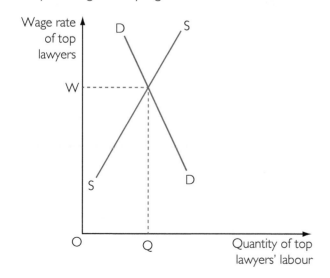

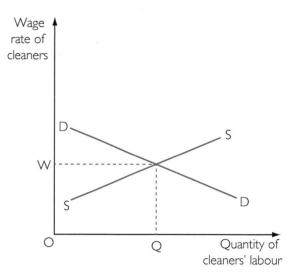

It is interesting to note the differences in the elasticities of demand and supply in the two labour markets. Most people could work as cleaners and so supply is elastic whereas not many people have the skills, qualifications and experience to be top lawyers. Demand for cleaners is more elastic as it is easier to reduce the number of cleaners required by introducing the use of more capital equipment.

Some individual workers are so skilful in a particular field and/or their services are in such high demand, that they can enjoy considerable economic rent. For instance, whilst there are many low paid actors, a few top actors earn considerably more than in their next best paid job. This is illustrated in the figure below.

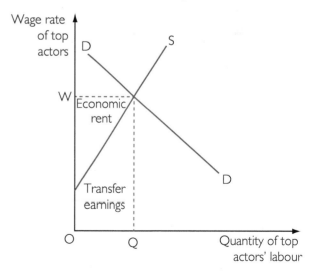

Whilst the need for particular skills or qualifications can act as a barrier to stop workers moving from low paid to high paid jobs, other factors can keep people in low paid jobs. They may not want to move from one region of the country to another region, perhaps because of family ties. Workers also base their decisions as to what jobs to do not just on the wage rate. They take into account, for instance, promotion chances, job security and working hours. Some nurses, for example, might earn more in other jobs but stay working as nurses because of the job satisfaction they gain.

Wage rates are also not determined just by demand and supply. Governments and trade unions may influence the wages and so the extent to which inequalities in wage rates occur. The gap between the highest paid and the lowest paid workers may be less in countries which operate a national minimum wage although the effects of national minimum wage legislation are somewhat uncertain. Governments also influence wage rates through the wages they pay public sector workers and the education and training they provide. The more educated and the better trained workers are, the greater their earning potential.

Trade unions engage in collective bargaining with employers. They seek to raise the wage rates of their members as well as trying to achieve other benefits for their members. How influential trade unions are in determining wage rates depend on a number of factors. These include what proportion of workers the union represents, whether the members are prepared to take industrial action, the buying power employers have and the relative bargaining strength and skills of the trade unions and employers.

Wage negotiations may take place under conditions of bilateral monopoly. This occurs when a monopolist trade union, representing everyone in a particular group of workers, and a monopsonist employer, the sole buyer of a particular group of workers. The following figure shows such a market.

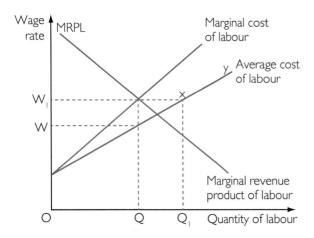

The employer will want a wage rate of W but the trade union may be able to raise the wage rate to W1. If the trade union is successful, it will not cause a loss of jobs as the new supply curve of labour will become W1XY. If, however, the employer operates in a competitive market, a trade union pushing up the wage rate above the equilibrium level may cause unemployment. The figure below shows that raising the wage rate from W to W1, in this case, causes the quantity of labour employed to fall from Q to Q1.

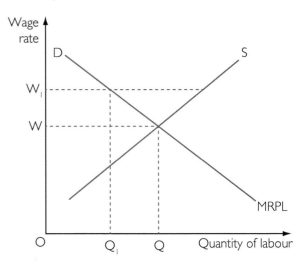

One group of workers may be paid less than another group if there is discrimination. If, for example, employers in a country think that female workers are less productive than male workers, they may pay them less. The following figure shows that the wage rate of female workers and their employment will be lower if there is discrimination.

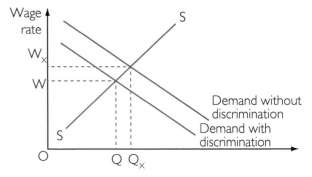

Workers and jobs differ and so demand for and supply of labour vary. Market forces, however, do not explain all of the wage differentials in an economy. Institutional factors and government policy also play a role. In addition, in some cases, discrimination may occur.

2 **a** Negative externalities are the harmful effects on third parties arising from the production or consumption by others. Those suffering from these adverse effects are not compensated through the market. So those who create these negative externalities by their production or consumption activities do not pay those who suffer as a result of their activities.

When private sector firms decide on their output and price they take into account private costs and benefits. For example, a chemical firm will consider its wage, fuel, advertising and other production costs and the revenue it will receive from selling the chemicals it produces. Without government intervention, it is unlikely to consider the external benefits, for example employment generated in the local area and the external costs such as the visual, air and noise pollution, it creates.

The following figure shows a firm seeking to maximise profits where marginal private cost equals marginal private benefit.

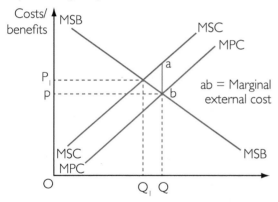

The output of Q is above the allocatively optimum level of Q_X. The price of P also fails to reflect the social cost and is below the allocatively efficient price of P_X.

b There are a number of measures which a government could introduce to reduce pollution. One measure is to seek to internalise the external cost of polluting by taxation. This means seeking to change pollution from an external cost into a private cost so that social cost equals private cost. To achieve this, the government would have to impose a tax on polluting firms which is equal to marginal external cost. The revenue raised could be used to treat pollution or compensate sufferers.

However, in practice, it is difficult to estimate external costs as they do not go through the market. There is the risk that a tax may add to inflationary pressure, especially if the demand for the products produced by the polluting firms is inelastic. A tax may also reduce international competitiveness and place a greater burden on the poor than on the rich.

An alternative approach is to regulate. Legislation could be passed which sets rules for the maximum permitted level of pollution emissions from different industries. As with a tax, this measure should internalise the external cost and shift the supply curve to the left. Regulation is more common than imposing a pollution tax but regulation also has its drawbacks. As with a tax, it is difficult to determine the 'right' level of pollution. Levels of pollution have to be checked and this involves a cost. Regulation also does not compensate the victims and does not provide firms with an incentive to reduce pollution below the maximum level.

One measure which does build in an incentive to reduce pollution is tradable pollution permits. This involves issuing permits to firms which allow them to pollute up to a certain level. Firms that pollute more have to buy additional permits. Those that pollute less can sell some of their permits. This should mean that high polluting firms will experience a rise in costs which should reduce their output whilst low polluting firms will gain extra revenue, encouraging them to expand. It is important that the level of pollution set reflects an efficient level. If, for instance, it is set too high, no firm would have to purchase additional permits. Money would have to be spent monitoring firms and, in practice, it can be difficult to determine where some pollution has come from. The measure is also more likely to be successful if it is introduced on a global scale as otherwise, firms may relocate to countries not operating tradable permits.

A measure that has become popular in some countries, including the US, is extending property rights. By giving local inhabitants ownership rights over, for instance, fresh air, rivers and the sea, it makes it easier for people to take legal action against a firm that pollutes. People could be given the right to sell pollution opportunities to firms. The allocatively efficient level of pollution might be achieved if they sell these rights at a price equivalent to marginal external cost. There may, however, be disagreements over ownership and it may be expensive for a firm to negotiate with a high number of people if the pollution is widespread.

A government might also decide to subsidise the installation of equipment which will generate less pollution. This will involve government expenditure. This might involve reducing spending on other areas. It might also involve higher taxes which will involve a transfer of income from tax payers to the firms which cause the pollution.

In the case of all the measures discussed, there is the problem of measuring external costs accurately. Each measure has a number of disadvantages and advantages.

Chapter 9

Answers to progress checks

A A country may have a higher GNI than another country but a lower value on the HDI due to lower life expectancy and people spending less time in education.

B External debt may hinder economic growth for a number of reasons. One is that some of the export revenue earned may have to be spent on servicing the debt rather than, for instance, buying imported capital goods to expand output. Another reason is that foreign financial institutions may be reluctant to lend to a country which has a high level of debt. This may restrict spending on, for instance, the country's infrastructure.

C A country may experience both an increase in employment and unemployment if there is a rise in the labour force. More people entering the labour force can increase both the numbers employed and the numbers of unemployed.

D A country may experience a decrease in production but an increase in labour productivity as a result of a rise in unemployment. With fewer people in work, total output may fall but if the best workers have been retained, output per worker hour may increase.

E Advances in technology may create jobs by increasing productivity and so raising international competitiveness. This may increase aggregate demand and real GDP and so may create jobs. In addition, advances in technology can lead to the development of new products, for example the ipad, and so can generate demand and jobs.

F Unemployment could cause unemployment as experiencing a period of unemployment may result in people losing the work habit, their skills becoming out of date and the longer people are out of work, the less attractive they will appear to employers.

G Among the reasons why someone may stop being unemployed are s/he may find another job, may emigrate, may retire, may enter full-time employment and may become a homemaker.

H A closed economy is an economy which does not engage in international trade. In such an economy, the injections are investment and government spending and the withdrawals are savings and taxation.

I A rise in the marginal rate of tax will reduce the size of the multiplier. More of extra spending caused by an injection will leak out of the circular flow. For example, if initially mps is 0.2, mrt is 0.1 and mpm is 0.1, the multiplier would be $1/0.4 = 2.5$. If mrt then increased to 0.2, the multiplier would fall to $1/0.5 = 2$.

J If there is a rise in liquid assets of $20 million with a credit multiplier of 20, bank loans will rise to $380 million ($400 m $-$ $20 m).

K Keynesians think that there may be large scale unemployment which will continue without government intervention. In contrast, monetarists think that in the long run, unemployment will return to the natural rate.

L The liquidity trap occurs when the rate of interest is so low (and the price of government securities is so high) that it becomes impossible to lower it further. A central bank may increase the money supply in a bid to reduce the rate of interest but if people think it will rise in the future and so the price of government securities will fall, they will hold all the extra money. This means that the rate of interest will remain unchanged.

Answers to revision activities

A

Country	Employed (millions)	Unemployed (millions)	Proportion of population in labour force (%)
China	770.232	33.768	57.43
Hong Kong	3.787	0.113	54.93
Maldives	0.176	0.024	50.00
New Zealand	2.355	0.145	56.82
Nigeria	43.7	13.8	31.77

  a Maldives

  b China

  c China

  d Nigeria

B **a** National income = injection × multiplier.

      Investment is the injection. The multiplier is $1/mps = 1/0.25 = 4$.

      So national income = \$50 bn × 4 = \$200 bn.

  b **i** mrt = 0.2 and mps = 0.25 × 0.8 = 0.2.
$k = 1/0.2 + 0.2 = 1/0.4 = 2\frac{1}{2}$.

      ii I + G = \$50 bn + \$70 bn = \$120 bn.

          National income = \$120 bn × $2\frac{1}{2}$ = \$300 bn.

      iii Tax revenue = 0.2 × \$300 bn = \$60 bn.

          Budget balance = tax revenue − government spending = \$60 bn − \$70 bn = −\$10 bn.

          There is a budget deficit of \$10 bn.

  c **i** mrt is 0.2, mps is 0.2 and mpm is 1/8 of 0.8 = 0.1.

      So $k = 1/0.2 + 0.2 + 0.1 = 1/0.5 = 2$.

      ii NY = J × k = I + G + X × k = \$50 bn + \$70 bn + \$40 bn × 2 = \$320 bn.

      iii The trade balance = X − M

          = \$40 bn − 0.1 × \$320 bn

          = \$40 bn − \$32 bn

          = \$8 bn.

          There is a trade surplus of \$8 bn.

      iv The budget position = T − G

          = 0.2 × \$320 bn − \$70 bn

          = \$64 bn − \$70 bn

          = −\$6 bn.

          There is a budget deficit of \$6 bn.

C **a** True. Current accounts are included in both measures. In contrast, deposit (time) accounts are only included in broad measures.

  b True. By engaging in credit creation, banks create more accounts than they have cash. This practice will not cause a problem as long as bank customers believe they could get the cash out of their accounts – which in fact they could not do.

  c True. The more liquid a bank's assets are, the less profitable they are. The bank's most liquid asset is cash which does not earn any money whereas its advances (bank loans) are profitable but not liquid.

  d True. Both sides represent total spending on goods and services.

  e False. A budget deficit may increase the money supply but it may not do so. If the government finances it by borrowing from the banking sector or from abroad, it will do so. If, however, it finances it by selling government securities to the non-bank sector, it will just be using existing money.

  f False. A credit crunch involves a shortage of bank loans which can lead to a recession.

D

	Keynesians	Monetarists
View on market failure	Significant	Not very significant
View on government failure	Not very significant	Significant
View on Quantity Theory	Reject	Support
Cause of inflation	May be demand-pull or cost-push	Excessive growth of the money supply
Main cause of unemployment	Frictional, structural and cyclical	Frictional and structural
Effect of government borrowing	Crowding in	Crowding out
Shape of LRAS curve	Horizontal, then upward sloping and then vertical	Vertical
Macroeconomic policy	Favour demand management	Favour supply side policies
Government intervention	Needed to ensure the smooth running of the economy	To be kept to a minimum. Main responsibilities = remove market imperfections and keep inflation low.

Answers to multiple choice questions

1 **B** The difference between GDP and NDP is depreciation. Net property income from abroad is the difference between a national and a domestic income measure. Net exports and consumer expenditure are included in both national and domestic measures.

2 **D** Real GDP in 2012 was $30bn × 100/125 = $24bn. Real GDP in 2002 per head was $20bn/20m = $1,000. In 2012, it was $24bn/22m = $1,090.91. Higher real GDP per head may increase living standards.

3 **A** Both average and marginal propensities to consume decrease.

Disposable income ($billion)	Consumer expenditure ($billion)	Average propensity to consume	Marginal propensity to consume
100	120	1.2	–
200	200	1.0	0.8
300	270	0.9	0.7
400	320	0.8	0.5
500	350	0.7	0.3

4 B A definition question. The monetary base forms the basis of bank credit.

5 D The sale of treasury bills to the banking system would increase the liquid assets of the commercial banks, permitting them to lend more. A, B and C would all be making use of existing money.

6 A Keynesians favour increasing aggregate demand to reduce unemployment. B contains a supply side policy. C contains two monetarist policy measures and a rise in the exchange rate is not likely to be favoured by either group as a measure to reduce unemployment. D also contains two monetarist policy measures and one measure, a rise in the rate of interest, which again would not tend to be favoured by either Keynesians or monetarists as solution to unemployment.

7 D The crowding out view suggests that a rise in government borrowing will push up the rate of interest and reduce the quantity of loanable funds available to private sector firms.

8 B Aggregate expenditure consists of C + I + G + (X − M). The difference between aggregate expenditure and C + I + (X − M) is G.

9 B In this case, mps is 0.1, mrt is 0.1 and mpm is 0.2. So the multiplier is 1/0.4 = $2\frac{1}{2}$. To raise national income by the $50 bn desired, the government would have to increase its spending by $50 bn/$2\frac{1}{2}$ = $20 bn.

10 C A definition question. A is a partial explanation of the multiplier. In terms of B and D, actual saving will always equal actual investment.

11 C A rise in bank lending would increase the money supply. Liquidity preference will increase as a result of more money being demanded for transactions purposes.

12 B In a closed economy, Y = C + I + G. In this case, C = 0.75 × $400 m = $300 m. C + G = $340 m, so investment must be $60 m.
$60 m = $(70 − 2 × ?) m. So the rate of interest must be 5%.

13 D The multiplier is 1/0.1 + 0.05 + 0.1 = 1/0.25 = 4. National income will increase by $200 m × 4 = $800 m. Consumer expenditure will rise by 80% of $800 m = $640 m. Note of

this $40 m will be spent on imports and $600 m on domestic products.

14 D Consumer expenditure is MN. Planned investment is PY. Firms make MP amount of consumer goods but only MN is sold. This means there are unsold stocks of NP. Actual investment consists of planned investment and changes in stocks, which in this case is PY + NP = NY.

15 D The closure of bookshops and the resulting unemployment of bookshop assistants is affecting one industry. It has resulted from a change in supply conditions – a structural change. A and C are types of frictional unemployment which arises when people are in between jobs. B is caused by a general lack of demand for all products.

16 A The natural rate of unemployment is the rate of unemployment which is consistent with a stable rate of inflation. This occurs when the aggregate labour market is in equilibrium with no upward pressure on wages and the price level.

17 B An increase in potential output raises the productive capacity. If real GDP does not rise in line, there will be unemployed resources.

18 D Increasing government spending would increase aggregate demand. This would reduce unemployment as firms will expand to produce the extra products being demanded. Higher aggregate demand, however, would increase demand-pull inflation. More government spending will raise GDP by a multiple amount. This will increase consumer expenditure, some of which will be spent on imports. This will increase a current account deficit and reduce the value of the currency.

19 B 55% of the country's working age population is in the labour force i.e. 55% of 50 m = 27.5m. Of the people who are in the labour force 8% are unemployed and so 92% are employed. 92% of 27.5m is 25.3m.

20 D An increase in the retirement age would mean that people would work for a longer period of their life. People will stay in the labour force for longer. C would reduce the size of the labour force. B does not change the size of the labour force, just its utilisation. A would mean that the size of the labour force is still decreasing but at a slower rate.

Answers to data response questions

1 a Economic growth is usually measured by increases in real gross domestic product (GDP).

   b A deflationary gap occurs when there is not sufficient aggregate expenditure to achieve full employment. Injecting government spending into the circular flow will cause a multiple increase in GDP. If the multiplier has been calculated accurately and sufficient government spending has been injected, a deflationary gap may be reduced. For instance, if there is a deflationary gap of $20 bn and the multiplier is 4, the government would have to increase its spending by $5 bn. In the following figure, there would be a deflationary gap of ab unless government spending rises to G_1.

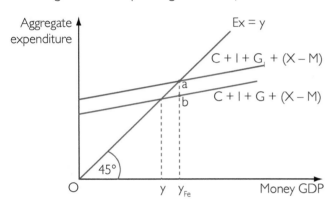

   c i   A large budget deficit will mean that the government will have to borrow a considerable amount to finance the gap between its spending and its revenue. The high demand for funds may result in a high interest rate.

      ii The information in Table 9.-04 does provide some evidence to confirm this relationship. Brazil had the largest relative budget deficit and the highest interest rate. The US had the lowest deficit and the lowest interest rate. The UK, however, had the second largest budget deficit but the fifth lowest interest rate. China and Russia, however, have similar budget deficits but markedly different interest rates.

   d Liquidity ratios are the percentages of liquid assets that commercial banks have to keep relative to their liabilities (deposits). For instance, a liquidity ratio of 10% would mean that a bank with deposits of $200 m would have to keep liquid assets of $20 m. If a central bank raises a formal liquidity ratio requirement from 10% to $12\frac{1}{2}$ %, this would mean that $20 m of liquid assets would only be able to support deposits of $160 m. This would reduce the amount the bank could lend from $180 m ($200 m − $20 m) to $140 m ($160 m − $20 m). A reduction in bank loans (advances) could reduce consumer spending.

      It is possible, however, that whilst a bank may have been able to lend $180 m, demand for loans might have only been, for instance, $120 m. In this case, the increase in the liquidity ratio would have no effect. Even if demand for loans is $180 m or more, an increase in the liquidity ratio, may not reduce bank lending if banks can arrange loans through their foreign branches. Consumer demand may also increase, even if loans are being reduced, if income is rising or consumers are becoming more confident.

2 a A fall in capital stock would be expected to reduce aggregate supply. This is because there will be a reduction in resources and so the economy would be capable of producing less.

   b i   It cannot be concluded that the output of Pakistan's economy was $248 bn in 2015. This is because although its GDP as measured by C + I + G + (X − M) was $248 bn, the information states that there was informal economic activity. Such undeclared output is not recorded in GDP.

      ii Domestic demand consists of C + I + G. In India in 2015 this amounted to $2,266 bn.

   c The size of the multiplier varies between countries because of the tendency to withdraw extra income from the circular flow. The marginal propensity to save, the marginal rate of taxation and the marginal propensity to import differ between countries. If people in a country save a higher proportion of their income, are taxed more and spend a higher proportion of their income on imports than in another country, the size of the multiplier will be smaller. Less of any extra income will spent on the economy's products. For example, if one country's mps, mrt and mpm are 0.2, 0.2 and 0.2, the multiplier will 1/0.6 = 1.67. In contrast, if another country has a mps, mrt and mpm of 0.1, 0.05 and 0.05, its multiplier will be 1/0.2 = 5.

d An output gap occurs when an economy is not producing at full capacity. A negative output exists when an economy's output is below its potential output.

e Consumer expenditure may increase in absolute terms if disposable income rises in Pakistan. Of course, there is the possibility that as income rises, the average and marginal propensities to consume may fall. This is because as people get richer they are more able to save.

Consumer expenditure might increase, even if income does not rise, if people become more confident about the future or if the rate of interest falls. In the latter case, the reward from saving will fall and it will become cheaper to borrow to buy items such as cars. In addition, a rise in wealth may increase consumer expenditure. If, for instance, the value of housing and/or shares increases, people may spend more as they will feel richer and will have more collateral to borrow against.

If, however, income falls, confidence declines, the rate of interest rises or the value of wealth decreases, it would be expected that consumer expenditure would decline.

Answers to essay questions

1 To decide whether people in the Netherlands enjoy living standards three times as great as that of people in Chile, more information than the GDP per head would be needed.

It would be necessary to know real GDP per head as the difference in GDP per head would be exaggerated if the Netherlands experienced higher inflation than Chile and would have been understated if Chile's price level had risen by a greater percentage.

It would also be useful to know what type of product is being produced. A country may have a high output relative to its population but if it devotes a significant proportion of its resources to its armed forces, its population may not enjoy many consumer goods and services. A country's output might consist of a high proportion of capital goods. This might mean higher living standards in the future, but relatively low living standards now.

It is also important to check whether the GDP per head figures have been compared using purchasing power parity, that is an exchange rate based on the cost of a given basket of products. This would prevent a misleading impression being given of the gap by the comparison being made when there has been a significant change in the market exchange rate which does not reflect the internal purchasing power of the currencies.

GDP per head takes into account differences in population size but it does not provide information about the distribution of income. If income is very unevenly distributed in a country with a higher GDP per head, only a small proportion of the population may enjoy higher material living standards than those in a country with a lower but more evenly distributed GDP per head.

Income plays a key role in determining the living standards people enjoy, but it is not the only determinant. A number of other measures of economic welfare take into account not only income per head but also other indicators. For instance, the Human Development Index (HDI) also considers the education people experience and the life expectancy they enjoy. A good quality education increases a person's career choices, earning capacity and often their interests. Higher life expectancy indicates better quality healthcare. The Index of Sustainable Economic Welfare (ISEW) includes in its measure income inequality, environmental damage and depletion of environmental assets.

It is difficult for a measure of a country's income to take into account all economic activity since not all such activity is declared. A country may have a smaller real GDP per head than another country but if it has a larger informal economy, depending on its composition, its citizens may enjoy higher living standards. The quality of the products produced and differences in working hours and working conditions also have to be considered.

In addition, cultures and climates vary between countries. People living in a non-materialistic culture may be satisfied with fewer goods and services. People living in cold climates may have to spend more on heating than people living in warmer climates, just to experience the same standard of living.

GDP per head figures give some indication of living standards but other factors have to be considered to gain a fuller picture of the quality of people's lives.

2 a Economic growth is concerned with output and the ability to produce output whereas economic development is concerned with welfare.

Actual economic growth occurs when the output of an economy grows. With higher output comes higher income and higher expenditure. Potential economic growth enables an economy to continue to produce more products and so earn higher incomes. It is achieved when the productive capacity of the economy increases due to a higher quantity and/or quality of resources.

Economic growth may lead to an increase in economic development but, depending on how it is achieved, it may reduce economic development. A country will experience economic development if its population achieves an improvement in their economic welfare. It is possible that a rise in real GDP, especially if it is evenly distributed, may improve the quality of people's lives. People will be able to enjoy more goods and services and this may be particularly important in the case of people lacking basic necessities. Higher income will also be expected to raise tax revenue, some of which may be spent on education and healthcare – key influences on economic welfare. A high GDP per head is one of the main indicators of a developed country. High incomes also enable more saving which, in turn, can increase investment and lead to further economic growth.

Economic growth, however, may come at the cost of economic development if it is accompanied by a rise in pollution, longer working hours and worse working conditions. Economic growth also involves change, with workers often having to develop new skills and some may find this stressful.

b Multinational companies (MNCs) often contribute to the economic growth of developing countries, at least in the short term. Their impact on economic development is, however, more debatable.

A MNC is one which produces in more than one country. It has its headquarters in one country but may have plants in a number of countries.

When setting up in another country, MNCs usually add to that country's output unless they replace domestic firms. MNCs' output may increase more rapidly than that of domestic firms and they tend to export a relatively high proportion of their output. They may also promote economic growth in a developing country by providing workers with transferrable skills, introducing new technology and working methods and sometimes building transport links.

Their contribution to the economic growth of a particular developing country may be short lived if, after a period of time, they decide to relocate their production to an economy with lower costs or a larger market. MNCs may be less committed to the country than domestic firms. It is also possible that the MNCs may deplete some of the country's natural resources, thereby reducing the country's ability to grow in the future.

MNCs may promote economic development by providing employment, higher wages, training and better working conditions. It may also raise economic welfare by introducing new products. The more skilled are the jobs on offer, the more economic development there is likely to be. In some cases, MNCS may offer mainly low skilled jobs which may not allow workers to make much progress. For instance, foreign owned hotels may employ managers from their own countries whilst employing waiters and cleaners from the developing country.

MNCs may pay workers less in a developing country than it pays workers in developed countries. If, however, it pays them more than the wages in the country, it may nevertheless promote economic development. Generic training is likely to be more beneficial than firm specific training as the workers will be able to make use of it in other jobs.

The working conditions provided by MNCs may not be as good as they provide in their home countries but again may be better than in the developing countries.

They may introduce products which help to make life easier and promote healthcare. Some of the products they produce and sell in developing countries, however, may be demerit goods and may clash with the culture of the countries. MNCs may also cause environmental damage and may take risks in terms of health and safety to save costs. They may also put pressure on national governments to pursue policies beneficial to them but not necessarily to the country's economic development.

The effect MNCs have on developing countries varies across the world and really needs to be considered on a case by case basis.

Chapter 10

Answers to progress checks

A A government may want its country's exchange rate to fall in value in order to reduce a current account deficit and to raise employment.

B The internal value of money may decline but its external value rises if the country experiences a lower inflation rate than its main rivals. The inflation will reduce the internal value. Its lower rate, however, may increase the country's international price competitiveness. This could increase demand for its currency and so raise its external value.

C Globalisation may increase tax competition. Governments may think they have to lower their spending on education and other areas so that they can reduce tax rates. They may consider that lower tax rates are needed to attract and keep MNCs in the country.

D A conventional Phillips curve would shift to the left if any given rate of unemployment is accompanied by a lower inflation rate. This could occur if workers press for lower wage rises when unemployment falls. This may be the result of reduced expectations of inflation.

E A supply constraint means that a lack of aggregate supply is limiting economic growth. When an economy is operating at full capacity, it will not be able to produce more unless there is an increase in aggregate supply. In contrast, a demand constraint occurs when a failure of aggregate demand to increase stops economic growth taking place.

F Unemployment might increase despite a rise in real GDP, if the rise in real GDP is below the increase in potential output. With improved education, training and advances in technology, an economy may be able to produce more with fewer workers. If aggregate demand rises but at a slower rate than productive potential, there is likely to be a rise in unemployment.

Answers to revision activities

A

Characteristic	Developed country	Developing country
GDP per head	High	Low
Population growth	Low	High
Proportion of population employed in agriculture	Low	High
Urbanisation	High	Low
HDI ranking	High	Low
Foreign debt as % of GDP	Low	High
Energy consumption	High	Low
Enrolment in tertiary education	High	Low
Life expectancy	High	Low
Population per doctor	Low	High
Labour productivity	High	Low
Savings ratio	High	Low

B Internal: **b**, **c** and **e**

External: **a** and **d**.

C **a** Cyclical   **b** Structural   **c** Frictional

    d Cyclical   **e** Structural   **f** Structural

D **a** $100 bn ($20 bn + $10 bn = $30 bn).

    b A surplus of $35 bn ($75 bn − $20 bn + $25 bn).

    c As GDP rises a government would gain more tax revenue to spend as people will earn and spend more, and so both direct and indirect tax revenue will rise. In addition, as income rises people demand a higher quality of publicly financed services. Indeed, demand for education, healthcare and roads, for example, is income elastic.

Answers to multiple choice questions

1 C An upward revaluation of the currency would raise export prices and lower import prices. This will reduce current account surplus if demand for exports and imports are elastic. Lower import prices will reduce the prices of some finished products produced, and may lower the prices of some domestically produced products if they use imported raw materials. Higher export prices do not affect the country's inflation rate as the country's population does not buy exports.

2 C India's current account would have benefited from $6m coming into the income section. The financial account covers direct investment, portfolio investment and bank loans. The $5m borrowed from Indian banks would come out of India's financial account. This would mean that the net currency flow would have been $6m − $5m = $1m.

3 C Country C has the second highest GNI per head, by far the longest life expectancy and the largest time spent in education.

4 D A definition question. An optimum population is the population which maximises output per head and so allows income per head to be maximised.

5 A Devaluation would reduce the price of exports and increase the price of imports. These price changes could result in an increase in net exports. Such a change would improve the current account position and the resulting higher aggregate demand would reduce cyclical unemployment.

6 A Some of the income taxed may have been saved and so one leakage will replace another leakage. For instance, a government spends an extra $100m and raises taxes by a $100m. If the savings ratio is 20%, the rise in taxes will reduce private sector spending by $80m and so there will be a net injection of spending of $20m. B would reduce the impact on aggregate demand. C is not true for most countries and is anyway concerned with absolute amounts rather than changes. D is true but does not explain why a rise in government spending matched by an equal increase in tax revenue is likely to increase aggregate demand.

7 C If inflationary expectations are at 5%, the economy is operating on the second short-run Phillips curve. To remove inflation from the system, unemployment would have to rise to the point where the short-run Phillips curve cuts the horizontal axis. In this case, this would be at an unemployment rate of 13%.

8 A A rise in taxation and a cut in government spending would reduce household spending. Lower spending may reduce demand-pull inflation and, by reducing spending on imports, may lower a current account deficit. Lower household spending would raise unemployment and may increase a current account surplus.

9 C The natural rate of unemployment is the rate of unemployment which exists when the labour market is in equilibrium and the rate of inflation is stable. An increase in unemployment benefit may put less pressure on the unemployed to find jobs. It may also push up wages as employers will have to make employment more attractive. A and D would tend to reduce the natural rate of unemployment as they would make work more financially rewarding and would make labour more mobile. B may reduce cyclical unemployment.

10 C A high marginal propensity to save would reduce the size of the multiplier and so reduce the impact of expansionary fiscal policy. A, B and D would all tend to increase the effectiveness of expansionary fiscal policy.

Answers to data response questions

1 a 47.36 million.

b Unemployment and poverty are usually directly linked. A rise in unemployment would be expected to increase poverty. Most people experience a fall in income when they lose their job. The longer they are unemployed, the more financial difficulties they may experience.

c There are pieces of evidence to suggest that USA is a developed country. Although there is a significant proportion of the population living in poverty, the poverty line is set at a relatively high rate. In many countries, an income of, for instance, $28,000 for a family of five would be considered to be a high income but in the US it would result in the family being classified as poor. Being ranked 8th in the Human Development Index (HDI) is a strong indicator that the USA is a developed country. The HDI takes into account GDP per head, education and life expectancy. An average income of $51,939 is high. Long life expectancy, such as the 79.6 years that USA enjoys, is a sign of a developed country. A high percentage of the labour force employed in the tertiary sector also provides evidence that the US is a developed country.

d The children of the poor tend to become poor adults because they are likely to have grown up in poor housing and may have only a few years of education. The resulting poor health and limited skills and qualifications reduces their earning capacity. They may also have lower expectations which will also limit the types of jobs they apply for.

e Achieving the macroeconomic objectives of full employment and steady and sustainable economic growth is likely to reduce absolute poverty but not necessarily relative poverty. With more people in work, more people may have access to basic necessities. Economic growth may result in a rise in income per head. It should also increase tax revenue and some of this may be spent on education, healthcare and benefits which may reduce absolute poverty.

Higher employment and economic growth may, however, be accompanied by a widening of the gap between those receiving a high income and those receiving a low income. Successful entrepreneurs and workers with skills in high demand may experience significant increases in their incomes during prosperous times. More people may be in work but some may be in low paid jobs and the standard of living that they are able to enjoy may be significantly lower than that of the highest paid. To reduce relative poverty, a government may have to pursue another macroeconomic growth, that is a redistribution of income.

2 a i Aggregate demand is the total demand for a country's products at the current price level. It consists of consumer expenditure, investment, government spending and net exports.

ii One reason why aggregate demand has increased in recent years is because of the rise in consumer expenditure. People have become richer and as a result they are spending more. Another reason for the increase in aggregate demand is the increase in government spending on investment.

iii Aggregate supply has increased because of the rise in the labour force. Having more workers available increases potential output. The increase in labour productivity has also increased aggregate supply. Workers are capable of producing more units of output per hour.

b India's growth in labour productivity exceeded the growth of global productivity and that of the USA and UK in all the periods shown. India's labour productivity grew by the second highest percentage in the period 1999–2006 but was 6.7% points below the growth of China's labour productivity. In the period 2007–2012 India again came second but this time its growth came close to the high rate achieved by China. India's growth in labour productivity between 2012–2014 slowed relative to the previous period. In 2012 India's growth was only third highest and in 2013 it was fourth highest.

c If the labour force increases without any rise in employment, output will not increase. More people will be unemployed and so government spending on unemployment benefit will increase. If the supply of labour exceeds the demand for labour, there may be downward pressure on wages. An increase in the labour force may also encourage some firms to continue to use very labour-intensive methods of production which may slow down the adoption of new technology.

A larger labour force, however, may bring significant benefits. It will increase the productive potential of the economy. If the extra workers are employed, output will rise. Expanding firms will be able to recruit new staff and if aggregate supply can rise in line with aggregate demand, inflationary pressure can be reduced. If the extra workers are young, they may be more mobile and may be more up to date with advances in technology. A larger labour force may also attract multinational companies to set up in the country as there will be a ready supply of labour.

1 a The natural rate of unemployment is the unemployment which exists when the labour market is in equilibrium with all those wanting to work at the going wage rate are able to find a job. As there is no shortage of workers there is no upward pressure on wages and so no upward pressure on the price level. The following figure shows the labour market in equilibrium at a wage rate of W. The aggregate labour force, however, is greater than those willing and able to work at the wage rate on offer. The natural rate of unemployment is $Q_1 - Q$.

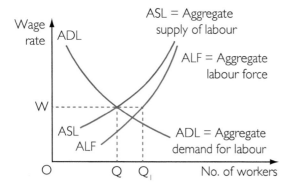

To reduce the natural rate of unemployment a government would implement supply side measures. One such measure would be to cut unemployment benefit. The intention behind this measure is to encourage the unemployed to look more actively for work and so reduce the search unemployment component of the natural rate.

A government might also reduce the gap between paid employment and benefits by reducing income tax. Such a reduction would increase disposable income and so would provide a financial incentive for the unemployed to take the jobs on offer.

In some countries, it might be thought that trade unions are pushing wage rates above their equilibrium levels and engaging in restrictive practices. These actions may be discouraging some employers from taking workers on and so a government may decide to pass laws to reduce trade union power.

The natural rate of unemployment may be reduced by increasing the occupational and geographical mobility of labour. The main way to increase occupational mobility is to promote education and training. This might be achieved, for example, by giving tax incentives to firms which undertake training. To increase geographical mobility a government might remove any restrictions on building homes in areas of the countries where industries are expanding so as to reduce the cost of housing there.

So there are a number of measures a government might take to reduce the natural rate of unemployment. The concept is, however, a somewhat controversial one and even its supporters admit, it can be difficult to determine what is the natural rate at any one time.

b According to the traditional Phillips curve, a decrease in unemployment will cause inflation. In the following figure, a fall in unemployment from 6% to 4% causes an increase in the inflation rate from 4% to 7%.

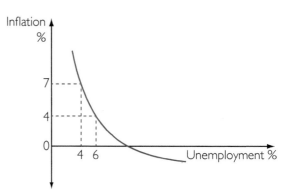

When unemployment falls, aggregate demand increases, firms compete more for labour and trade unions become more powerful. These forces can push up the price level.

The expectations-augmented Phillips curve suggests that attempts to reduce unemployment below the natural rate will cause inflation. It also suggests that, in the long run, unemployment will return to the natural rate but with a higher inflation rate. In the figure that follows, the economy is initially operating at the natural rate of unemployment of, in this case, 6% and on the short-run Phillips curve (SPC). A government attempt to reduce unemployment succeeds in the short run in lowering unemployment to 3%. It does, however, also cause inflation of 5%. When some workers realise that with inflation the real wages they are being paid have not risen, they leave employment. Some firms will also realise that their real profits have not gone up and so will reduce the number of workers they employ.

In this case, unemployment returns to 6%. Having experienced an inflation rate of 5% workers and firms will anticipate that inflation will continue. As a result they will behave in a way, for instance by asking for wage rises and by increasing prices, that will cause inflation to continue. The economy will move on to a higher short-run Phillips curve (SPC1). Now any further attempt to reduce unemployment below 6% will generate even higher unemployment.

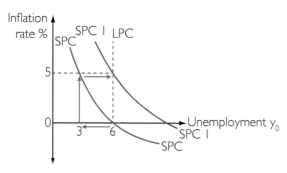

It is, however, possible to argue that a fall in unemployment will not necessarily cause inflation. Unemployment may decrease because workers become more educated or better trained. In this case, the higher aggregate demand which will result from more people being in work may be matched by the higher aggregate supply resulting from the increase in labour productivity. Aggregate supply may also be increased by advances in technology which again may offset any inflationary pressure arising from lower unemployment. In addition, increased global competition may make it difficult for firms to raise their prices even if domestic demand is increasing. It is possible that the nature of the relationship between unemployment and inflation may be changing in some countries. The following figure shows a new type of Phillips curve with a reduction in unemployment from 6% to 3% having no effect on the inflation rate which remains at 5%.

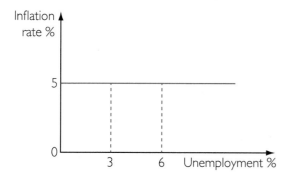

There are reasons to think that a fall in unemployment may contribute to inflation by raising both aggregate demand and costs of production but the relationship is not clear cut.

2 a An increase in taxes would reduce national income. Higher income tax would reduce disposable income. Lower disposable income would be likely to reduce consumer expenditure. Higher indirect taxes would also probably result in lower consumer expenditure. A decline in consumer expenditure, ceteris paribus, will reduce aggregate demand. Lower aggregate demand can reduce real GDP as shown in the figure here.

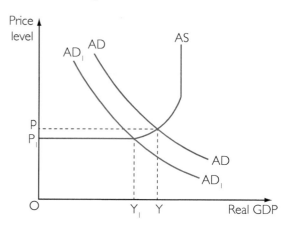

The extent to which an increase in taxes will reduce national income will be influenced by the size of the rise in taxes, which taxes are raised and how firms and households react. A small increase in taxes will not have much effect. A rise in the top rates of progressive taxes may also not cause national income to fall significantly. If the rich have to pay higher taxes they may reduce their savings rather than their spending. Higher direct taxes may increase tax evasion and, as a result, not increase tax revenue. A rise in indirect taxes on products with inelastic demand or on products with substitutes that are not taxed may also mean that consumer spending does not fall by much.

It is even possible that during periods of high inflation or large government debt, a rise in taxes may increase consumer and business confidence and so raise aggregate demand.

b Whether the aims of government policy will conflict will be affected by the time period under consideration, the current state of the economy and the type of economic policies pursued. If there is a conflict, which aim should be given priority will again be influenced by the current state of the economy, future predictions, the costs involved and which aim the government thinks it will be most effective in achieving.

In the short run, if an economy is operating close to full employment, there may be a conflict between reducing the inflation rate or at least ensuring the inflation rate remains stable. If a government seeks to reduce unemployment by expansionary fiscal policy, the higher aggregate demand may result in inflationary pressure. In the diagram as aggregate demand (AD) increases, output is increased rises closer to the vertical part of the aggregate supply curve (AS) and the price level rises from P to P_1.

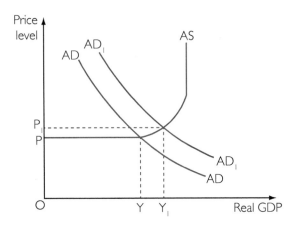

If, however, the economy has considerable spare capacity, with a noticeable output gap, it may be possible to reduce unemployment by a noticeable amount without causing inflationary pressure.

In the short run, the objectives of economic growth and a stable inflation rate may also conflict. As the previous diagram shows, higher AD causes real GDP to rise but it also pushes up the price level. As an economy's AD increases, more resources are used and they become in shorter supply and the rising competition pushes up their prices. Firms know they can charge more for their products and so they are willing to increase their prices.

Economic growth may also conflict with a balance on the current account of the balance of payments. If economic growth occurs, incomes will rise. This may result in demand

for goods and services. As a result, imports of finished products and raw materials may increase. Some products originally intended for the export market may also be diverted to the home market. Of course, it is possible that economic growth may be export led and in such a circumstance may be accompanied by a declining current account deficit.

In the long run, if a government follows effective supply side policy measures it may be able to achieve all of its objectives. This is because such policies, such as improved education and training, will shift the aggregate supply (AS) curve to the right enabling AD to increase, lowering unemployment, achieving economic growth without causing inflation. Effective supply side policy measures can also improve the current account position by improving the quality and price competitiveness of domestic products. Of course, a government may also have to ensure that both AD and AS increase in line with each other. In the diagram below, both AD and AS rise. These shifts keep the price level at P and raises real GDP from Y to Y_1.

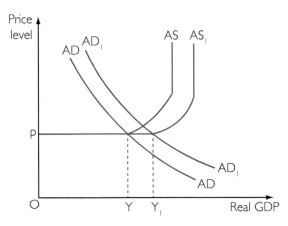

In practice, a government is likely to need to use a range of policy measures to achieve its objectives. In the short run, whilst unemployment and economic growth are likely to be helped by an increase in AD, a reduction in AD may be needed to reduce demand-pull inflation and a current account deficit. In the long run, however, all the objectives should benefit from an increase in AS which matches an increase in AD. This is why some economists claim that sustained economic growth should be given priority. If both aggregate demand and aggregate supply shift to the right, inflation and unemployment should be kept low and the current account close to balance. In the short run, if there is significant and rising unemployment whilst inflation is low and stable, there is still positive economic growth and the current account position is close to balance, a government is likely to prioritise reducing unemployment. If, however, unemployment is of a short-term duration and on a downturn trend whilst inflation is unanticipated and of a cost-push nature, a government may decide to concentrate on reducing inflation.

3 a There are a number of indicators which can be examined to determine whether a country should be classified as developed or developing. It does, however, have to be remembered that no country's characteristics will fit entirely into one of these two categories.

One of the key indicators is real GDP per head. A developed country would be expected to have a high GDP per head, giving its citizens the ability to consume a high number of goods and services. A developing country would be likely to have a low GDP per head. This does not mean that everyone in the country will be poor. Indeed, a developing country may contain a number of rich people but, on average, income will be low.

A higher proportion of the labour force would be expected to be employed in the primary sector and it would be anticipated that this sector would make a larger contribution to GDP in a developing country than in developed country. In contrast, the tertiary sector would usually make a larger contribution to employment and output in a developed country.

Primary products may also form a high proportion of the exports of developing countries. There may also be a narrow range of products forming those exports.

The labour force in developing countries usually has a lower productivity than that in developed countries. With lower income, the amount spent on education and training per head is likely to be lower, leading to lower skilled workers and hence lower productivity. In turn, lower productivity can result in lower income which can keep saving and investment low. This vicious circle of poverty is illustrated in the figure here.

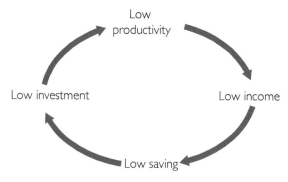

One of the reasons why spending on education per head may be low is because of high population growth. Developing countries tend to have higher population growth than developed countries. Their birth rates and death rates tend to be higher in developing countries, giving them a pyramid shaped population pyramid as shown here.

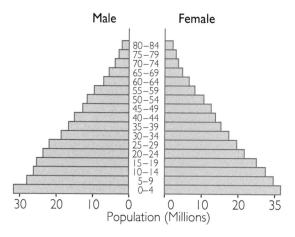

This contrasts with the typical population pyramid of a developed country which has a narrower base and wider apex as shown in the following figure.

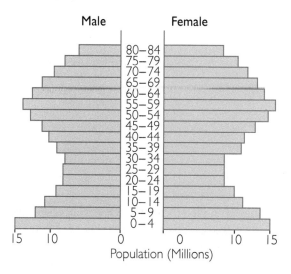

The population structure of developing countries leads to a higher dependency ratio. This means that a high proportion of economically inactive dependants rely on a relatively small proportion of economically active workers to supply them with goods and services.

Migration patterns may also be examined to decide whether a country should be classified as a developing country or developed country. Developing countries tend to experience net emigration as some people leave the country in search of employment and higher incomes abroad. Many are also experiencing rural to urban migration as people leave the countryside to move to towns and cities, again in search of employment and higher income. In contrast, many developed countries experience net immigration and have already achieved a relatively high level of urbanisation.

Countries might also be classified according to a composite measure of living standards such as the Human Development Index. In practice, developing countries have differences as well as similarities. These differences include, for instance, disparities in factor endowment, the inequality of income and economic growth rates. Developed countries also exhibit a range of differences.

b One advantage claimed for the adoption of a floating exchange rate is that it will free a government to concentrate on internal problems. Whilst, however, it is likely to give a government more influence over its domestic performance, it does not mean that a government can neglect the balance of payments. Some, but not all, developing economies have large deficits on the current account of their balance of payments.

In theory, under a floating exchange rate, the balance of payments or at least the current account will always move to an equilibrium position. This is because if, for instance, there is a current account deficit, the exchange rate will float downwards and, in theory at least, export revenue will rise and import expenditure will fall until an equilibrium is again restored. This will occur without any government action. So a government wishing to concentrate, for example, on raising employment may not regard the balance of payments as a constraint when it decides to increase demand. For even

if a reflationary policy initially results in an increase in demand for imports, the resulting depreciation of the exchange rate will reduce the number of imports purchased.

It is also claimed that a floating exchange rate enables a government to have more control over its interest rate policy. With a fixed exchange rate, a government may have to use interest rate changes to maintain the exchange rate at the set value.

A floating exchange rate, however, whilst giving a government more opportunity to concentrate on internal problems will not in practice mean that it can neglect the balance of payments. This is because a floating exchange rate does not always guarantee a balance of payments equilibrium and because movements in the exchange rate will have an impact on the economy and the government's internal policy objectives.

If there is a balance of payments deficit, the exchange rate will float downwards. The depreciation, however, will not restore a current account equilibrium if demand for exports and demand for imports is inelastic. This is because, in this case, a fall in the price of exports will result in a smaller percentage increase in demand for exports and hence, a fall in export revenue. Also, a rise in import prices will cause a smaller percentage fall in demand for imports and so expenditure on imports will rise.

A balance of payments deficit may also arise due to a net outflow from the financial account. Higher interest rates abroad, lower taxes and better economic prospects may cause direct and portfolio investment to leave the country.

A government may be concerned that a fall in the value of the exchange rate may give rise to inflationary pressures since the rising import prices may increase raw material costs and may stimulate wage demands. One disadvantage of a floating exchange rate is the ratchet effect. This is that when the exchange rate floats down workers, experiencing rises in the cost of living, press for wage rises but when the exchange rate floats upwards and the workers experience a reduction in the cost of living, they do not ask for a wage reduction. So the pressure over time is for wage rises.

A government may also want to use the exchange rate to stimulate economic growth and employment. Lowering the exchange rate from the free market value may increase aggregate demand, raise output and create more jobs. A number of developing economies have sought to promote economic growth and development by operating a low fixed exchange rate.

The exchange rate of a developing country may be very volatile if the country is a large exporter of primary products. This is because the revenue earned may fluctuate by large amounts due to changes in both demand and supply conditions. A volatile exchange rate could discourage the inward investment which may promote development.

So although a floating exchange rate may be used as a policy measure rather than a policy objective, the government cannot ignore the balance of payments position nor can it presume that a floating exchange rate will guarantee a balance of payments equilibrium.

Index